THE MOST

EVIL

MOBSTERS

IN HISTORY

THE MOST
EVIL
MOBSTERS
IN HISTORY

LAUREN CARTER

MICHAEL O'MARA BOOKS LIMITED

First published in Great Britain in 2004 by
Michael O'Mara Books Limited
9 Lion Yard
Tremadoc Road
London SW4 7NQ

Copyright © Michael O'Mara Books Ltd 2004

A CIP catalogue record for this book is available from the British Library

ISBN 1-84317-107-4

www.mombooks.com

Designed and typeset by Design 23

Printed and bound in Singapore by Tien Wah Press

CONTENTS

Introduction   **7**

JOSEPH BONANNO THE MAN OF HONOR   **11**

AL CAPONE SCARFACE   **23**

PAUL CASTELLANO THE POPE OF TODT HILL   **36**

FRANK COSTELLO THE PRIME MINISTER OF THE UNDERWORLD   **47**

CARLO GAMBINO THE DAPPER DON   **59**

VITO GENOVESE DON VITONE   **69**

SAM 'MOMO' GIANCANA THE BUTCHER OF CHICAGO   **80**

JOHN GOTTI THE 'TEFLON DON'   **92**

SAMMY 'THE BULL' GRAVANO THE UNDERBOSS   **105**

MEYER 'LITTLE MAN' LANSKY THE CHAIRMAN OF THE BOARD   **119**

'LUCKY' LUCIANO THE FATHER OF ORGANIZED CRIME   **132**

GEORGE MORAN THE BUG   **143**

DEAN O'BANION CHICAGO'S ARCH KILLER   **156**

DUTCH SCHULTZ THE FLYING DUTCHMAN   **167**

BENJAMIN 'BUGSY' SIEGEL THE KING OF LAS VEGAS   **179**

Picture Acknowledgements   **191**

Acknowledgements   **192**

INTRODUCTION

'Mafia, Maffia, mä' fe-a, n. a spirit of opposition to the law in
Sicily, hence a preference for private and unofficial rather than
legal justice: a secret criminal society originating in Sicily,
controlling many illegal activities, e.g., gambling, narcotics, etc.,
in many parts of the world, and particularly active in the U.S.'

Chambers Twentieth Century Dictionary,
W & R Chambers Ltd, 1977

'The Mafia is oppression, arrogance, greed, self-enrichment,
power and hegemony above and against all others. It is not an
abstract concept, or a state of mind, or a literary term . . . It is a
criminal organization regulated by unwritten but iron and
inexorable rules . . . The myth of a courageous and generous
'man of honor' must be destroyed, because a Mafioso is
just the opposite.'

Cesare Terranova, Italian Magistrate murdered in 1979

In many ways, the history of the Mafia (or Cosa Nostra, as it is frequently called)
is as shady as the organization itself. Commonly believed to have originated in
Sicily during the Middle Ages, it was initially created in order to protect the
poorer sections of society from invading forces, home-grown bandits, over-zealous
landlords and, in later years, from government agencies such as the police. In this
way, the myth of the autonomous Mafiosi boss as a kind of Sicilian Robin Hood –
doing good for his neighbors and friends – grew. From this came the idea that they
were somehow 'men of honor' who were acting for the greater good of their
community. It may also be supposed that the Sicilians' natural dislike and suspicion
of legitimate law enforcement, together with their hatred of the aristocracy and the
old feudal system, all combined to create the type of conditions within which the
Mafiosi flourished.

By the mid-nineteenth century practically every town had a chief of operations or
'capo', although when Mussolini came to power in 1922 he had his aptly named 'Iron
Prefect' – Cesare Mori – imprison the majority of these men. In truth, Mussolini's
dislike of the Mafia probably stemmed from the fact that the Fascists had a lot in
common with their underworld counterparts and Mussolini did not appreciate the
competition. During the Second World War, when the Allies invaded Sicily, most
Mafiosi were on the side of the Americans, and after the end of the war the Americans
made several Mafiosi bosses mayors of their respective towns. But if Sicily was the
breeding ground for this organization, America soon proved to be the place where it
thrived best. During the 1880s a mass migration took place, with thousands of

Italians and Sicilians seeking out a new life across the Atlantic. The majority came from southern Italy and were of peasant stock. Used to a tough life back home at the hands of their lords and masters, they instinctively shied away from officialdom and viewed organizations such as the police and local government with deep distrust. Instead, they relied on and placed their trust in their immediate families and afterwards with their local community bosses. 'The migrant,' according to the author Henk van Woerden, 'is an uncertain and incomplete man. He lives in an inveterate state of unease. The ultimate measure of his success is the extent to which he manages to adapt himself.'[1] As with nearly all émigrés, however, assimilation by the Italian/Sicilian community was well nigh impossible due to the brutal type of prejudice they had to endure. Instead, most of the immigrants preferred to stick to their own kind and abide by their own rules as laid down by 'La Cosa Nostra', a rough translation of which is 'our thing' or 'this thing of ours.' Although the Mafia had its roots in these purely Italian/Sicilian communities, it soon grew into a nationwide alliance of criminals that had little or nothing to do with protecting their own people, but everything to do with organized crime.

In the 1920s men like Giuseppe 'Joe the Boss' Masseria and Salvatore Maranzano arrived in America and, along with the likes of Joseph Bonanno, Lucky Luciano, Joe Profaci and Carlo Gambino, established a criminal enterprise on a massive scale. Ironically, the biggest boost to Cosa Nostra came from none other than the US government which, after the end of World War One, in order to reduce crime figures and to improve the health of the American nation, decided to eliminate the consumption of alcohol. Called the 'Noble Experiment' by Herbert Hoover, the 18th Amendment to the Constitution, better known as either the National Prohibition Act, or the Volstead Act, went into effect on 17 January 1920 banning the manufacture, sale, transportation and consumption of all intoxicating substances. Naturally, although some sections of society such as the Women's Christian Temperance Union and the Anti-Saloon League upheld the new law, the majority of the public openly flouted it, thus providing gangsters with the perfect opportunity to make huge sums of money. Speakeasies – illicit drinking clubs – sprang up in nearly every community, often providing not only alcohol, but also illegal gambling and prostitution, and with so much at stake, with so much to be won or lost, it was only a matter of time before violence became part and parcel of this underworld landscape. Gangland killings grew to be, if not an everyday occurrence, then all too frequent for comfort. The gangsters and Mafia bosses also began investing their ill-gotten gains in other businesses, some of which were legitimate. Bribery began to run rife, with law enforcement officers and government officials only too willing to take money in exchange for turning a blind eye. In effect, the 18th Amendment, far from improving the nation's health, granted organized crime a stranglehold over the whole country; one that, even after the Act's abolition in 1933, continued to grow and make inroads into practically every industry, every stratum of society.

Of those Mafiosi who are presented in this book, virtually all of them, save perhaps for John Gotti and Sammy 'The Bull' Gravano, were directly or indirectly involved in bootlegging. While the manufacture and supply of alcohol is by no means the most heinous of crimes, the brutal world which sprang up around it did America no favors. But what, apart from bootlegging, did all the men collected in this volume have in common?

Again with the exception of the two most recent Mafiosi, Gotti and Gravano, it is their backgrounds that speak volumes. As émigrés to a foreign country, men like Joseph Bonanno, Frank Costello, Lucky Luciano, Meyer Lansky and Vito Genovese were immediately set at a disadvantage due to the reluctance of their parents to assimilate with their adoptive country and their adoptive country's equal reluctance to accept the new settlers. The slums, such as Little Italy in Manhattan and Little Hell in Chicago, in which the settlers formed ghettos to make themselves feel 'at home' in their new surroundings, served only to isolate them further. No wonder, then, that old-world organizations such as the Mafia thrived and that hundreds of youngsters, seeing the easy riches and street credibility they could acquire by joining a gang, did so in droves. The Mafia, or in the case of Dean O'Banion and George Moran, the North Siders' Gang, provided not only camaraderie, but the type of power about which most newcomers to America could only dream. Even John Gotti was affected. 'My life,' he once said, though somewhat overstating the facts, 'dictated that I take each course that I took. I didn't have any multiple choice. My time, all the doors were closed.'[2] Sadly, far from being 'men of honor' as the Mafia liked (and still likes) to think of itself, the opposite was far nearer the truth.

With their worship of the word 'tradition' and with the establishment of organizations such as the Commission (initially set up by Lucky Luciano and Joseph Bonanno) one might be forgiven for thinking that the Mafia did act with propriety. Consider, for example, the following extract from Joseph Bonanno's autobiography:

A man of our world was held strictly accountable for his actions. If he did something of a violent nature against another Family member he had to be sure he was doing the right thing.

But on closer inspection such a pompous statement reveals nothing more than a perverted code of conduct, which when put into operation was simply a license to kill. There was no honor amongst these thieves; they intimidated and bullied their way into making hundreds of thousands of dollars off the back of ordinary citizens through racketeering, through the manipulation of the unions, through bribery and corruption of police and politicians, not to mention the countless murders which they committed. In fact, all of the gangsters included in this volume did nothing other than trade in violence, and although some Mafiosi, perhaps Frank Costello or Meyer Lansky, were a little less sanguine than others, it still didn't pay to cross them.

In this respect Sammy 'The Bull' Gravano's story is more interesting than most for, having served as John Gotti's underboss for many years, he eventually turned State's evidence, flouted the Mafia's sacred rule of Omerta (roughly translated as meaning an oath of silence) and testified against his former employer. Not only that, but Gravano also wrote (with the help of author Peter Maas) an autobiography that blew open the doors on the Mafia's secretive world. Yet, although he attempts to justify his despicable acts by insisting he had no choice in the matter, what the book successfully reveals is his and, by association the Mafia's, total and utter disrespect for humanity. There are no excuses for the type of behavior any of the men in this book display, no possible justification other than that they were avaricious, self-serving individuals who, through terrorism and corruption, inveigled their way into the heart of America's social, economic and political power bases.

In 1969 a book appeared in the shops which, when it was subsequently made into a film in 1972, caught the public's imagination like no other. *The Godfather* instilled in all of us the perception that we somehow knew the Mafia first hand, how it operated, what its secret codes of conduct signified in respect to membership. *The Godfather* became part of our popular culture, part of our psychic experience; the blueprint of what we thought it was like to be a gangster in twentieth-century America. *The Godfather* also came out at a time when the media, but in particular television and glossy magazines, had begun hyping everyone who was anyone, and soon fame and infamy blended into one amorphous beast. Men like John Gotti became media celebrities, the type of man who not only graced the front cover of publications such as *Newsweek*, but who could also lay claim to a worldwide fan club.

Surely it would have served us all better if, instead of relying on films such as *The Godfather* with its romanticized version of the truth (complete with haunting theme tune and impossibly handsome actors), we remembered that most normal citizens do not know or have never known a mobster. Most people are not familiar with gangsters and the iconic image we have built up bears little resemblance to the reality. Mobsters are not tragic anti-heroes, glitzy fantasy figures or celebrities who have done something exceptional. They are thugs. The false image we harbor is further enhanced by the secretive sub-culture the mobsters have woven around themselves. Although interesting on one level, it is really no more noteworthy than the milieu within which any common criminal operates.

Why then devote a whole book to their antics? Because to understand the twentieth century, particularly in America, one must acknowledge the tremendous influence the Mafia has wielded both socially and psychologically. And, as the old saying goes, by learning about one's enemies one will always stay one step ahead of the game.

---

[1] *The Assassin*, Henk van Woerden, translated from the Dutch by Dan Jacobson, Granta, 2000.
[2] *Mob Star: The Story of John Gotti*, Gene Mustain and Jerry Capeci, Alpha Books and Pearson Education, Inc., 1988.

JOSEPH BONANNO
The Man of Honor

'Our life-styles centred on our Family. A Family (with a capital
F to distinguish it from one's immediate household), in the
Sicilian usage of the term, is a group of people, allied friends as
well as blood relatives, held together by trust in one another.
Regardless of their varied individual activities, Family members
support each other any way they can in order to prosper and
to avoid harm.'

A Man of Honor: The Autobiography of Joseph Bonanno, 1983

Joseph Bonanno, bootlegger, gunman, loan shark, extortionist and Mafia Don, always thought of himself first and foremost as a man of honor, a man to whom tradition was all important, one whose good name and reputation came before anything else. Widely believed to be the model for Mario Puzo's Don Corleone in the blockbuster novel, *The Godfather*, Joseph Bonanno embodies all that is unforgettable about Mafia lore, and perhaps more than any other gangster in history best sums up what it was to belong to La Cosa Nostra.

Born on January 18, 1905 in Castellammare del Golfo in western Sicily, Bonanno first came to the United States with his parents, Catherine and Salvatore Bonanno, when he was three years old; hence his earliest memories were not of his native Sicily but of America. He wouldn't to stay long on foreign soil, however, for when he was seven years old his parents decided to move back to their native Sicily. Here the young Bonanno enjoyed a relatively peaceful childhood until his father was called up to serve in the First World War. Returning home on sick leave, Salvatore Bonanno died in 1916. Three years later his mother also passed away and Joseph went to live with his uncle. Shortly afterwards Joseph decided he wished to make a career at sea and he was enrolled at the Joeni Trabia Nautical Institute. It was not too long before the young man crossed swords with authority and was suspended, along with his cousin, Peter Magaddino, for not wearing a black shirt in support of Benito Mussolini, then leader of the Fascist movement, which was better known as the Black Shirts. It was now that Bonanno decided he wanted to return to the States and, together with Peter, he traveled to Paris to stay with another cousin, Salvatore. Neither Peter nor Joseph had the relevant documents to complete the last stage of their journey, so instead they decided to enter America illegally by way of Cuba. From Cuba the two cousins took a boat that dropped them in Tampa, Florida, but they were soon picked up by immigration officers and detained. Luckily for Joseph, he had an uncle (his mother's brother) living in New York whom he rang and who posted bail. He and Peter were then escorted from Florida up to New York where his uncle Bonventre offered to put them both up. Initially, Joseph stayed with his relatives, but after a few weeks he decided to move to a boarding house in Brooklyn's Williamsburg-Greenpoint section, which was heavily populated by Castellammarese who all knew the Bonanno name and, therefore, assured Joseph a warm welcome. Among these were heavyweights such as Stefano Magaddino (yet another of Joseph's cousins), and Gaspar DiGregorio, who was running a large bootlegging operation which he asked Joseph Bonanno to join. Bonanno didn't hesitate and immediately agreed. Nor was it long before he became a valuable member of the team, particularly because he was extremely successful in reorganizing the operation. At the same time, in 1926, Bonanno also became partners with his uncle Bonventre in a bakery. Joseph worked hard in both businesses, slowly but surely building up a reputation as someone who was going places. This reputation was only enhanced when Joseph met up with a long-time hero (and childhood acquaintance) of his from Sicily, Salvatore Maranzano:

> I found him irresistible, he found me refreshing. I was twenty-one years old, and he was about forty. He must have liked having a disciple around him. I liked being around a man of experience. He could talk to me on a high level, as he could with few others among the Castellammarese because they lacked schooling. With me, Maranzano could expand and elaborate and not stint in his vocabulary.[1]

Maranzano was a Mafiosi and would have a massive influence over organized crime in America. Soon he was setting up businesses all over New York, including a real estate company, an import-export operation and, of course, the obligatory bootlegging enterprise. Completely in awe of him, it wasn't long before Bonanno was in Maranzano's employ, traveling around the country inspecting his whisky stills. Bonanno then began carrying a gun. He needed it for protection and also, as he points out in his autobiography, occasionally he 'undertook missions for Maranzano that required the use of force.' Still Maranzano wasn't yet a 'made' member of the Castellammarese Family, that honor was later bestowed on him in 1929, when he attended a formal dinner to officially welcome him into the fold. Not long afterwards, Joseph Bonanno became involved in what would come to be known as the Castellammarese War; a vicious feud that ended with the slaying of his beloved leader as well as Maranzano's opponent, a pug-faced little man by the name of Giuseppe 'Joe the Boss' Masseria.

Giuseppe Masseria, at the age of forty-five, was the head of the most powerful crime Family in New York, a Family which at one time included among its members Peter 'the Clutching Hand' Morello, Frank Costello, Vito Genovese, Lucky Luciano and Joe Adonis. Masseria was an unlikely leader of men, being short and fat with bloated cheeks. Bonanno describes him as follows:

> Though he was known as 'Joe the Boss,' his insatiable appetite could have won him the nickname 'Joe the Glutton.' He attacked a plate of spaghetti as if he were a drooling mastiff. He had the table manners of a Hun.[2]

Despite his appearance, however, Masseria was a vicious killer with a reputation for always getting his own way. Masseria also had a vision of consolidating all the most powerful Families in New York under his overall direction, but there was one Family that resisted his plans, the Maranzanos, and it was this resistance that triggered an all-out war. By this point, in the early 1930s, Maranzano had become the boss of his own Family and Joseph Bonanno was his right-hand man. The Castellammarese War lasted for approximately a year-and-a-half, during which time there were casualties and fatalities on both sides, including Tom Reina (boss of the third most powerful Family in New York) and Peter Morello, Masseria's chief advisor. But the Maranzanos didn't make any real progress in the conflict until Charles 'Lucky' Luciano – one of Masseria's own men – decided to switch allegiances (see chapter on Luciano). According to Bonanno's memoirs, Maranzano let it be known that if, or rather when, Masseria was finally killed he would seek revenge on all Masseria's men, implying that their best option for survival was to cross over to enemy lines and betray their boss. The ruse appeared to work, for Luciano arranged to meet with Maranzano and a deal was worked out to the effect that he would kill Masseria in return for immunity. There was also another reason, perhaps a more acceptable motive, why Luciano wanted to see his boss dead. Being young and headstrong it is said that Luciano had grown irritated by Masseria's reluctance to

Bonanno always liked to give the impression that he had nothing to do with organized crime, but this 'Family Tree' chart, prepared for a 1963 US Senate crime investigation, clearly shows that the authorities thought otherwise.

change his ways, to look into the future and grab new opportunities. In his eyes, the best way forward would be to see Masseria into an early grave. Whichever version one believes (and the truth probably lies between the two), Luciano had Masseria killed on April 15, 1931 in the Nuova Villa Tammaro Restaurant.

With Masseria out of the way Maranzano, according to legend, declared himself 'boss of all bosses' and began throwing his weight around in a manner that quickly grew unacceptable. Far more dangerously, it is said he drew up a list of those men he thought were a threat to his supremacy; on that list was the name of Lucky Luciano.[3] Whether Luciano caught wind of this or whether he simply possessed second sight, the result was the same. On September 10, 1931, Joseph Bonanno's beloved boss was shot dead at his offices by four men posing as IRS officers.

In Maranzano's wake, his underboss Angelo Caruso was said to have no inclination to take his place as head of the Family. Instead, with the support of his cousin Stefano Magaddino, Joseph Bonanno was elected to the post:

> I think Italiano [Bonanno's opposition] got about seven votes to about three hundred for me. Bonanno was Father. Henceforth, what I said and what I decided would affect many people. I always had to keep in mind that my personal sentiments did not matter as much as the interests of the Family. I had lost the privilege of selfishness.[4]

Bonanno's first job as the new boss was to meet with Luciano and come to an agreement to settle their differences. Afterwards, other Family bosses realigned themselves to suit the new political landscape, recognizing Bonanno as one of the most powerful Family leaders in the whole of the country. At the same time, Bonanno approached his immediate family with the news that he was going to wed his long-time girlfriend, Fay Labruzzo. The couple were married at St Joseph's Church in Brooklyn on November 15, 1931. Just over a year later, Fay gave birth to a son who was christened Salvatore in honor of Joseph's late father.

Taking his responsibilities as the new boss of the Castellammarese very seriously, Joseph Bonanno, together with Lucky Luciano, now put into place what became known as the 'Commission,' a board of leading Mafiosi overseeing all the different crime factions to settle any disputes that might arise. The first Commission is said to have included the bosses of all five leading New York Families together with the boss of Chicago and that of Buffalo. Bonanno was also an astute enough businessman to know that his illegal earnings from bootlegging, numbers rackets, loan sharking and protection rackets needed to be hidden behind several legitimate enterprises on which he could pay tax and appear to be acting within the law. To this end he invested money in several ventures, becoming a partner or stockholder in the B&D Coat Co, together with another garment business, a funeral parlor and even a company that produced cheese – the Grande Cheese Company, which was located in Wisconsin.

For several years after Bonanno took over the leadership of his Family, relative peace reigned in New York, with each group operating their own businesses in their own territories. It was during this time that Bonanno concentrated on establishing his

Family's long-held traditions, traditions that he was at pains to point out were exceedingly close to his heart. He wrote in his autobiography that:

> All societies, whether the unit of cooperation be that of the family, the tribe, the city or the nation, use force, at some level, to enforce the rules of that society . . . In discussing the role of violence in my world I don't expect outsiders to condone or approve of the rules by which we lived. I would only ask the outsider to appreciate the context of our lives. The first step is to recognize that traditionally a Sicilian has a personal sense of justice. If a 'man of honor' is wronged it is up to him to redress that wrong personally . . . One of the inviolate rules of our old Tradition was that no Family member should fool around with another Family member's wife, or female relative. If a Family member discovered that his wife had gone to bed with another Family member, he was justified in killing him.'[5]

There were also countless other reasons for killing fellow and non-fellow Family members and soon enough several such cases occurred which, though not directly linked to Bonanno, gave him serious pause for thought.

On May 31, 1945, Vito Genovese, an early member of Lucky Luciano's gang when both had worked for Giuseppe 'Joe the Boss' Masseria, returned to the States after a period of temporary exile in Italy in order to stand trial for a murder that had been committed ten years previously. The case never actually came to court and Genovese was released. It was around this time, however, that Luciano was himself being deported back to Italy, prior to which he had bequeathed the leadership of his Family to Frank Costello. Genovese now sought to depose Costello and take his place at the head of the Luciano Family. Over the next few years there was considerable friction between and maneuvering within all five major Families in New York, with allegiances being made mostly in the name of survival. Joseph Bonanno made overtures towards Joe Profaci and Joe Magliocco – leaders of the Colombo Family – while Carlo Gambino (who was an up-and-coming young buck in the Mangano Family) was establishing links with Vito Genovese and Tommy Lucchese. Frank Costello, on the other hand, was veering towards Albert Anastasia – a man whom Bonanno often referred to as the 'Earthquake' owing to his fearsome temper. 'New York was a firecracker,' wrote Bonanno of this period, 'which could go off at any time. We conservatives on the Commission viewed these developments with dismay. The Commission was supposed to alleviate such discord, but things seemed to be getting increasingly out of control.'[6]

Nowhere was this more evident than in 1951 with the murder of Philip Mangano, brother of Vincent and joint leader of the Mangano tribe. Following his brother's death, Vincent then vanished into thin air – believed to have become the victim of what Sicilians call a 'white death,' that is death by disappearance. A meeting of the Commission was convened during which Albert Anastasia (according to Bonanno) stated that both the Mangano brothers had been plotting against him. The inference was clear; that Anastasia was behind both hits. Nevertheless, he was voted in as the

Claiming that he had been kidnapped, Bonanno disappeared the night before he was due to be questioned by a federal grand jury in 1964. He is pictured here talking to a news reporter when he reappeared and surrendered to the authorities in New York in May 1966.

new Mangano Family boss and thereafter took his place on the Commission.

During this period, Frank Costello allied himself as far as possible with Anastasia, which in turn made Costello's right-hand man, Willie Moretti, increasingly jealous. Moretti's behavior grew ever more erratic and eventually, on October 14, 1951, he was shot dead in New Jersey. But that wasn't the end of the scheming and plotting. Again according to Bonanno, he was asked to mediate between Tommy Lucchese and Frank Costello, who believed Lucchese was planning to assassinate Anastasia. Extraordinarily, Lucchese confessed that this was indeed what he wished to do, but only because he thought Anastasia was in turn plotting to kill him. Consequently, Bonanno advised Lucchese to throw himself on the mercy of Anastasia and beg his forgiveness, advice that Lucchese took to heart and acted upon swiftly. Bonanno had diffused a very tricky situation, but unrest still existed amongst the Families, the type of discord that would eventually erupt and see many men dead.

By the mid-1950s, despite all the earlier intrigue and the occasional murder, Joseph Bonanno was personally in a very comfortable position. Within New York's underworld he was highly respected, and he was a man of considerable property, owning houses in Brooklyn, on Long Island and in Arizona, as well as a mansion in New York State. He had a good marriage with three children – two sons and a daughter – and owned shares in an assortment of lucrative legal businesses, as well as earning substantial rewards from running various illegal gambling institutions.

In 1956 Bonanno threw a huge wedding for his eldest son, Salvatore, who was marrying Rosalie Profaci, niece of Joe Profaci (boss of the Colombo Family). Hundreds of people attended the ceremony and hundreds more attended the party at which Tony Bennett sang. But Bonanno's love for his blood family had a jealous mistress with which to contend – his first love was for his Mafia Family. How better to celebrate this sinister union than to trace its roots back in Sicily. Bonanno, along with his wife, Fay, took a trip to the old country in 1957. In his absence he left his cousin, Stefano Magaddino, in charge of the Family.

While in Italy, Bonanno met up with Lucky Luciano and several other Mafia heavyweights, and over a period of several days, they discussed Mafia matters arising on both sides of the Atlantic. In particular, it is believed they agreed on a set of ground rules for the import and distribution of heroin into and around the United States[7] – an NYPD report dated October 1963 states that one out of every three members of the Bonanno family had been arrested on narcotics' charges.

Also rumored to have been under discussion during these meetings was the assassination of Albert Anastasia who, despite being the boss of the Mangano Family, had become an increasing threat to the rest of the Mafiosi. Whatever the truth behind this suggestion, the fact remains that two weeks later, by the time Bonanno returned to America, Anastasia was dead, gunned down while having a haircut in Midtown Manhattan.

Erratic and psychopathic, Anastasia was a Bugsy Siegel without the charm. He had hurt and threatened so many people that, once it had happened, his violent end could be seen to have had a certain inevitability – even a certain justice – about it.[8]

Returning to the States, Bonanno insisted he knew nothing about the Anastasia murder, or what was to come next – a national meeting of all the major mob Families that was to be chaired by Joe Barbara (who was associated with the Bufalino crime Family from Pennsylvania) on his estate in Apalachin, New York.

In total, approximately 120 Family members from around the country attended the gathering at Apalachin, although Joseph Bonanno was noticeably absent. In his autobiography he states that, 'Although I knew none of the details, my instincts told me the peace, the Pax Bonanno, that I was so proud of having forged was on the verge of disintegration.' That being the case, he decided to stay away. After all, with Anastasia's death things did look increasingly unstable and, in the long run, Bonanno was proved right. The Apalachin conference was a disaster, though not for the reasons Bonanno had initially thought, for no sooner had the convention begun than it ground to a halt when police raided the estate and rounded up approximately sixty-three delegates.

The raid made headline news and forced the authorities (who had formerly, under the direction of J. Edgar Hoover, stated that there was no such thing as organized crime in America) to change their views and set up a 'Top Hoodlum Program.' One other consequence of Apalachin was that Joseph Bonanno now became a subject of intense interest for the FBI. Despite not having attended the conference, newspapers had named him (owing to a mix-up with a driving license) as one of the delegates. Suddenly, Bonanno, who had prided himself on keeping a low profile, was under intense pressure, and in 1959 he was indicted on charges of conspiracy to obstruct justice. The investigators hoped to uncover the reason why the Apalachin conference had been held. As luck would have it, however, Joseph Bonanno was never tried, for before his case came to court he suffered a massive heart attack and retired to Arizona in order to recuperate.

It is pehaps not surprising to learn, with the approach of the 1960s, that drugs had increasingly become the name of the Mafia game. On April 17, 1959, Vito Genovese was convicted of narcotics trafficking and sent to prison (where he would die a little less than ten years later). But this was the least of the Mafia's problems for, in 1961, things further disintegrated when internal warfare broke out within the Colombo Family (whose boss was still Joseph Profaci). The Gallo brothers, Albert, Joey[9] and Larry, headed the insurrection, and in turn sought the support of Carlo Gambino – now head of his own Family. On February 27, 1961, the Gallos kidnapped Joseph Profaci's brother, Frank, along with the Profaci underboss, Joseph Magliocco, who was a close friend of Bonanno's and one of Profaci's personal bodyguards. Profaci himself escaped capture and headed for Florida from where he negotiated a peaceful resolution, promising the Gallos a bigger share of the Family's profits. But as soon as the hostages were released, Profaci back-tracked. The Gallos were incensed and between fall 1961 and fall 1963 there ensued a bloody tit-for-tat war as the two sides vied for power. All through this, Joseph Bonanno sided with Profaci, but as he points out in his memoirs, not many others did. 'Profaci was having trouble with the Gallos,' he wrote. 'The Gallos were close to Gambino. Gambino was very close to Lucchese. Lucchese was flirting with Magaddino. The center was not holding.' As a result the Commission tried to pressurize Joseph Profaci into resigning, but he declined. Not long afterwards, however, on June 2, 1962, Profaci died of cancer. His second-in-command, Joe Magliocco, was then voted in as boss. This might have been a fresh start for all concerned, but the Gallos pursued their grievances in the certain knowledge that they now had the backing of the majority of the Commission.

It is around this period in 1963 that Joseph Bonanno is thought to have plotted the murder of three of his biggest rivals, Tommy Lucchese, Carlo Gambino and his own cousin, Stefano Magaddino, whom he increasingly distrusted. Sources believe he passed his plans through Joe Magliocco who would consequently enjoy equal control of the Commission with Bonanno himself. Magliocco is then thought to have suggested Joseph Colombo for the contract, but Colombo apparently had second thoughts. Instead of carrying out the hits, he went to Carlo Gambino and spilt the beans, sparking off what later became known as 'The Bonanno War.' There are different versions of these events, some maintaining that it was Magliocco who decided to have Gambino, Magaddino and Lucchese taken out, but the end result was the same – all-out war. Before this kicked off, however, Joseph Magliocco died of a heart attack on December 28, 1963. In his place, Joseph Colombo was nominated head of the family. This then gave Lucchese and Gambino a strong ally on the Commission.

According to Joseph Bonanno's memoirs, he was by now feeling increasingly disillusioned with his fellow mobsters on the Commission and decided to take a back-seat role. He traveled to Canada with his wife to set up a new business, the Saputo Cheese Company. So fed up was he of the internecine squabbling back in New York that he decided to settle in Montreal and applied for a Canadian immigration card. Only a few weeks later, however, he was arrested for not disclosing his criminal history on the official documentation forms for immigration. In fact, the only criminal conviction he had was for a minor violation of a wages-and-hour law to do with one of his clothing businesses. Nonetheless, the Canadians kept Bonanno in prison for three months before deporting him back to the States. Clearly, they didn't want him living in their country.

In October 1964, having returned to New York, Bonanno faced further problems. He was subpoenaed to appear before a federal grand jury which was conducting an investigation into organized crime. Bonanno had already faced one of these federal juries, at which time he had taken the Fifth. Bonanno also faced increasing internal warfare within his own Family, certain members of which were set on deposing him in favor of Gaspar DiGregorio. The night before Bonanno was due to appear in court things came to a head when he was supposedly kidnapped by his cousin Stefano Magaddino's brother and son, Peter and Nino. But there were certain Mafia people who believed Bonanno had orchestrated the whole event himself, either to gain sympathy from within his own Family or to confuse government officials who had been monitoring his movements. Bonanno, unsurprisingly, stuck to his own version of events and said that he had been taken to Buffalo where he was kept in a farmhouse for weeks on end. Eventually, Stefano Magaddino released Bonanno – after what type of agreement was struck, no one can be certain – and Bonanno returned to his residence in Arizona where he hid out for a further few months. Once again, this story differs from that which was circulating in New York at that time. The New York version was that Bonanno was hiding out in Haiti where he had several gambling concessions arranged with the blessing of the then president, Papa Doc Duvalier.

By 1965, Gaspar DiGregorio appeared to have established himself as the 'official' boss of the Bonanno Family, no one being able to pin down Joseph Bonanno's true whereabouts. Having taken over the leader's mantel, DiGregorio began handing a lot of power over to Paul Sciacca, whom Bonanno described in extremely unflattering terms as a 'nobody.'

Joseph Bonanno didn't resurface again until late in 1965, making contact with his sons, if not with his other, larger Family. Then, on January 28, 1966, at a house on Troutman Street in Brooklyn, a meeting was convened between those who supported Joseph Bonanno and those who were with Gaspar DiGregorio to see if a compromise could be worked out. The meeting turned out to be nothing but a set-up. Gaspar DiGregorio never showed up, but a handful of his gunmen did. They began firing on Bonanno's men, including his son, Salvatore. Miraculously, no one was killed, but as a result of Troutman Street, the situation within the Family grew even worse.

Having kept a low profile for almost two years, Bonanno officially resurfaced on May 17, 1966 when he surrendered himself to the authorities at the Foley Square courthouse. Released on bail, he went to stay with his son Salvatore on Long Island, from where he began to try and re-establish himself as head of the Family.

The first casualty of the ensuing war was one of DiGregorio's top gunmen, Frank Mari, who was wounded by a Bonanno hitman while out walking in Brooklyn. Other casualties included two of Bonanno's men, Vincent Cassese and Vincent Garofalo (again both survived) and three associates of DiGregorio, Thomas D'Angelo, Jimmy D'Angelo and Francisco Terelli, who were all killed outright while they were dining in a restaurant. In March 1968 another leading light in the DiGregorio camp, Peter Crociata, was shot in the neck, although he survived the attack. On March 11, the same year, one of Salvatore Bonanno's bodyguards was shot and killed. And so the war continued with countless others succumbing to the bullet until finally on February 6, 1969, Thomas Zummo, a DiGregorio supporter, was shot to death in Queens. At this point, both sides decided the violence had to stop. Bonanno was concerned about all the adverse publicity the killings were attracting and DiGregorio, who had already suffered several heart attacks, was now diagnosed as having cancer.

With the war over, it soon became clear that Joseph Bonanno was no longer

When this photograph was taken at his home in Tucson, Arizona, in 1977, Bonanno had retired as head of his Family, but he was not beyond the long arm of the law. He was eventually jailed for five years in 1980 for conspiracy to obstruct justice.

interested in continuing as head of the Family. In his memoirs he puts his disillusion down to the fact that during the 1960s and 1970s 'my Tradition in America had become a gross parody of itself.' He also suffered his third heart attack, after which it is said he called the Family together and announced that he was going to retire to his home in Tucson, Arizona.

Joseph Bonanno's cousin, Stefano Magaddino, died of natural causes in 1974 having ruled over the Buffalo branch of the crime Family for many, many years. Practically all of Joseph Bonanno's rivals and enemies eventually died before he did, including DiGregorio, who succumbed to his cancer on June 11, 1970, Tommy Lucchese who died of a cerebral hemorrhage in 1967, Carlo Gambino, Paul Sciacca and Joseph Colombo.

But Bonanno's life in Arizona was not all easy-going, either. Over the next five years several government departments continued to investigate him, resulting in a conviction on a charge of conspiracy to obstruct justice in 1980. 'The trial proper lasted from April to July 1980,' wrote Bonanno. 'I had to put up with all sorts of vile accusations, fully knowing that I could not speak on my own behalf. I could have taken the stand, of course, but it would have been suicide. With my rotten English, the prosecutors would have chopped up my words and made me seem foolish.' Convicted, Bonanno was sentenced to five years in prison. It was a terrible blow to a man who had deluded himself all his life that he'd been no part of organized crime. But an even heavier blow was shortly to befall him, for just before he entered prison his wife, Fay, died.

Joseph Bonanno was eventually freed from jail in 1986. He retired for a second time and lived a further sixteen years, before dying at the ripe old age of ninety-seven on May 11, 2002. At the end of his autobiography he wrote:

I have learned that true power comes from self control.

I have learned that true strength comes from a clear conscience.

I have learned that true wealth comes from a good family and good friends.

These fine sentiments seem fitting words to write towards the end of one's life, but perhaps less than convincing coming from one of the most notorious Mafia bosses in history.

[1] *A Man of Honor: The Autobiography of Joseph Bonanno*, Simon & Schuster, 1983.

[2] Ibid.

[3] Bonanno later reveals that Luciano believed Vincent Coll had been hired by Maranzano to carry out the hit.

[4] *A Man of Honor: The Autobiography of Joseph Bonanno*, Simon & Schuster, 1983.

[5] Ibid.

[6] Ibid.

[7] In his autobiography Bonanno states on more than one occasion that he never had any dealings in the narcotics' trade, that it was against his tradition. However what he says must be taken with a pinch of salt, and given that there were huge profits to be made in drug trafficking, it is more likely than ever that he was involved.

[8] *Little Man: Meyer Lansky and the Gangster Life*: Robert Lacey, Little Brown Inc, 1991.

[9] Joey 'Crazy Joe' Gallo was one of those whom the police identified as being the possible assassin of Albert Anastasia – which in turn would explain how he became a 'made' member within the Colombo Family.

AL CAPONE

Scarface

'Once in the racket, you're always in the racket.'

Al Capone, quoted in the *Philadelphia Public Ledger*, 1929

If you were to ask anyone to name one famous gangland mobster, either living or dead, Al 'Scarface' Capone would undoubtedly be the first name on everyone's lips. Forever linked with the St Valentine's Day massacre and with bootlegging, speakeasies and brothels, more films have been made about Al Capone than about any other mobster in history. Rod Steiger played him in the 1959 classic *Al Capone*, Kevin Costner painstakingly hunted him down in *The Untouchables* (1987) and Capone's story even inspired Billy Wilder to give *Some Like it Hot* (1959) a gangster-led subplot. Capone's popular and often romanticized movie image is, however, far removed from the sinister truth behind this semi-mythical figure.

Alphonse Capone was born on January 17, 1899 in Brooklyn, New York. His parents, Gabriel and Teresa, had emigrated from Naples in Italy several years earlier and both were granted American citizenship in 1906.

The area in which the young Capone grew up was a rough, yet close-knit, vibrant neighborhood, mostly populated by Italian immigrants. Street markets vied for space with pawnshops, dance halls and tenement buildings, and the skyline above the dock area was dominated by the Williamsburg Bridge.

Capone's early schooling showed him to be a boy with some promise, and up until the sixth grade he maintained a respectable B-average, but at the age of fourteen he was reprimanded for truancy and, losing his temper, he struck out at a teacher. He was swiftly expelled. As luck (or fate) would have it, it was also around this time that the young Capone fell under the influence of a Neapolitan gangster by the name of Johnny Torrio. Torrio was seventeen years Capone's senior and belonged to a notorious Manhattan gang called the Five Pointers. Soon Capone was running errands for Torrio; ' "I looked on Johnny as my advisor and father, said Capone in middle age, "and the party who made it possible for me to get my start." '[1]

By the time he was eighteen, Capone was working for another gangster, Frankie Yale, who hired Capone to work in his bar, the Harvard Inn. The job included using his fists and, on occasions, a gun to rid the club of unwanted customers, but even with Yale's backing, things did not always go Capone's way. One evening a local thug by the name of Frank Galluccio dropped in to the Harvard Inn for a drink with his sister. Legend has it that Capone made an offensive remark towards the young girl, a remark Galluccio couldn't let pass. Picking up a knife, he slashed Capone's face three times, leaving Capone scarred for life and earning him the nickname 'Scarface.'

This disfigurement seems to have had little effect on Capone's romantic aspirations as, early in 1918, he met and fell in love with a young Irish girl called Mae Coughlin. The two were married on December 18, and the following year Mae gave birth to their only child, Albert Francis, nicknamed Sonny. Johnny Torrio, Capone's mentor and best friend, was immediately named Sonny's godfather.

Capone now had a family to support, a task he took very seriously. Handing in his notice at the Harvard Inn, he went to work as a bookkeeper for a construction company. At the same time, Johnny Torrio had decided to move to Chicago where his uncle, James 'Big Jim' Colosimo, owned several lucrative businesses. It soon made sense for Capone to join his mentor; after all, he was never going to make much money working as a bookkeeper, and his criminal activities had led to the police now suspecting him of being involved in a murder.

The mainstay of Big Jim's business ventures was a club called Colosimo's Café, which was a melting pot for the famous and infamous of the city. Gangsters mixed with politicians, hustlers, movie stars and businessmen; Al Jolson frequented the place, as did John Barrymore. But Johnny Torrio had plans of his own and while helping his uncle run his businesses he began setting up clubs of his own, the most notorious of which was known as the Four Deuces. The Deuces contained gambling rooms, a saloon, a large brothel and a sealed-off area in the basement that was to become synonymous with the torture and death of errant associates and business rivals. It was into this shady, yet glamorous world that Al Capone stepped in late 1919.

Initially Capone's duties didn't amount to much. He was a bartender, a bouncer, a chauffeur and bodyguard, but not long after Capone moved to Chicago there occurred an historic change in the law that spawned an orgy of illegal and violent activity. At 12:01 a.m. on January 17, 1920, the 18th Amendment of the National Prohibition Law brought the Volstead Act (named after the Republican congressman, Andrew Volstead of Minnesota) into force, effectively putting an end to the legal brewing, distilling and distribution of alcohol.

To some, Prohibition spelt disaster, but to the likes of Johnny Torrio, it represented the most profitable business opportunity ever to come his way. Torrio was certain he could 'persuade' the Chicago police to turn a blind eye to his bootlegging activities and in some cases even enlist them to protect his business interests. Four months after the Prohibition Act became law, on May 11, Torrio's uncle, 'Big Jim' Colosimo was gunned down in the vestibule of Colosimo's Café. Rumors spread that the man behind the execution was none other than Johnny Torrio himself. The story was that Torrio had become infuriated at his uncle's preference for old-time rackets such as prostitution over the new business of bootlegging. With 'Big Jim' out of the way, Torrio immediately began expanding his empire. This was good news for Capone, who soon took over the management of the Four Deuces and was also rewarded with a 25 per cent share of all the profits from Torrio's many brothels. Torrio further promised Capone a 50 per cent share in all the profits from the bootlegging business as soon as it started earning revenue. It was not long before Capone was banking substantial amounts of money, which allowed him to buy a large

Posing proudly like any other father and son, Capone and his son, Sonny, are pictured here in 1928, by which time Capone's bootlegging business had made him a very rich man.

house in Chicago. The house immediately became home to various members of the Capone family. Capone's father had died back in 1920 after suffering a heart attack, but a family posse, including Al's mother, sisters and two of his brothers, Frank and Ralph, were soon relocated to Chicago.

In 1923 Johnny Torrio decided to take a long holiday and set off on a tour of Europe, leaving Capone in sole charge of their combined business ventures. Torrio's absence provided Capone with the ideal opportunity to further his own interests. He set up his head office in a building known as the Hawthorne Inn, in a suburb of Chicago called Cicero. On Torrio's return in 1924, Cicero was due to hold key local elections and it was around this time that Torrio and Capone were approached by representatives of Joseph Z. Klenha, the presiding mayor, with an offer neither man could resist. If they could ensure a Klenha victory, the authorities would turn a blind eye to all their business enterprises, with the exception of the brothels. Capone and Torrio's men were set to work intimidating and bribing not only Klenha's opposition, but also the voters. Several people, including a Democratic candidate, a policeman and a Democratic campaign worker, were wounded or received severe beatings but, ironically, it was Capone who suffered the greatest loss when, in a shoot-out outside

a polling station on Twenty-Second Street in Cicero, Frank Capone was gunned
down by police.

The funeral that followed was a grand affair by anyone's standards, and was
attended by some of the biggest names from the underworld including 'Dago Mike'
Carozzo, Julian 'Potatoes' Kaufman and Hymie Weiss. The *Chicago Tribune* ran the
following article:

> Before noon the entire interior of the [Capone] house was banked with a
> profusion of blossoms. When every nook and cranny from the kitchen to the
> attic had been fairly choked with these delicate tributes, they were heaped up
> on the front porch and hung from the balcony . . . Finally the lack of space
> made it necessary to festoon the trees and lamp posts in front of the house with
> wreaths, immortelles and hanging baskets.[2]

Despite his brother's violent and untimely death, Al Capone saw no reason to
change his ways or curtail his criminal activities – quite the opposite, in fact. With the
successful re-election of Klenha, Torrio and Capone were able to set up several
gambling houses in Cicero, fully confident that the police would not attempt to close
them down. Perhaps this over-confidence in his own invulnerability and a desire to
provide a show of strength following his brother's death were what led to what can
only be described as a foolhardy display of violence. Capone committed murder in
full view of several witnesses.

Jake 'Greasy Thumb' Guzik was an old friend of Capone's from his days at the
Four Deuces. Not given to violence, Guzik was best known as a brilliant accountant.
On May 8, 1924 a petty thug by the name of Joe Howard insulted and slapped Guzik
in a bar-room brawl. Unable to defend himself, Guzik went straight to Capone,
whose reaction was excessive and surprising, even given his predilection for violence.
He followed Howard to a saloon bar down the street from the Four Deuces and,
when he was close enough, shot Howard in the head at point-blank range.

Three witnesses were questioned by police who subsequently named Capone as
their chief suspect. The following day, the *Chicago Tribune* ran a photograph of
Capone saying he was wanted for questioning over the death of Joe Howard. If the
police thought they had cornered their man, however, they were sorely mistaken for
by the time of the first inquest, two of the chief witnesses said they were unable to
identify Capone and a third witness had gone missing. Eventually Capone handed
himself in to the authorities, but he denied all knowledge of Torrio, Guzik or Howard.
When the final inquest took place a few days later, the jury concluded that Joe
Howard had been shot by an unknown white, male assailant.

Free to resume his illegal activities, Capone returned to Cicero and to Johnny
Torrio with another, much larger, battle now looming on the horizon. This showdown
involved the North Side Chicago gang leader Dean O'Banion.

When Prohibition first become law, Torrio had sat down with all the chief gang
leaders in Chicago to try to carve out mutually agreeable terms for the smooth
operation of their individual businesses. O'Banion's specialty was running illegal

whisky down from Canada, whereas Torrio was more interested in beer. For a long time both leaders kept out of each other's areas and several other gangs were also given a share of the trade. Eventually, however, Torrio's carefully balanced division of the trade began to disintegrate, with one gang undercutting another and/or invading another gang's turf with the sole purpose of flooding the market with cheaper and cheaper alcohol. It was a recipe for a disaster that was to bring down O'Banion and see Torrio imprisoned.

O'Banion had grown increasingly irritated by Capone and Torrio's supremacy in Cicero. He had lent the two men several of his 'heavies' for their campaign to ensure Klenha was elected mayor, but hadn't received the courtesy of any payment. Bearing this and other grievances in mind, O'Banion decided to set up Capone and Torrio. His act of treachery was to take place on May 19, 1924. As luck would have it, Capone was in hiding, having just killed Joe Howard, but Torrio was not so fortunate and fell straight into O'Banion's trap. O'Banion told Torrio that he wanted to retire and sell his liquor-running business. In a gesture of kindness he said he would help Torrio in one last alcohol shipment, but the deal was rigged because O'Banion already knew that the police planned to raid this particular consignment. He also knew that, because this would be Torrio's second offence as a bootlegger, he would receive a prison sentence, whereas it would be a first offence for O'Banion and he would not go to jail. Torrio was arrested (though shortly afterwards he was released on bail), along with many other gang members, and while he was incensed at O'Banion's daring to double cross him, he would have his revenge. On November 10, 1924, while O'Banion was arranging flowers (he owned a florist shop), three men entered the premises and gunned him down.

A huge funeral was held, attended by all the Mafia bosses *including* Torrio and Capone, both of whom pretended to look grief-stricken. Later Capone was to tell the press:

Deany was all right and he was getting along to begin with better than he had any right to expect. But like everyone else his head got away from his hat. Johnny Torrio had taught O'Banion all he knew and then O'Banion grabbed some of the best guys we had and decided to be the boss of the booze racket in Chicago. What a chance! O'Banion had a swell route to make it touch for us and he did. His job had been to smooth the coppers and we gave him a lot of authority with the booze and beer buyers. When he broke away, for a while it wasn't so good. He knew the ropes and got running us ragged. It was his funeral.[3]

No one was charged with Dean O'Banion's murder, but no sooner was the funeral over than Hymie Weiss took over as boss of the North Siders, swearing revenge on Torrio and Capone.

Johnny Torrio, still out on bail while awaiting trial, decided to take a short trip round America, once again leaving Capone in sole charge of their business. With Torrio away, Weiss attempted to assassinate Capone, but only succeeded in wounding Capone's chauffeur, Sylvester Barton. When Torrio returned to Chicago to face trial, fearful of being killed by Weiss, he pleaded guilty to all the charges laid against him, hoping that he would be safe in prison. His plan might have worked had the judge in the case not given Torrio five days in which he could go home and sort out his affairs before sentence was passed. Seeing a window of opportunity, Weiss planned a second assassination attempt on those he saw responsible for O'Banion's murder. He succeeded in badly wounding Johnny Torrio, but didn't manage to kill him and eventually Torrio, having recovered in hospital, served nine months in Lake County Jail at Waukegan.

Perhaps the attempt on his life had a salutary effect on the gangster or perhaps he could only foresee more bloodshed and internecine warfare for which he was rapidly losing his taste, but shortly after entering prison Johnny Torrio announced to Capone that he wanted to retire. He intended to divest himself of all his business interests. Effectively, this left Capone in command of a huge empire with a turnover of tens of millions of dollars, but it also left him to deal with the growing anarchy among the rival gangs, none of whom trusted each other and all of whom were quite willing to stab each other in the back. For Capone to succeed he would have to stamp his authority on Chicago like never before. Shortly after he took over the reins of power, however, he was involved in another murder and was forced to go into hiding.

William H. McSwiggin was one of the toughest prosecutors working on State

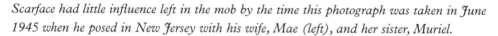

Scarface had little influence left in the mob by the time this photograph was taken in June 1945 when he posed in New Jersey with his wife, Mae (left), and her sister, Muriel.

Attorney Robert E. Crowe's staff. Capone maintained that McSwiggin was his close friend. Shortly after Capone took over from Johnny Torrio, he met with McSwiggin at the Hawthorne Inn. Capone never divulged the nature of the conversation, but it seemed to confirm Capone's friendship with the State Attorney's prosecutor. Their friendship, however, would not be allowed to stand in the way of Capone's business. A few days after the meeting, McSwiggin met up with a handful of his Irish friends, including two brothers by the name of Myles and Klondike O'Donnell and another man by the name of Jim Doherty. All three were minor figures in the Irish underworld, but McSwiggin had grown up with these hoodlums, as they had all been childhood friends, and the friendship had lasted even though they were now on opposite sides of the law.

The small group set out for an evening's drinking in Cicero, finally ending up in a place called the Pony Inn. For months Capone had been trailing the O'Donnells in the hope of finishing them off. They had been damaging his beer operation by undercutting his prices, which not only deprived him of income, but also showed him up in front of his other business associates. As soon as Capone heard that his prey were drinking at the Pony Inn, he equipped himself and a group of his triggermen with guns and set out to eliminate them. Parking outside the Pony, Capone didn't have long to wait before the O'Donnells, Doherty *and* McSwiggin appeared. The resulting bloodshed was terrible; both Doherty and McSwiggin suffered horrific injuries, but neither O'Donnell brother was hit. The Irishmen bundled both Doherty and McSwiggin into the back of their car, hoping that they could get them to safety and find a doctor to attend to their wounds. Before the car reached Klondike's apartment, however, both Doherty and McSwiggin were dead. The bodies were dumped in a remote roadside area and both brothers now fled Chicago. They weren't the only ones to leave town. Capone, realizing he had shot a state prosecutor, also disappeared for three months.

Although convinced that Capone was responsible for these latest executions, the police could garner no direct evidence on which to charge him. Instead, under Crowe's direction, they concentrated their efforts on raiding Capone's many businesses. They smashed up his nightclubs, his slot-machine franchises, roulette wheels and crap tables as well as hundreds of thousands of barrels of alcohol. They arrested prostitutes and one establishment, having first been ransacked by the police, was later burnt to the ground by a rival gang. Capone lost hundreds of thousands of dollars in revenue, but the police's biggest coup was the discovery and confiscation of several of Capone's ledgers. In his absence (the police had searched for Capone as far afield as New York) Capone was charged with violations against the Prohibition Act.

Unlike Capone, the O'Donnells were captured and charged to testify before a grand jury investigating the death of William McSwiggin. Unwilling to admit they were present during the shoot-out, they said that they were nowhere near the scene. They denied all knowledge of how McSwiggin and Doherty's bodies had ended up dumped in the middle of nowhere. Their story seemed to satisfy the authorities (though some said the O'Donnells had bribed their way out of trouble), and both men were released.

For Capone, the outcome was more complicated. Having gone into hiding, he reappeared some time later in Indiana announcing that he was ready to turn himself over to State Attorney Crowe. He claimed that he was entirely innocent of the Doherty/McSwiggin murders, and that it would only take a short time to prove this. He was arrested and forced to appear before Justice Lynch in Chicago but walked free because, as Assistant State Attorney George E. Gormon noted, there was not enough evidence to secure a conviction.

On Capone's return, rather than keeping a low profile after his near-imprisonment, he and Hymie Weiss resumed their very public war against one another. The first two assassination attempts occurred in August 1926 and were made by Capone against Weiss, but miraculously the latter escaped. Strike number three was subsequently perpetrated by Weiss against Capone. It took place at the Hawthorne Inn, but Capone was as lucky as his rival and survived the attack. Capone's next move was to try for peace talks, but these came to nothing. Finally, on October 11, while returning to his office on State Street, Hymie Weiss (together with two of his henchmen) was gunned down and killed by assailants who had rented some rooms opposite. Once again, Capone denied any involvement in the execution, and despite the police suspecting the whole set-up was down to him alone, they had no direct evidence linking him to the murders.

With his most dangerous rival now but a distant memory, Capone initiated a second round of peace talks. This time they were to involve not just one or two gang leaders, but every mobster-boss in the Chicago area. Like Johnny Torrio before him, Capone wanted all these underworld bosses to operate side by side without constantly believing they were going to be killed. There were enough rich pickings for everyone and after several days negotiating, a treaty was drawn up and agreed upon.

The treaty lasted a grand total of seventy days, only to be broken with the murder of a beer runner named Hilary Clements who had encroached on rival (Saltis-McErlane) territory. In retaliation, and to show that this type of execution should not have occurred without his consent, Capone ordered the death of two Saltis-McErlane men, Lefty Koncil and Charlie 'Big Hayes' Hubacek. But the bloodshed didn't stop there. Still smarting over the death of their beloved boss, Dean O'Banion, and frustrated by the constraints of the new Capone treaty, the new O'Banionites decided enough was enough.

Theodore 'the Greek' Anton was one of Capone's dearest friends. He owned a restaurant and one winter's night while dining there, Capone witnessed the kidnap of his host by two O'Banionites. Later, Anton's body was found covered in quicklime; it was obvious from its condition that he had been tortured prior to death. Capone was inconsolable and, predictably, vowed revenge.

First, however, there was the small matter of yet another mayoral election. Capone was supporting the Republican William 'Big Bill' Thompson against the present incumbent Mayor Dever, and to this end employed every means possible to secure a win for his man. It is ironic that the first killing during the campaign was not actually planned by Capone although he was the one who reaped most benefit from it.

Politically, the O'Banionites were on the same side as Capone, through their support of Big Bill. Schemer Drucci had taken over from Hymie Weiss as O'Banionite leader and, in pursuit of their campaign for the election of Big Bill, Drucci and a few of his henchmen burst in to State Attorney Crowe's offices (Crowe was a Dever man). Failing to find Crowe, they attacked his secretary instead. On leaving the building, the police attempted to apprehend this group of thugs, and in the ensuing brawl, Drucci was shot four times and killed. Capone could not have been more pleased; yet another O'Banionite boss[4] had been murdered and he hadn't had to lift a finger.

Capone's luck was running high. Big Bill was returned to office and with his man in place, Capone now had free run of the city. Business could not have been better but despite, or perhaps because of, this Capone still had many enemies eager to see him dead. One such rival was Joseph Aiello, the head of a large Mafia family. Aiello spread the word that he would pay $50,000 to anyone able to assassinate Capone. Suddenly four freelance hitmen appeared in Chicago, only to be unceremoniously dispatched by Capone's own henchmen. The Aiellos then tried poisoning their target, but this plot failed miserably. More freelance assassins were hired, but no one seemed able to touch Capone. Eventually, the police arrested Aiello on suspicion of attempted murder. Having been taken down to the station, someone tipped Capone off that his arch-rival was there. Suddenly a fleet of cars appeared outside the station building. When Aiello eventually obtained his release, he refused to venture out into the street as he knew he'd be gunned down. Instead, he turned to the police and begged them for protection. But his pleas fell on deaf ears and he was told in no uncertain terms to flee Chicago, better still the country. Surprisingly, Aiello took the advice of the authorities and, along with his brothers Tony and Dominic, he decamped to New Jersey.[5]

Al Capone now turned his attention to a different enemy, his one-time friend and former employer from his days as a youth in New York, Frankie Yale. Since 1926, Capone had been building up his bootlegging business not just in Chicago and its satellite suburbs, but further afield in places like Detroit, St Louis and Philadelphia. It was Yale's job to oversee the shipments from Canada to Long Island then deliver them to Chicago, but the only trouble was that consignments were being hijacked on a regular basis and Capone couldn't rule out the suspicion that Yale was double-crossing him.

On July 1, 1927, Frankie Yale was having a drink in a local speakeasy when the barman said there was a phone call for him in one of the booths. Whatever it was that Yale heard on the other end of the line sent him scurrying out to his car. He drove away at top speed, but his vehicle was intercepted by another and penned in on Forty-Fourth Street. In a matter of seconds Yale's body was riddled with bullets.

For years, bootlegging remained the mainstay of Capone's very lucrative business, but he was well aware that at some point he would have to diversify, especially if Prohibition was ever repealed. Capone chose to add to his business ventures by going into racketeering.

A 'racketeer' may be the boss of a supposedly legitimate business association; he may be a labor union organizer; he may pretend to be one, or the other, or both; or he may be just a journeyman thug.

Whether he is a gunman who has imposed himself upon some union as its leader, or whether he is a business association organizer, his methods are the same; by throwing a few bricks into a few windows, an incidental and perhaps accidental murder, he succeeds in organizing a group of small businessmen into what he calls a protective association. He then proceeds to collect what fees and dues he likes, to impose what fines suit him, regulates prices and hours of work, and in various ways undertakes to boss the outfit to his own profit.

Any merchant who doesn't come in or who comes in and doesn't stay in and continue to pay tribute, is bombed, slugged or otherwise intimidated.[6]

Slowly but surely Capone began to take over the majority of Chicago's racketeering business, until some government officials reckoned he controlled 70 per cent of the overall market. But there was one fly in the ointment; the new O'Banionite boss 'Bugs' Moran. Ever since Moran had taken overall control of the North Siders gang, he had made it his mission to hijack as many of Capone's liquor deliveries as possible. He also attacked several saloons that were purchasing Capone's beer and began to encroach on the core of Capone's racketeering business. Enough was enough.

Capone took a holiday in Miami from where he began phoning his old friend Jake Guzik back in Chicago. According to telephone records, the conversations were lengthy but suddenly, on February 11, 1929, the phone calls stopped.

On February 13 'Bugs' Moran received a phone call asking him if he wanted to purchase a truckload of whisky at the knockdown price of $57 per case. Moran couldn't refuse and so it was arranged that the deal should take place the following morning at a garage warehouse at 2122 North Clark Street. On February 14, St Valentine's Day, Moran set off to do business but, as chance would have it, on his way there his car was sideswiped by a truck. The accident made him late for the appointment. Meanwhile, at the warehouse, seven of Moran's men sat waiting for their boss to arrive when what looked like a police car containing three uniformed officers and two plain-clothes detectives, pulled up outside. Believing it to be a police raid, Moran's men did everything the officers asked, lining up against a back wall with their hands raised above their heads. In barely two minutes it is estimated that over 150 bullets were fired directly at Moran's henchmen. Six of them were killed outright, but the seventh was still breathing when the 'officers' left the building. 'Bugs' Moran, the main target for the hit, eventually arrived for the meeting, but when he saw the police car parked outside he, like his men, thought it was a

A photograph of a relaxed Al Capone enjoying the sunshine with his mother, Teresa, on the dock of his Florida mansion in the mid-1940s.

legitimate raid. He drove swiftly away, little realizing at the time that his collision with the truck had saved his life. Finally, the real police arrived at the scene. They found Frank Gusenburg (who had been shot fourteen times) still breathing. The officers asked Frank to tell them who had done this to him and his friends, but Frank wouldn't talk. His last words were said to be, 'I ain't no copper.'

The St Valentine's Day massacre, as it soon become known, shocked even the violence-hardened citizens of Chicago who, together with the Association of Commerce, the City Council and the State Attorney's office, put together a $100,000 reward for the arrest and conviction of the killers. Naturally, no one came forward to name Capone, who was still in Miami at the time of the shootings. A man by the name of Jack McGurn was arrested and charged on the evidence of a witness who identified him as being one of the five 'officers' who had entered the garage. Despite this witness, however, under Illinois law if a defendant demands a trial at four separate court hearings and the prosecutors fail to meet these demands, then the case must be dropped. Amazingly, this is precisely what occurred. By December 2,

McGurn was a free man. By this time the police had decided that rather than being one of the five assassins at the garage, he was most likely the man who had organized the whole operation.

Capone returned from Miami seemingly oblivious to the political furor that had occurred after the massacre. More than ever before, government officials were now determined to bring Capone down. Capone, on the other hand, had more pressing things on his mind; namely three men by the name of John Scalise, Albert Anselmi and Joe Giunta, all of whom Capone believed had been disloyal. On May 7, the three men were invited to a dinner held by Capone at the Hawthorne Inn. As was the old Sicilian tradition – 'Hospitality before Execution' – Capone treated his guests to a sumptuous meal, one they all appreciated. Immediately afterwards the three of them were beaten (later the coroner said there was hardly an area of their bodies that was not covered in bruises or suffered broken bones), before being shot through the back of the head.

Not long after this, Capone was arrested in Philadelphia for carrying a concealed weapon. Some have suggested that it was his wish to be imprisoned because he was growing tired of staying one step ahead of his rivals and needed a break. Whatever the case Capone was sent to jail, during which time the Internal Revenue Service under a man named Eliot Ness – a twenty-six-year-old University of Chicago graduate – began an investigation into Capone's business activities. Progress was incredibly slow, and at one point it seemed they would find nothing of any consequence, until a man by the name of Frank J. Wilson discovered a package in a dusty filing cabinet which contained three ledgers that had been confiscated from Capone's property in 1926, after the McSwiggin murder. It was the moment everyone had been waiting for and a triumph for the IRS.

In 1931 Al Capone was charged on two counts of tax evasion and one count of violating the Prohibition Act. If convicted on all three charges, Capone could have faced a thirty-four-year prison sentence. Bearing this in mind, he tried to bargain with the prosecutors, saying that he would plead guilty if they would reduce his sentence. But just before Capone was to enter his plea, Judge James H. Wilkerson informed him that there was going to be no bargaining when it came to passing sentence. On hearing this, Capone withdrew his guilty plea. The trial was then scheduled to begin on October 6.

Given the evidence stacked against him and the fact that Capone was used to persuading people to act in his best interests, it was hardly surprising that the summer before the trial began, he and his men began intimidating and bribing all twelve members of the jury. Had James H. Wilkerson not been such an astute judge of character this plan might have worked. As it was, on the opening day of the trial Wilkerson openly swapped juries with another trial starting the same day. Capone's plans were scuppered and it was only a matter of time before the axe fell.

On October 24, Capone was sentenced to eleven years in prison together with fines totaling $80,000. Initially he was sent to the US Penitentiary in Atlanta (it was here that Capone was diagnosed with syphilis) where he managed to establish a privileged lifestyle thanks to his money and to influential friends and acquaintances. Johnny Torrio visited him in jail as did fellow hoodlums Dutch Schultz and Lucky Luciano, but this fairly comfortable existence was not to last long. Someone reported Capone to the Justice Department, accusing him of taking advantage of the prison system. As a consequence, Capone was shipped out to Alcatraz where a much tougher regime was in operation and where only family members were allowed to visit him. Cut off from the outside world and unable to buy a more comfortable lifestyle, Capone served out his remaining sentence which, due to good behavior, was reduced to a little over five years. The last year of his stay was spent in the prison hospital and when he was eventually released in November 1939 he was immediately admitted to a hospital in Baltimore until the spring of the following year.

Al Capone's last days were spent living at his Palm Island estate in Florida. They were relatively peaceful, although some friends said that he was paranoid about being gunned down in the streets of Miami and he could never totally relax.

On January 19, 1947, at the relatively young age of forty-eight, Al Capone suffered a massive brain hemorrhage, which he survived only to develop bronchial pneumonia within a week. On January 25, with his whole family gathered around his bed, Capone died after suffering a heart attack.

Capone's funeral, held at Chicago's Mount Olive Cemetery, was not a big affair; indeed Johnny Torrio was not even present. His headstone reads:

QUI RIPOSA
Alphonse Capone
Nato: Jan. 17, 1899
Morto: Jan. 25, 1947

[1] *The Life and World of Al Capone*, John Kobler, First published by Fawcett Publications Inc. New York, 1972.
[2] Ibid.
[3] Ibid.
[4] After Schemer Drucci was killed, George 'Bugs' Moran took over as boss.
[5] Jospeh Aiello was eventually killed on October 23, 1930. It was thought, though never proved, that Capone was behind the murder.
[6] Extract taken from the Chicago *Journal of Commerce*, December 17, 1927.

PAUL CASTELLANO
The Pope of Todt Hill

"'But, Mr Perdue," said Joe O'Brien, "what made you think that
Paul Castellano might be able to help in the first place?"
For the first time in the conversation, the chicken magnate looked
slightly at a loss. Was this some sort of trick question? If not, why
ask it, since the answer was so obvious?
"Why," said Perdue, giving forth a somewhat nervous cackle,
"because he's the Godfather."'

Boss of Bosses: The Fall of the Godfather, Joseph F. O'Brien & Andris Kurins

Occasionally known as the 'boss of bosses', or alternatively as 'The Pope', 'Big Paulie' or 'Meaty Curtains', Paul Castellano was, nevertheless, a name not to be messed with. Vain, violent and, unlike almost every other mobster in history, painfully reclusive, he ruled over the Gambino Family for nine long, bloody years.

Born Constantino Paul Castellano in Brooklyn on June 26, 1915 to Giuseppe and Concetta Castellano, both of whom hailed from Sicily, Paul was the last of three siblings. Cosseted throughout his childhood, he dropped out of school in the eighth grade, instead preferring to start work in his father's meat-cutting business. Giuseppe Castellano was not just a butcher, however, for he also ran several small-time racketeering enterprises and it was these that most fired Paul's imagination. Never one who enjoyed getting his clothes dirty cutting up carcasses, he preferred the clean-cut image of the local wise guys who hung around New York's bars. By 1934, at the age of nineteen, he effortlessly joined their ranks, having been arrested for the armed robbery of a clothing store. Sentenced to one year in Hartford County Jail, he served only three months and four days in prison, returning to Brooklyn a local hero among his fellow hoodlums.

Subsequent to this short spell in prison, as far as any law enforcement agency was concerned, Castellano disappeared from view for over twenty years. This did not mean, however, that he had decided to go straight – far from it. It simply confirmed that he preferred to stay well out of the limelight and operate from the shadows.

Castellano set up a meat-cutting business of his own, which did surprisingly well, and by the 1950s he began a wholesale operation called Blue Ribbon Meats which was also extraordinarily successful. But as with anyone who had friends of a dubious nature, there was naturally a dark side to these enterprises. Knowing that to get ahead he had to have connections, Paul had made it his job to ingratiate himself with the Brooklyn Mob. Not only that, in 1937 he married Nina Manno – sister-in-law of Carlo Gambino (head of the Gambino crime family) who, as luck would have it, was also one of Castellano's cousins. This last connection ensured Castellano's future successes; not for him any small-time rackets or street-corner scams. He was heading for the big time and when Carlo Gambino fell ill in the mid-1970s, it naturally assumed that Paul Castellano would step into his shoes to become boss of the entire Family.

In the interim between his marriage and his promotion, Castellano built up his meat businesses and tried to keep a low profile, which wasn't always easy. On November 14, 1957 his cover was completely blown when he became involved with the notorious Apalachin meeting, which was held at the home of Joseph Barbara. Apalachin, as the authors Joseph F. O'Brien and Andris Kurins point out in their book *Boss of Bosses*, was a watershed event in the history of the mob. ' . . . it is hardly an exaggeration,' they wrote, 'to say that Apalachin was the dividing line between the "old" Mafia of Al Capone and Salvatore Maranzano and the "new" Mafia that would eventually be headed by Paul Castellano. Involved in the event was not only a changing of the guard but, more subtle, a shift in approach, in self-perception. The Mob, while retaining its essential thuggishness, was taking on a veneer of sophistication. Apalachin was evidence of this process, notwithstanding the fact that, as with many pivotal events in La Cosa Nostra history, the meeting ended in a total and utter debacle.'[1]

Convened in order to allow the Mob's top bosses to try to work out a peaceful resolution to some long-term internal battles – especially those within the Genovese Family – Apalachin (or the 'big barbecue' as it soon became known) was also supposed to deal with a recruitment crisis within the Mafia. Back in the 1930s it had become, so several old-timers believed, too easy for anyone to become a 'made' member of a Family. Tradition (and with it precaution) was being thrown to the wind, as a result of which the five main Families had closed their doors to new members. Then, in the 1950s, recruitment began again to make up the number of foot soldiers required to run such large organizations. Frank 'Don Cheech' Scalice (an Albert Anastasia man) had begun selling membership into his family, outraging everyone to the point that something had to be done. Drugs were also on the Apalachin agenda or, to be more precise, the Bureau of Narcotics, which was making a nuisance of itself interfering in and disrupting the Mob's activities. These, then, were the three main reasons for the 'big barbecue' to which over one hundred mob bosses and underbosses from all over the States had been invited.

As Carlo Gambino's right-hand man, Paul Castellano was included on the list, however, as the history books show, Apalachin was destined to be a disaster. This was due, in the main, to one man, a New York State trooper called Sergeant Edgar D. Crosswell, who began noticing an unusual number of enormous black limousines on the roads. When he realized the cars were congregating outside the home of Joseph Barbara, a man who was known either to be associated with or a member of the Mob, Crosswell alerted his superiors. Reinforcements were immediately sent to stake out the Barbara estate but, having spotted a roadblock, the mob bosses panicked and tried to run. Suddenly, the police had in their custody sixty-three Mafiosi; one of whom was Paul Castellano. In 1959 Castellano, along with all the others who had been arrested, was made to appear before a grand jury in New York City to explain his presence at the conference. All of the mobsters stuck to more or less the same story; that they had been visiting their sick friend Joseph Barbara. Castellano even elaborated on the tale by saying he shared a heart condition with Barbara and was, therefore, wishing to seek his advice. The prosecutor in the case was naturally dubious; after all, wasn't it strange that all sixty-three men had decided to visit their sick friend at exactly the same time? Castellano answered in the affirmative but said little else, and as a result he was sentenced to five years in prison for refusing to cooperate with the investigation. As luck would have it, he served only seven months of his sentence because at that time, before the 1970 Racketeer-Influenced and Corrupt Organizations Act (RICO), the Apalachin Conference could not be regarded as 'constituting a criminal conspiracy.' Castellano's conviction was overturned.

Paul Castellano was once again a free man, only this time he was even more popular within the Mob for having neither talked nor implicated anyone else while being questioned in court.

Throughout the 1960s, with his increasingly good contacts as well as the goodwill he had drummed up within the Gambino Family itself, Paul's meat enterprises became ever more successful. Undoubtedly this also had something to do with the arsenal of tricks Castellano employed to pass tainted meat off as fresh.

> He was familiar, for example, with the process known as 'bleaching,' in which spoiled meat is drained of its foul-smelling juices, then soaked overnight in white preservative powder known in the trade as 'dynamite,' which makes it look red and appetizing again. He understood the value of formaldehyde in masking the stench of decay. He was conversant with the use of counterfeit Department of Agriculture stamps to put a fraudulent grade or expiration date on a carcass. He knew that 'beef' did not always come from cows and that 'pork' had not necessarily been the property of a pig.[2]

Paul Castellano's success was also due to an uncanny ability to muscle in on other Families' territories, including those of the Lucchese, Genovese and Bonanno Families, who between them enjoyed overall control of almost all New York's fish and meat markets. Furthermore, Castellano enjoyed the company of several men whose services he bought, among whom was Pasquale Conte, one of the directors of the Key Food Cooperative chain of supermarkets, who soon became a Gambino Family capo. Another major player in the supermarket game, the millionaire Ira Waldbaum, also became a close acquaintance of Castellano, as did Irving Stern who was vice-president of the United Food and Commercial Workers Union. In 1970, Castellano once again displayed his business acumen by setting up two of his sons, Joe and Paul Jnr, in a meat wholesale business called Dial Meat Purveyors Inc (better known as Dial Poultry). With his sons providing the product and his friends in high places purchasing it to put on the shelves of their supermarkets, Castellano thought of everything. Even in the late 1970s when other crime families, including the Lucchese Family headed by Carmine Tramunti, the Colombo Family headed by Carmine Persico and the Bonanno Family headed by Paul Sciacca, were coming under increasing pressure from various government organizations, the Gambinos and Castellano weren't among those who were prosecuted. Instead, when Carlo Gambino fell seriously ill in 1975, Castellano's star rose even higher when Gambino named him as his successor, a move which alienated several Gambino members who thought that Aniello Dellacroce – his underboss since 1965 – should have been given the job.

Variously known as the 'Tall Guy', 'Mr O'Neill' or just plain 'Neil', Dellacroce's service to the family stretched back to the days of Albert Anastasia. Dellacroce also enjoyed the support of the Gambino Family's strongest crew, whose members numbered among them the up-and-coming John Gotti. Nevertheless, it was Castellano who was given the top job, a post he undertook while Carlo Gambino was still alive, providing him with the added bonus of Gambino's guidance. Thereafter, Castellano

When Castellano was forced to attend a State Commission of Investigation in New York following the famous Apalachin meeting, he claimed he had called in at his friend's house to discuss their respective heart conditions and had no knowledge of the other 120 guests.

rapidly gained the acceptance and respect of other mob bosses although, as has been pointed out by various commentators, he did not receive his official 'confirmation' as head of the Gambino clan until after Neil Dellacroce, who was serving a five-year prison sentence for tax evasion, was released. On November 24, 1976 a small ceremony was then held in Bensonhurst as a coronation for the new 'King.' Paul Castellano was now at the top of the tree. No one, or so it seemed, could assail his position, but believing this may well have precipitated his downfall because several special investigators, infuriated at his apparent impregnability, now made it their mission to bring 'Big Paulie' to justice.

In this respect no one was keener than Bruce Mouw (also see chapter on Sammy Gravano), who was overall supervisor of the FBI's Gambino squad. University educated, Mouw was a quiet, methodical man to whom organized crime was a personal affront. But for all his intelligence, for all the resources he had at his disposal, Mouw was going to find Paul Castellano a tough nut to crack. Over the years, the Gambino boss had become more and more of a recluse, preferring to remain in the seclusion of his mansion, nicknamed 'The White House,' on Staten Island, and conduct all his business affairs (which now numbered among them holdings in construction companies, sanitation companies, food, clothing and gambling rackets) over the phone.

This reluctance to step outside his own premises was a big mistake on Castellano's part for, although it made it difficult for the FBI to catch him out, it also made him an aloof boss, a boss who consciously divorced himself from the nitty-gritty of everyday mob politics, whose foot soldiers rarely if ever had a chance to speak to their leader. Should anyone doubt his power, however, they need only look to his own family to see how terrifying he could be. His only daughter, Connie, married a small-time hood by the name of Frank Amato who at some point in the marriage beat up his wife. It is also alleged that Amato was responsible for Connie miscarrying her first child. After the couple were divorced around 1973, the errant husband disappeared, never to be seen or heard from again.

Just as Castellano stayed close to his blood family, so he grew further away from his Mafia Family. His decision to try to rule from a distance soon placed him in a vulnerable position for, having removed himself from his soldiers, it gave the likes of John Gotti the chance to ingratiate himself with the troops behind the boss's back. Later, Gotti would go so far as to persuade the majority of the Family to side with him against the boss. One man, nevertheless, remained loyal to Castellano from beginning to end. Starting out as 'Big Paulie's' chauffeur and bodyguard, Thomas Bilotti, much to everyone's surprise, soon became the boss's favorite employee and protégé. Uneducated, uncouth and with more than the average thug's penchant for violence, Bilotti was a strange choice of man to represent Castellano out on the streets. 'Talking to Bilotti,' wrote O'Brien and Kurins, 'was like talking to the dog.' He was a 'yes' man, whose only mission in life seemed to be to please his master. But Castellano took to him like no other and soon Bilotti was the boss's chief representative. In fact, the more

Castellano hid out at the White House, the more public the face of Thomas Bilotti became.

Meanwhile, Bruce Mouw was slowly coming to the realization that Castellano's reluctance to leave home gave him the ideal opportunity to bug the Gambino boss's premises and listen in to all his conversations, including those he conducted over the phone.

The planting of a residential bug is the Rolls-Royce of surveillance techniques. On the scale that runs from casual observation, to systematic study, to the development of informants, to the tapping of phone lines, the bugging of a house reaches an entirely different level of intimacy.[3]

All Mouw required was what in legal parlance is known as 'probable cause' – in other words a good reason to carry out such an operation legitimately. And, as if God were watching over him, in June 1982 he suddenly stumbled over precisely the right kind of evidence.

Earlier in the year, the FBI had acquired a license to bug the home of Gambino Family foot soldier, Angelo 'Quack Quack' Ruggiero – nephew to Aniello Dellacroce. Ruggiero belonged to the John Gotti faction of the Gambinos; those who were disillusioned with Castellano, who believed Dellacroce should have, on Carlo Gambino's death, been made boss. The FBI caught Ruggiero on tape bad-mouthing his superior, calling him and his children all manner of insulting names. Ruggiero, along with John Gotti's brother, Gene, had also been trafficking heroin. When Paul Castellano had taken over as boss, this was an offense that he had ruled would be punishable by death. If anyone was in any doubt that Castellano was serious when laying down this edict, they only had to look at the case of Family member Pete Tambone. When Castellano discovered Tambone was dealing in drugs, he immediately issued instructions that Tambone should be executed. Ruggiero was subsequently caught on tape telling Tambone to get out of town as quickly as possible and to take his wife with him.

Naturally, with all this on tape, the FBI had enough 'probable cause' to enter and bug Castellano's estate. Not long afterwards, district court judge Henry Bramwell signed the appropriate documentation to allow for eavesdropping equipment to be put in place.

The results were extraordinary. Suddenly, the FBI was in possession of hundreds of hours of incriminating evidence and, although it took painstaking work to piece all the relevant bits of information together and decipher the numerous oblique references, it was more than worthwhile. Castellano, so it appeared, had his finger in so many pies it was hard to keep track. Construction, nightclubs, car-jacking, gambling halls, the garment industry, the meat industry (retail and wholesale), cement, liquor, the trade unions, the pornography industry, extortion rackets; the list was seemingly endless. But for all the hours of recorded material that the FBI garnered, they soon realized something was amiss inside the Gambino Family. Despite being 'Big Paulie's' underboss, Aniello Dellacroce had yet to be heard speaking in any of the conversations.

This discovery, perhaps more than anything else, pointed to the fact there was a rift inside Castellano's ostensibly tight-knit world and if there was a rift, it was only a matter of time before internal warfare broke out. Bruce Mouw also had the taped conversations of Angelo Ruggiero bad-mouthing the boss as well as another Gambino Family soldier, Robert Di Bernardo doing much the same and coming down in support of John Gotti.

By 1984, now in his mid-sixties, Paul Castellano was enjoying splendid isolation in The White House. His wife, Nina, had left the family home and Castellano was having intimate relations with one of his servants, Gloria Olarte. There was less and less reason for him ever to leave his mansion. He could have his food delivered, his mistress was in residence and Tommy Bilotti could report to him every day on what was happening out on the streets. But 1984 was not to be a good year for the Godfather. A Gambino foot soldier called Roy 'The Killing Machine' DeMeo would see to that. DeMeo had run a notorious crew of killers and car thieves who were said to have concentrated on stealing luxury cars that were shipped out to the Middle East (Kuwait being the most popular destination) to be sold. Legend also has it that this crew was

This mugshot of 'Big Paulie' was taken when he was arrested in 1975 along with eight others on loan-sharking charges. By this time, Carlo Gambino was seriously ill and had named Castellano as his successor at the head of the Gambino Family.

responsible for the deaths of thirty-seven men. Back in January 1983, however, DeMeo's bullet-ridden body had been discovered frozen in the boot of his car. This was enough for the then US Attorney in Manhattan, Rudy Giuliani to make his move on Castellano who, as head of the Family, was seen as being ultimately responsible for the actions of his foot soldiers. On March 30, 1984 'Big Paulie' (along with twenty-one others) was indicted on charges of car theft, child pornography, prostitution, racketeering and murder.

The charges were a bloody lesson on how quickly the Family kills, and not just its own. The defendants were accused of varying roles in thirty murders tied to the ring's car-theft enterprise. Most of the victims were hoodlums, but one was a twenty-year-old man who happened to witness a double homicide; a second was the nineteen-year-old girlfriend of a suspected informer.[4]

Paul Castellano then had to suffer the indignity of being taken down to FBI headquarters in full view of the press. The photographers and TV cameras had a field day, snapping at 'Big Paulie'. Until this date his face was practically unknown in America, but now and forever more his name and image would be linked with the Mafia.

Bail was set at $2 million, a sum which Castellano duly paid, putting the White House up as collateral. He was then allowed to go home. In the meantime, a Mafia Commission meeting had been called to take place at a house on Cameron Avenue in South Beach. In attendance were, amongst others, acting Colombo Family boss Gennaro Langella, Tommy Bilotti, Frankie De Cicco, the Lucchese underboss Salvatore Santoro and the *capo di tutti capi*, Paul Castellano. The FBI (thanks to an informant) had photographed everyone as they exited the building. Nor could they have been more pleased with themselves for not since Apalachin had so many Mafia men been recorded by the authorities while attending a get-together.

In addition to Castellano's indictment on the above charges, it seemed that he was also going to stand as a defendant in what became known as the 'Commission Case.' On February 25, 1985, law enforcement agencies blitzed every mob Family in New York, causing one newspaper to comment that February 25 would be 'the Mob's worst day ever.'

Fat Tony Salerno would be pulled in, as would the jaunty Gerry Lang, Tony 'Ducks' Corallo, boss of the Luccheses would be pinched, as would Colombo chieftain Carmine 'The Snake' Persico. Scopo, Santoro, Gambino underboss and peacekeeper Aniello Dellacroce – they would all be herded in that evening.[5]
Also included was the Pope of Todt Hill, Paul Castellano himself.

By the spring of 1985, having reached the grand old age of seventy, Paul Castellano was awaiting two trials. It was understood that his underboss and erstwhile enemy within, Neil Dellacroce was suffering from cancer, and on December 2 of that same year he died. With his passing went the last reasonable hope of a peaceful resolution to the war that had been brewing between the differing Gambino Family factions. Perhaps not realizing quite how acute the bad feelings were among the ranks, or

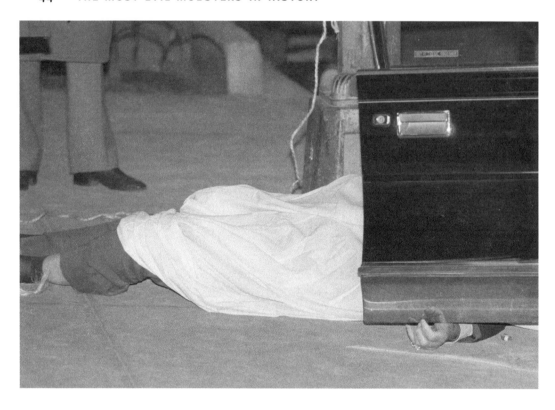

On December 16, 1985, Paul Castellano and his bodyguard, Thomas Bilotti, were executed amid crowds of Christmas shoppers on East Forty-Sixth Street in New York. Each man was shot six times in the head and upper body.

perhaps because he wanted to leave his mansion even less than before (by this time the Pope's first trial on charges of car theft and murder was underway), Paul Castellano failed to turn up at Dellacroce's wake. The rank and file were appalled. Paying one's last respects was an absolute 'must' in Mafia circles. To put it another way, not paying one's last respects would be seen by one and all as an enormous insult.

But Castellano was about to make an even worse mistake; with Dellacroce's job now vacant, he named Thomas Bilotti as his new underboss, thus disregarding all Family protocol by promoting someone whom most people regarded as a joker over the likes of Tommy Gambino or John Gotti. Bilotti was not leadership material; he had no class, he was simply a 'yes' man. And yet, if John Gotti and friends were outraged at their Godfather's decisions, Castellano himself was none too pleased with Gotti & Co – for after Aniello Dellacroce died, Paul Castellano was handed the tapes on which Angelo 'Quack Quack' Ruggiero had been heard to rubbish the boss. Ruggiero was a pal of Gotti's brother Gene, not to mention of John Gotti himself. It wouldn't have been beyond the realms of possibility, therefore, that Castellano might want to see both these men dead.

Once the DeMeo cars-and-killings trial got under way it quickly developed into a complete farce. Prosecution witness Vito J. Arena, having gone into minute and grisly detail concerning three murders that Roy DeMeo and friends had committed, subsequently announced that he'd never in his life seen Paul Castellano before. The final straw that broke the prosecution's back, however, was the announcement by Judge Kevin Thomas Duffy that they were unprepared for the case. Yet all this paled into insignificance when compared to what happened next.

On December 16, 1985, two weeks after Aniello Dellacroce's death and three days before his current trial was due to recess for the Christmas holidays, Paul Castellano was padding around his home on Staten Island. No doubt he was thinking of his upcoming holiday (sanctioned by the judge) in Pompano Beach, Florida, where he could relax with his mistress and forget all the tribulations of the past few months. By mid-afternoon he dropped by his lawyer's office in Manhattan to give 'Christmas envelopes' to the office secretaries after which he decided to stop off and buy a bottle of perfume for a particularly helpful secretary. That done, Castellano headed towards Sparks Steak House at 210 East Forty-Sixth Street, also in Manhattan. At the restaurant, he was due to meet with Gambino captain James Failla and Frank DeCicco for dinner. Sparks was something of an institution in New York, popular with office workers, businessmen and the diplomats who worked in the United Nations complex two blocks away. 'Big Paulie' was well known there too; in fact not so long before, he had engineered a 'sweetheart union contract'[6] for the owners. Driving Castellano to his meetings was Thomas Bilotti.

The car maneuvered its way through the late afternoon traffic until it turned the corner onto East Forty-Sixth Street. Waiting there was a whole bevy of men dressed identically in trench coats and Russian-style fur hats. Neither Bilotti nor Castellano, so later reports were to say, were carrying guns. It was a rule of Castellano's that no-one attending a Family meeting should show up armed. The car slowed down and parked directly outside the restaurant, but even before either Bilotti or Castellano had managed to exit the vehicle, two men had approached the car each firing directly at their assigned victim. Suddenly, with the firing of two semi-automatic guns, there was blood and bone spattered everywhere. Paul Castellano and Tommy Bilotti each received six bullets to the head and upper torso – an onlooker later recalled one of the gunmen leaning over and pumping a final shot into the Pope's head. Afterwards, the assassins calmly tucked away their weapons and walked towards Second Avenue. In what seemed like less than a minute the street was swarming with police and FBI agents.

Thomas Bilotti is buried in the Moravian Cemetery on Staten Island where his gravestone is marked with two interlocking hearts, underneath which appear the words 'Thomas 1940-1985.' In stark contrast, Paul Castellano, though laid to rest in the same cemetery, wasn't allowed a public Mass and isn't buried in the sort of style one might have expected. Only a small blank stone in amongst several others marks his passing.

As for the Roy DeMeo cars-and-killings trial, with the main defendant dead there could be no conviction. If anyone harbored any doubts that the Pope might have ordered killings from on high while at the White House, however, then the FBI's tapes surely put paid to that notion.

'Look,' the Godfather was recorded as saying to Gambino Family member Joe 'Piney' Armone, 'when we sit down to clip a guy, we have to remember what's at stake here. There's some hazard. Guys forget that. They get a guy behind in his vig payments, they get a hard-on about it, right away they wanna whack him. Why? Just because they're pissed off . . . I'll tell ya, Piney, any time I can remember that we knocked guys out, it cost us. It's like there's a tax on it or some shit. Somebody gets arrested. Or there's a fuck-up, which means we gotta clip another guy, maybe a guy we don't wanna lose.'

Sadly for Castellano, this time it was his turn to be clipped. The number-one suspect for the murder, John Gotti, did not attend his wake, which was conducted in the same funeral parlour that had held the wake for Castellano's predecessor, Carlo Gambino. By boycotting the wake, of course, Gotti had made it clear that, just as Castellano had snubbed Aniello Dellacroce, so he was snubbing the Pope of Todt Hill.

[1] *Boss of Bosses: The Fall of the Godfather*, Joseph F. O'Brien & Andris Kurins, Simon & Schuster, 1991.

[2] Ibid.

[3] Ibid.

[4] *Mob Star: The Story of John Gotti*, Gene Mustain and Jerry Capeci, Alpha Books and Pearson Education Inc., 1988.

[5] *Boss of Bosses: The Fall of the Godfather*, Joseph F. O'Brien & Andris Kurins, Simon & Schuster, 1991.

[6] *Mob Star: The Story of John Gotti*, Gene Mustain and Jerry Capeci, Alpha Books and Pearson Education Inc., 1988.

FRANK COSTELLO
The Prime Minister of the Underworld

'"Do you want to know what kind of a man Frank Costello was,"
an old-time Tammany Hall politician asked rhetorically during an
interview. "Well, I'll tell you, he was a prince of a fellow.'"

Uncle Frank: The Biography of Frank Costello, Leonard Katz

On January 26, 1891 there was born into abject poverty a sixth baby to Don Luigi Castiglia and his wife, Maria. They lived in Lauropoli in the hills of southern Calabria, a region of outstanding beauty situated at the toe of Italy. This was an area where poverty was endemic and where ignorance and superstition was rife. Less than seven miles away, across the Straight of Messina, lay Sicily. Along with the Sicilians, the Calabrese shared not only grinding poverty, but also a history of foreign invasion that had brought with it murder, rape and every conceivable type of torture. In turn this cruelty had contributed to a legacy that the Calabrese held dear, a code of honor that spoke of resistance and vengeance; one which overshadowed all the hardship, ignorance and squalor they had had to suffer and ultimately culminated in the founding of a secret society – a government within a government – the Mafia. The baby born into this environment was baptized Francesco Castiglia.

Two years later, Luigi Castiglia, had managed to raise enough money to buy a passage for himself and some of his children to leave Italy for America. He left behind his wife, two daughters and the baby. After a further two years, he sent for Maria and another daughter as he had saved up enough money for their passage. Maria also brought Francesco with her because he was young enough to travel for free. Francesco was four years old. He used to reminisce that all they took with them on the long, arduous journey was a huge iron cooking pot in which a blanket was kept for the young Francesco to sleep on.

Starting out his American life in an Italian ghetto in the East Harlem area of Manhattan, New York, Francesco quickly learned that it was the immigrant men who were left to do all the dirty jobs in the city. In contrast to his rather ineffectual father, his mother possessed great strength and determination. When Luigi started his own business by opening a hole-in-the-wall grocery store, she helped out. Despite his wife's aid, Luigi still proved to be an incompetent businessman and the grocery shop failed to prosper. The family were constantly hungry and the children quickly learnt to become streetwise and to steal in order to assuage their hunger.

One day, when he was about seven or eight years old, Francesco wandered into a Jewish neighborhood where a man with a beard offered him a penny to light his stove, it being the Sabbath. Frank (about this time he anglicized his first name) began his first ever organized business to earn money, doing just this for the Orthodox Jews on their Sabbath when they were forbidden to work. Later he upped the price to a nickel.

He started school late, at nine years of age, probably because he was very slow to learn English but when he was thirteen he openly defied his parents and quit. In later years, he recalled how he had hated school. Instead, he enjoyed the freedom of the streets and told his parents that he would one day make good. It was about this time that he anglicized his surname, too, choosing Costello, which was an Irish name, though the reasoning behind his choice is unknown.

By the age of thirteen Frank Costello was indistinguishable from all the other hoodlums running wild on the streets of New York. The first twenty years of the twentieth century were undoubtedly the best breeding ground and finishing school that America had ever known for racketeers of all kinds from petty criminals upwards. Costello was an eager and willing participant. Gang rule in New York was made up mainly from three sets of immigrants – the Irish, the Italians and the Jews. The Irish had colonized the Westside, while the Italians and the Jews ran the Eastside. Frank Costello avidly soaked up the lessons these two environments taught him – their morality and their ideals – and within the Italian community he also learned all about the old country, the Mafia of Calabria and of Sicily itself. All important was the code of silence – no matter how you were cheated, robbed, or beaten, you were less of a man if you went to the police. You took your own revenge in your own time and in your own way. He also learned the all-important lesson that to do someone a favor was like making a deposit in a bank. You could draw on it when needed.

From about 1908, when he was seventeen years old, he and later his brother, Eduardo Costello, became 'hold-up' men with crude, violent methods of robbery, including attacking women in the street. They were really nothing but cheap, small-time hoodlums. Later in life, Costello did not like being reminded of these early years. His comment on his younger days being, 'Tough times make monkeys eat red pepper.' Not too much shame here.

He and his brother went on to become stevedores at the docks and managed to muscle their way into becoming hirers and firers for all the on-site work. Needless to say, they made their money by becoming the source of all the available employment – you had to pay the Costellos in order to get a job. It was also during this period, around 1914, that Frank Costello met a girl, Loretta (Bobbie) Geigerman. She was small, dark, attractive and had a little-girly voice which stayed with her into old age. Frank was immediately smitten and wanted to marry her. On the marriage license she gave her age as nineteen, but according to Immigration she was still only fifteen; nor was this the only lie on the document, for Frank gave his occupation as 'plumber.' Bobbie was Jewish, but the wedding ceremony was conducted by an Episcopalian minister, perhaps because a priest from Frank's birth religion or a rabbi from hers might have asked too many questions about the validity of their union. Neither family was very happy about the wedding but, although childless, Frank and Bobbie enjoyed a long life together and the marriage was, as far as anyone can tell, a success.

Over the next few years Frank continued to hustle with the same hooligan element in any way he could. Then, in January 1920, there appeared on the horizon the greatest business opportunity imaginable. Prohibition. Prohibition began with the passing of the Volstead Act. Although no one realized it at the time, it would signal the start of twenty years of outrageous lawlessness. In 1917, when the USA was still at war in Europe, the manufacture of liquor was taking up too much of the precious grain harvest, which was sorely needed for the running of the country. Many religious zealots seized on the idea of Prohibition as being a cure-all for mankind's (and particularly American) ills, both moral and physical. As Joseph Bonanno commented in his autobiography:

Prohibition was championed by the rural ladies of America, who considered booze the cause of dissipation among their menfolk. These ladies of the Women's Christian Temperance Union had no confidence in their men's ability to resist temptation.[1]

By 1919 all thirty-six States had ratified the Act and by 1920 it came into effect. At that point, however, the war had ended and it was peacetime in America. What would have been acceptable during the war as a valid sacrifice became, in peacetime, completely intolerable. The majority of the American people ignored the new law. Even ordinary housewives purchased liquor by the crate load. Because of this adverse reaction, rum-running quickly became a goldmine for criminals, from small-time hoodlums to organized gangsters. The field was wide open. Many bootleggers became national heroes and passed into American folklore. But alas, Prohibition also encouraged the corruption of politicians, judges, policemen and lawyers, so that while providing a service to the public, it also began undermining the very fabric of society. Speakeasies and nightclubs proliferated and were frequented by men and women from all walks of life. The drinking of illegal alcohol soon became the 'fashionable' thing to do. The American people would not stand for a law which interfered with their social life and they openly flouted it, very quickly making Prohibition unenforceable. But behind the relatively fun scenes in the drinking clubs, activities behind closed doors were growing ever more dangerous. Huge fortunes were being made in the world of the gangster, which were fought over to the death. The bootleg wars were lethal and during the 1920s more than a thousand gangsters died in these battles.

Frank and his brother, Eddie, became very much part of this bootlegging scene. It was their golden opportunity; Frank supplied the brains, Eddie the brawn. Frank was wily, ruthless, and he instinctively knew the right time to take a gamble; above all he had imagination. Prohibition enabled him to enlarge his contacts from small-time peddling through to wholesale deals and finally to a partnership with William Vincent Dwyer, a New York Irishman known as 'Big Bill' on account of his huge bankroll. With money behind him, Frank began importing liquor, which was where the really big money could be made. Frank's business interests quickly expanded. He bought the illustrious Club 21 where, so the story goes, he designed and set up the electrically controlled bar that could be 'disappeared' at the touch of a button whenever a police raid began.

Importing was a complicated business. It involved the purchasing of cheap liquor in bulk in such places as the Bahamas, and the financing of ships to transport the liquor close to American shores where it would then be transferred onto a flotilla of speedboats located all along the east coast of the United States. The contraband was then dropped off at a host of tiny docks from where it would be driven overland by trucks to be sold to the wholesalers. Operations of this type were risky in the extreme, but in spite of deadly competitive hijacking and the work of the undermanned Federal Government Enforcement Agency, the rewards when the liquor was delivered were enormous. A successful importer became instantly wealthy.

Frank was making huge profits from his involvement in the illicit import operation. He hired the crews for the ships, equipped the speedboats, bribed whoever needed to be bribed (police, coastguards, agents, politicians) and recruited gunmen to protect his interests. When the money flowed in, he began to invest in other, often legitimate, businesses and real estate. Success required a great deal of self-confidence in his own judgment. Never a threatening type of man in his general behavior, he gained the friendship of respectable business people. His influence grew and he became the man to see in New York.

He called himself 'Mr Schedule' and used the world-famous Waldorf Hotel in Park Lane as his office. His favorite nightclub was Club 21, but the whole glittering panorama of night life in the city became, as it were, his drawing room. Business and pleasure took place there and anyone who was anyone attended. Bobbie would accompany him and she loved the excitement and glamor of it all. Unlike many Mafiosi, he took pains to avoid the trappings of the 'Men of Respect', such as bodyguards and chauffeurs, and never used them in his day-to-day life, preferring instead to walk or use cabs. He also took great care with his appearance, traveling daily to the barbershop to be shaved and manicured. Three times a week he indulged in a Turkish bath. Rather like the court of the kings of old, surrounded by subjects seeking help and advice and paying their respects, Frank Costello lorded it over his minions. For many years he lived in the aptly named Majestic Apartment building to the west of Central Park (where he liked to walk his dogs, a miniature Doberman and a toy poodle – no big fierce dogs for him) and at the height of his success he would have a string of some of the best-known New York names – Wall Street magnates, politicians, judges, lawyers, famous show-business personalities and newspapermen – calling on him including, so it was rumored, Joe Kennedy.

"When I [one of Costello's lawyers] arrived in his apartment," he said, "Costello was on the phone. He waved to me and continued talking. He was in the midst of cussing someone out like I never heard before. This went on for a few minutes, and then he hung up. I was curious. Since he hadn't made any secret about the phone call, I decided to be a little impolite and asked him, 'who were you talking to like that?' He just looked at me and gave this little laugh and said, 'Oh, just that Kennedy fella from Boston.'"[2]

Costello's other world – the underworld – also loomed large in his life. In fact, he cast a giant shadow over the entire history of organized crime in America although, by 1928, he had begun to realize (along with most of his gangster contemporaries) that it would only be a matter of time before liquor would again be made legal. Bearing this in mind, Costello began searching round for a new source of income, a different racket that would enable him to maintain the standard of living to which the huge profits from bootlegging had allowed him to grow accustomed. He settled on gambling. Arthur Rothstein, who was best known as the underworld's financier and New York's most successful racketeer during the 1920s, had the bookmaking side of gambling sewn up, but Costello soon realized that slot-machine gambling was still available for exploitation. He quickly set about muscling in on the business, in his usual methodical style. He founded the Triangle Mint Company and with a trusted friend and associate, Dandy Phil Kastel, he claimed New York City as his exclusive territory. He also promised Joe 'The Boss' Masseria some of the profits and made certain that several high-ranking police officers were on his payroll. He was, which was his forte, a master of organizational ability, as any successful legitimate businessman must be. He gloried in this aspect of his life. He entered the slot-machine business with as much verve and enthusiasm as he had approached any business and eventually, in 1930, he even thought up an idea of pure genius in order to bypass the anti-gambling laws of the day – he fixed his gambling machines to throw out packets of mints every time a coin was inserted. When a jackpot was achieved, along with the mints the machine spewed out counters, which could be redeemed for cash. This successfully flouted the law and for some years it legitimized the small man's gambling habits. It was very profitable, in particular for the owner of the machines, and eventually the profits from the gaming machines surpassed even Costello's bootlegging endeavors.

In the meantime, on November 4, 1928, Arnold Rothstein was shot in the groin while in the Park Central Hotel (later to became known as the Park Sheraton – where Albert Anastasia would be murdered on October 25, 1957) and soon afterwards died of his injuries. The underworld was in total shock for with Rothstein gone, his whole empire was up for grabs. Without further ado, Frank Costello took over all Rothstein's gambling enterprises. Lucky Luciano was rumored to have taken command of the narcotics side of Rothstein's business, while Lepke Buchalter grabbed control of the union rackets.

Frank Costello installed a close friend, Frank Ericson, to handle the 'lay-off' bets and between them – with some respectful handouts to other underworld bosses – the two prospered. At the same time, however, a huge war (the Castellammarese War) broke out within the underworld. Costello, true to his character, decided to take a step back and watch and wait from the sidelines rather than join in the main fray. In fact, Costello was greatly in favor of a scheme to carve up the whole of the United States into slices, with each participant getting an equal share of the profits in a 'peaceful' manner. Several gangland bosses actually held a series of crime conventions, just as though they were participating in any other section of the legitimate business world. Costello was always thought to be the biggest influence in these meetings; indeed they elevated him to a position of real power in the country as a whole. But the scheme never came to fruition and war continued much to Costello's disapproval.

Especially since the success of his businesses, Frank had become an advocate of non-violence, believing that killing was only to be used among their own kind, as the supreme punishment for breaking one of the sacred rules of the Mafia. So he concentrated on his slot-machine business. It was said he had some 5,000 machines around New York which were being patronized by all and sundry. Costello even had wooden platforms made, to allow shorter kids to be able to play just like their elders. It was estimated that the daily gross takings were $50,000. Expenses, of course, were heavy – half the police force and probably all of Tammany Hall were on the payroll. (Tammany Hall was founded in 1786 when it was established as a social, ceremonial outfit representing the common man, but it soon grew to be the guiding force behind Jeffersonian politics and later became synonymous with the Democratic Party's political machine in New York.)

Fully aware of the press photo opportunity, Costello hands some cash to a down-and-out. Costello liked to play the philanthropist and once donated $40,000 to a New Orleans charity, although a local politician had promised in return that he could move his slot machines into the city.

By 1929, after many killings and near-killings in the Castellammarese War, after mutual agreements between Mafia bosses back in the old country, after the crash of the Stock Exchange and in 1933 with the repeal of the drinking laws making it legal to consume alcohol again, the climate for gangster crime had changed. Depression took over in America and morals began to return.

Also in 1933, a stout little man with a high, squeaky voice appeared on the New York scene. Fiorello La Guardia was sworn in as Mayor and almost immediately went after the gambling fraternity. Over the radio he said, 'Let's drive the bums out of town.'[3] He was, of course, referring to Costello and Ericson. La Guardia – 'Little Flower' – meant business. He set about smashing the slot-machine business in spite of its legitimacy. Although not always lilywhite himself, during his twelve years in office La Guardia nevertheless reduced organized crime in ways no one had been able to manage before him.

In the meantime, Frank Costello, ever patient, decided to start living the life of a gentleman of means and joined the upmarket Lakesville Country Club in Long Island. His golfing colleagues enjoyed listening to his stories about his bootlegging days (which were boldly cleaned up in the recounting), never once thinking the less of him as everyone was known to have been involved in similar ventures during Prohibition. He became popular; he was a 'proper gentleman', quiet, well-dressed and honest in his play and dealings at the club. No one guessed he was also a ruthless racketeer.

Then, in 1936, a bombshell to rival the assassination of Arnold Rothstein hit the underworld; Charles 'Lucky' Luciano was arrested by Special Prosecutor Thomas E. Dewey and indicted on charges of compulsory prostitution. The case went to trial and, having been found guilty as charged, Luciano was sentenced to between thirty and fifty years in jail. His imprisonment caused a power vacuum within Luciano's Family and it was said that, calling Costello from his prison cell, he now requested his old friend to take over as acting boss. Suddenly Frank was *capo di capi*, a position he undertook very seriously and during his so-called reign it is said that the leading Mafia Families of New York enjoyed relative peace mainly because Costello's philosophy of the non-violent resolution of problems prevailed. Costello became so well known for his subtle handling of situations that he was called the Prime Minister of the Underworld among his own kind.

In 1935 Costello, much to his chagrin, had a warehouse full of slot machines that were doing nothing but gathering dust. With La Guardia still in power there was nothing to be done about the situation, no way he could go back into business. Instead, he had to be patient and wait for a miracle; and eventually one happened to come his way in the guise of Huey Pierce Long.

Long (who was better known to his friends as 'The Kingfish' was one of the most charismatic but dangerous politicians ever to have entered public life. He invited Costello and his slot machines to New Orleans on Costello's promise that he would give $40,000 to charity. According to Frank, Long would then guarantee to have slot machines legalized in New Orleans. The plan worked, using the same old trick of vending mints in the machines. Business blossomed and charity gained the promised amount.

But for every silver lining, there is a cloud and in 1935, Huey Long was murdered by an idealistic doctor, Carl Austin Weiss, who felt obliged to put a stop to The Kingfish's dictatorial reign. His death complicated the whole of the New Orleans set up. So many people wanted a piece of the action, and once the pieces were all shaken up, a different set of characters emerged. Costello was still overall boss; until, in 1939 the unthinkable happened. The Internal Revenue Service initiated its first attempt to indict Frank Costello and his latest partner-in-crime, Dandy Phil Kastel, on charges of income tax evasion. The government case proved to be weak and the jury returned a 'not guilty' verdict, but during the next few years the moral appetite for cleaning up gambling enabled the Louisiana Supreme Court, along with the support of the general public, to rule in 1946 that candy-mint slot machines were indeed illegal. That was the end of this particular racket.

This was not, however, the end of operations in New Orleans. Frank Costello, now in his mid-forties, along with Kastel and others, purchased a nightclub and called it The Beverly. It became one of the most lavish nightclubs and gambling casinos in the country, presenting such top talents of the entertainment world as Sophie Tucker, Joe E. Lewis and Tony Martin. It also offered the best of everything else to its patrons; top cuisine, beautifully appointed rooms with the finest tableware, napery and crystal, the most lavish of decoration crowned with enormous chandeliers, under which the top bands of the time performed for the guests. In fact, The Beverly became very profitable right up until 1951 when the anti-corruption Kefauver Committee forced its closure.

New Orleans was not the only area of operation for Costello during these years. He had returned to his New York haunts several times and had built up a powerful base in the political life of the city. His political influence was so strong that he enjoyed a role as a power broker. This pleased his large ego which, though it rarely showed on the outside, was definitely very much part of his character. Costello understood power, didn't abuse it, knew its limitations and respected its compromises. Nonetheless, in 1943 a political scandal broke out that revealed the extent of Costello's influence in Tammany Hall, some going as far as to name Frank Costello as the real boss of this establishment. Despite the furore, Costello weathered the storm with the help of a coterie of highly-paid lawyers. In fact, Costello usually enjoyed the company of legitimate business people such as lawyers and politicians – often at the expense of the Mafiosi who kept themselves to themselves and weren't always the most educated of men. Some people belived that Costello would have preferred his power base always to have been legitimate.

Notwithstanding this view, the reign of Frank Costello, underworld boss and criminal mastermind, continued unabated. But by the late 1940s, his power had begun to wane. A young blood by the name of Vito Genovese had been snapping at

Seated behind a microphone with his famous 'dancing hands' hidden from view, Frank Costello is put under pressure by Rudolph Halley, chief counsel for the Kefauver Committee investigation into organized crime, which held its television audience in thrall in 1951.

his heels ever since Costello had taken over from Lucky Luciano in 1937.

Don Vitone [Vito Genovese] was not an imposing man in appearance. He was short, stocky, had a full face, and amber-tinted glasses. He wore expensive, conservatively-cut clothes, and could easily be taken for a successful accountant or small businessman. His most outstanding feature was the cold, hypnotic stare of his eyes. They seemed able to look right through you.[4]

And look right through Frank Costello they did; enviously eyeing up the seat of power and needling Costello every which way he turned. Sadly for Costello, Genovese was by no means his only problem during these years, for it was also around this time that he began suffering from long bouts of depression and insomnia. Unable to bear these illnesses, Costello consulted a psychiatrist, Dr Richard H.

Escorted by a police detective, Costello leaves the Roosevelt Hospital in New York in May 1957 with his head heavily bandaged. Earlier that evening, he had narrowly escaped death when a would-be assassin shot him in the head outside his apartment building.

Hoffman, who treated Frank for a little over two years. In addition to his mental problems, Costello also had to face other fights, the most important one being the Kefauver Committee, which had been set up specifically to investigate organized crime. Held in front of TV cameras, the whole of America   from suburban housewife to leading politicians – was gripped by the proceedings and never more so than when Frank Costello took the stand. Focusing on Costello's hands, the TV cameras revealed a remarkably nervous individual who couldn't stop his fingers from dancing, especially when he was asked a particularly tough question. The Kefauver Committee, and in particular Rudolph Halley, the committee's chief counsel from New York, wanted to scrutinize every part of Costello's life, in order to see what crimes it might uncover. Halley questioned Costello about names he had used prior to his naturalization in the United States, whether he had lied during his naturalization (thereby committing fraud), whether he had run a bootlegging operation, as well as all manner of other enquiries. Costello, who initially had waived his right to silence, suddenly, in the middle of proceedings, invoked the Fifth Amendment. He had had enough. It was a risky strategy, for if found guilty of contempt by the Committee, he stood a good chance of being jailed. Due mainly to his bull-dog attitude during questioning, he emerged from the investigation as one of the best-known racketeers in America. Everyone wanted a piece of Frank Costello, but in particular the Justice Department now came after his blood. Costello was now being attacked from every quarter. Vito Genovese was still after his job and the weaker Costello grew, the stronger Genovese became.

On October 4, 1951, Costello's close ally, Willie Moretti, was gunned down at a restaurant called Joe's Elbow Room. Costello was devastated and also in no doubt that Vito Genovese was behind the hit. But Costello had other, more pressing, concerns to deal with; namely the fallout from Kefauver. In 1952, Frank Costello was sentenced to eighteen months on a charge of contempt of the Senate. True to his style, he was a model prisoner and with time off for good behavior he served only fourteen months, being released at the end of October 1953. But the Internal Revenue Service hadn't finished with him yet. They now planned to build a tax evasion case against him. Several attempts failed but eventually, in 1954, after much careful detective work, Costello was put on trial again. This time he was found guilty and given five years and a $30,000 fine. He fought for two more years to appeal against the sentence but in 1956 he surrendered and went to prison. Again Costello bounced back. After eleven months he was released on a $25,000 bail while the Court of Appeal agreed to review his case. But his appeal was turned down and he went back inside once again to serve forty-two months, after the maximum reduction for good behavior had been allowed.

During his incarceration, attempts were also made to have him deported back to Italy and these continued well into the 1960s. In 1961, however, the Supreme Court overturned the deportation order. Frank Costello was by then seventy years old.

Throughout all this time, as he traveled backwards and forwards from jail, as lawyers fought his corner and others tried to put him away for life, Frank Costello was also constantly under threat from Vito Genovese. On May 2, 1957, this ongoing battle finally came to a head. Costello had been dining at a restaurant called L'Aiglon when, on his way back to his apartment in the Majestic, a long black Cadillac drew up. As he entered the vestibule, an assassin shot him at point-blank range. This marked the official end to Frank's already waning power and influence.

Costello was taken to hospital where he was swiftly dealt with – the shot not having been fatal – although he remained adamant that he didn't know who his attempted killer had been. Ever faithfull to the Mafia code of silence, he is believed to have told police that, 'I haven't an enemy in the world.'

The courts, however, continued to try to make him name names, but in Frank Costello they found a formidable adversary. Within the Mafia itself, Costello was quickly losing his grip on power, and although he sued for peace with Genovese, the price he paid was high. Costello had to promise never to become involved in racketeering again. He was stripped of all his gambling assets and reduced to the lowly position of soldier within the Family's ranks. Fortunately, he had no children to support and had enough money to live comfortably for the rest of his life.

Indeed, Costello lived a long life, continually engaged in fighting many tax evasion charges. He died in bed at half past seven on the morning of February 18, 1973, aged eighty-two.

Costello was something of an enigma. He genuinely seemed to believe that he was nothing more than a successful businessman giving people what they wanted or needed, and doing so efficiently and quietly. He admired integrity and loyalty and prided himself on keeping his word. Against this backdrop, however, it must be acknowledged that he was undoubtedly a master criminal – and a dangerous one at that.

Costello's funeral was, in keeping with his wishes, quiet and straightforward. A Roman Catholic priest said a prayer over his coffin. It was over in a few minutes. The legacy Frank left Bobbie, however, was a tangle of tax problems. She had never had to deal with anything like it before, having always been shielded by her husband from such activities. She became depressed, fleeing New York and it was said that within a few months of his death she transformed from an attractive, vital woman into a frail little old lady, with the whole fabric of her life torn away.

[1] *A Man of Honor: The Autobiography of Joseph Bonanno*, Simon & Schuster, 1983.
[2] *Uncle Frank: The Biography of Frank Costello*, Leonard Katz, W. H. Allen & Co. Ltd, 1974.
[3] Ibid.
[4] Ibid

CARLO GAMBINO
The Dapper Don

'In the beginning was the Father. Without him nothing can be done. A Family of friends coalesces around the Father, from whom flows all authority. The Family which a Father holds together embodies an ancient way of life, a mode of cooperation which precedes the formation of city-states and later of nations.'

Joseph Bonanno

In old age, photographs of Carlo Gambino show an elderly man with a kind, almost comic face similar to that of the comedian Jimmy Durante. With his hooked nose and twinkling eyes he could have been the quintessential grandfather, yet beneath the smiles and behind that gentlemanly façade lay a far harder version of the man who was one of the most perfidious of Mafia murderers. Known to the FBI by a number of pseudonyms such as Carlo Stane, Harry Stone, Mr O'Conner, T. Goldberg and Carlo Seaman; Carlo Gambino was the very epitome of a Mafia Don.

Born on August 24, 1902 into a moderately wealthy family in Palermo, Sicily – an area which was heavily dominated by the Mafia – Carlo Gambino enjoyed an unremarkable childhood. It was only when he reached his teens that he became involved in any real trouble. During these years, the young Gambino was influenced by Don Vito Cascio Ferro, perhaps the most powerful boss in the whole of Sicily and certainly one of the most formidable. Don Vito, more than any other individual, was responsible for establishing close ties between the Sicilian Mafia and their counterparts in the United States. He was revered on both sides of the Atlantic as a 'true man of respect.' Early on in his life, Carlo Gambino's relatives introduced the youngster to the 'Honor Society' and by the age of twenty he was fully initiated into its ranks. Desperate to leave Sicily and earn his fortune abroad, Gambino managed to smuggle himself onto the SS *Vincenzo Florio,* which was bound for Newport News in Virginia, arriving on December 23, 1921.

Once on American soil, it was relatively easy for the young Gambino to find work in one of Joe 'The Boss' Masseria's gangs by using contacts he had already made through the Family while still in Sicily. Masseria was at that time the head of the most dominant Family in New York. He had built up a huge liquor business since the introduction of Prohibition. A small, fat-faced man, his enemies often referred to him as 'The Chinese', as his flabby cheeks considerably narrowed his eyes. Despite his appearance, Masseria was quite nimble on his feet. During the early part of the 1920s he was involved in several violent gunfights from which he miraculously always seemed to escape unscathed. He earned the reputation of a man who could successfully outwit death, no matter what the odds.

At the time Carlo Gambino went to work for Masseria, he was at his zenith. It was a great schooling for the young Gambino who was eager to advance through the ranks, but when the Castellammarese War broke out between Masseria and Salvatore Maranzano (see chapters on Bonanno and Luciano), Gambino sided with Luciano. When Masseria's luck ran out and he was murdered, Gambino went to work for Maranzano. Maranzano would not last long either and, subsequent to his boss's murder, Gambino, along with his brothers-in-law Peter and Paul Castellano, joined Vincent Mangano's Family. Mangano had helped Luciano rid the underworld of the 'Mustache Petes' – old-timers, including both Masseria and Maranzano, who wouldn't or couldn't accept change within the Mafia – in exchange for which Luciano nominated Mangano onto the board of the all-powerful Commission, which he himself had established with Joseph Bonanno, amongst others.

> The most consequential aspect of this post-Maranzano era was our adoption of a new form of leadership consensus . . . We opted for a parliamentary arrangement whereby a group of the most important men in our world would assume the function formerly performed by one man. This group became known as the Commission. It originally consisted of the five New York Fathers and the Fathers from Chicago and Buffalo.[1]

For Carlo Gambino, working for Masseria, then Maranzano and ultimately for Vincent Mangano meant that his Mafia apprenticeship was unlike any other. Mangano's sphere of influence ran the length and breadth of New York, but was concentrated on the Brooklyn waterfront, which he ran with his brother and Albert Anastasia. They charged all the dockworkers a fee for working there each day, which in turn enabled them to keep an eye on all the imports and exports so they could choose which cargos to hijack. No doubt Gambino was involved in these activities, all the time learning how to wheel and deal with the best of them. By the age of twenty-nine he was so good at his job that he became a capo of his own crew, after which he recruited Paul Castellano to be his right-hand man. So successful was Gambino at running his own crew that when the Mangano brothers disappeared mysteriously in 1951 (most people believe they were killed by Albert Anastasia) and when Anastasia famously took over as head of the Family, Gambino was the natural choice for the position of underboss.

In 1932, at the age of thirty, Gambino married his first cousin, who also happened to be Paul Castellano's sister, Catherine (sometimes spelt Kathryn), and moved into his first real home on Ocean Parkway – an unprepossessing street in Gravesend, Brooklyn, although the house itself was far more elegant than the others in that area. To all intents and purposes, Gambino's marriage was a happy one, with the couple producing three sons and one daughter.

By this point Gambino had already made a substantial amount of money, part of which he invested in his domestic life, while the rest financed a variety of businesses, including several bars that were mostly frequented by the gay community. But for all

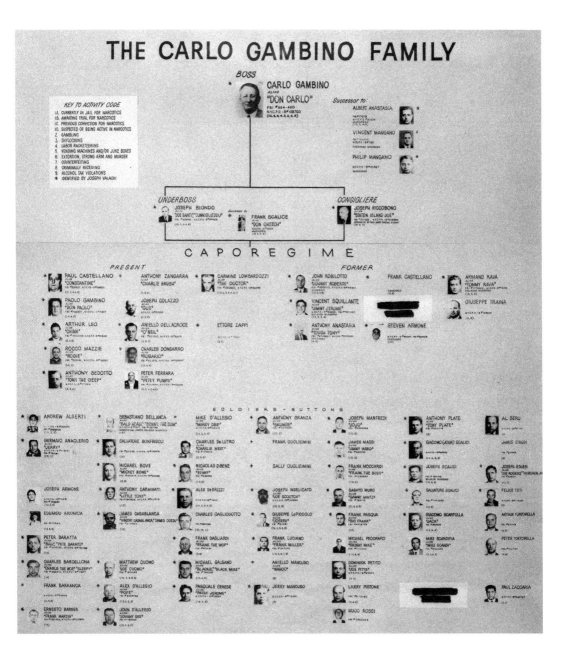

This Gambino Family Tree, used at a Senate inquiry into organized crime in 1963, shows how the authorities had identified the hierarchical structure of Gambino's organization and managed to chart known criminals in their proper place within the Family.

his good fortune, in 1939, several years after Prohibition was repealed, Gambino suffered a setback. He was handed a twenty-two-month prison sentence plus a $2,500 fine for conspiracy to defraud the United States government of liquor taxes. This was a bitter blow to Gambino, although eventually he only served eight months of the sentence, after his lawyers managed to have the conviction overturned.

With the Manganos out of the way and Anastasia now in charge, Carlo Gambino's role within the Family became ever more important. Anastasia was, if not the most prolific killer in La Cosa Nostra's history, then probably its most notorious (it is said – namely by Joseph Bonanno – that some time in the early 1930s he even plotted to kill Thomas E. Dewey who was then a special prosecutor, who later ran for president), earning him the nickname of 'Lord High Executioner.' As one of his group, Gambino was said to have bathed in his glory. Others have been less kind, painting a portrait of Gambino as nothing more than a mere lackey, a small-time nobody. Joseph Bonanno described him as follows:

> He [Gambino] was not a warrior. Given a choice, he avoided violence. He was a squirrel of a man, a servile and cringing individual . . . Albert used to use Gambino as his gopher, to go on errands for him. I once saw Albert get so angry at Carlo for bungling a simple assignment that Albert raised his hand and almost slapped him. In my Tradition, a slap on the face is tantamount to a moral offense [sic]. Another man would not have tolerated such public humiliation. Carlo responded with a fawning grin.[2]

Nevertheless, Gambino learnt from Anastasia how to be utterly ruthless, which stood him in good stead when he was later approached by another Family boss, Vito Genovese, to help murder Anastasia who had begun to cause Genovese problems by siding with a third powerful Mafia supremo, Frank Costello. Carlo Gambino jumped at the chance, which is probably what Anastasia himself would have done in the same position, and on October 25, 1957, while Anastasia was busy being pampered in a Manhattan barbershop, two men walked in and gunned him down. For a Mafia boss, Annastasia's funeral was relatively understated, costing in the region of $900. He was buried in Green Wood Cemetery in Brooklyn although few people attended the ceremony and later his wife left America to seek peaceful retirement in Canada.

Immediately after Anastasia's death, Carlo Gambino achieved the position he had coveted ever since he was a teenager, to be a Mafia boss just like the man he had idolized as a child, Don Vito Cascio Ferro. The Mangano Family was now renamed the Gambino Family, which was a source of great pride for Carlo. On November 14, 1957, Gambino represented his new Family at what soon became known as the Apalachin Conference, a national meeting of all the Mafia bosses. In his autobiography, Joseph Bonanno cites Anastasia's murder, and the desperation of Vito Genovese (amongst others) to have Gambino recognized officially in his new position of boss, as one of the main reasons for this gathering. This was important because Gambino was a Genovese man and made a good ally for Genovese in his ongoing fight with Frank Costello. 'If I [Joseph Bonanno] had been around I would have definitely lobbied against a national meeting. Such a conference would have the effect of giving official sanction to Gambino, pulling the rug out from under any dissidents within his Family. Of course, that's exactly what Lucchese and Genovese wanted.'[3]

As it happened, however, Apalachin was a disaster; the conference being broken up by the unexpected arrival of the police. Both Carlo Gambino and Vito Genovese were among those detained and convicted on charges of obstructing justice, although later these convictions were overturned when several of the mobsters' lawyers pointed out that meeting up together in one place, however it was perceived, was not in itself a crime.

But by promoting Gambino's rise to the position of boss, if Vito Genovese thought he had acquired a docile 'yes' man whom he could manipulate at will, he was sadly mistaken. Having taken over, Gambino was eager to make his own mark on the world, which included taking out two Anastasia loyalists. On September 7, 1958, John 'Johnny Roberts' Robilotto was shot in the face four times at point-blank range and his body dumped in the East Flatbush section of Brooklyn. Later in the same month, Armand Rava was apparently shot dead while playing cards, although his body was never discovered. As well as ridding himself of certain Anastasia men, Gambino was astute enough to realize he would have to bring on board several others, including one of Anastasia's most faithful supporters, Aniello 'Neil' Dellacroce. Dellacroce, a long-time Mafia member, sadistic killer and keen racketeer was made Gambino's underboss to try to avoid any trouble and, according to Sammy Gravano (later to be John Gotti's underboss), Gambino also kept on Anastasia's brother, Tough Tony Anastasio[4], as overall leader of Local 1814 of the longshoremen's union. This proved to be a wise move. Not only did it avert an internal power struggle, it also allowed the Gambino Family to carry on controlling the Brooklyn docks. When Tough Tony eventually died, Gambino saw to it that his son, Anthony Scotto, succeeded his father in the job at Local 1814.

Carlo Gambino was in his element and from the start made a huge success of running the Family. Although he would always keep his hand in where old-time racketeering was concerned (hijackings, illegal gambling and protection rackets), Gambino also set his sights on new money-making ventures such as the construction industry, Wall Street, garbage contracts and trucking. These were all potentially more profitable than anything that had gone before and, better still, were areas of gang activity as yet unmonitored by the authorities. Gambino knew that the more secretive he could be while pursuing his business affairs, the better. Hence his stance against drug trafficking – any soldier found to be dealing in narcotics would be sentenced to death. This was not due to any moral crusade, but was because Gambino loathed unwelcome public attention and drug trafficking was sure to attract the unwanted attention of the authorities.

'Gambino's reliance on personal family relationships, replete with marriages of in-laws as well as cousins, reflected his inbred, secretive ways, his profound wariness' wrote Sammy Gravano in his memoirs[5]. Gravano also described how Gambino cleverly combined his new stranglehold over trucking with his dominance of New York's thriving garment industry, an area where he shared the business with the Lucchese Family. (In 1962 Carlo's eldest son, Tommy, married Lucchese's daughter which further strengthened the links between the two families.) The clothing manufacturers were always under threat from hijackers eager to steal either cloth or fully made-up garments, but by using Gambino's trucks, which no one would dare hold up, they averted this problem. Gambino, of course, charged a premium rate for such guaranteed safe transport. But perhaps his biggest coup early on as Family boss was, in true Mafia style, double-crossing his former partner-in-crime, Vito Genovese. Along with the likes of Frank Costello, Sam Giancana and Meyer Lansky, who had all begun to feel uncomfortable at Genovese's megalomaniac tendencies, Gambino came up with a scheme to bring Genovese down by having him arrested on charges of drug trafficking. The plan was a great success, and Genovese was subsequently arrested and given a lengthy jail term from which he never emerged, as he died while still in prison.

With Genovese permanently removed from the picture, Carlo Gambino was now in an even stronger position than before. On the Commission, he and Tommy 'Three Fingers Brown' Lucchese (the nickname was derived after a policeman fingerprinted Lucchese and called him Tommy Three Fingers with reference to Mordechai (Tommy) Brown, a baseball pitcher) ruled almost without opposition alongside Joseph Colombo and Stefano Magaddino, much to the disapproval of Joseph Bonanno. By the early 1960s Gambino's advice was being sought not only by members of his own Family, but also by those from opposing Families. One such approach came from the Gallo brothers (Albert, Larry and Joey) who belonged to the Colombo Family, which was at that time run by Joseph Profaci. Normally, internal disputes would be dealt with by the Family itself. There were procedures that had to be followed, protocol to be observed. In short, Gambino didn't have to pay attention to the Gallo brothers' request, but he made a conscious decision to do so and granted them an audience. When Profaci discovered the betrayal he was incensed, but this didn't stop Gambino calling for a meeting of the Commission at which he announced that the Gallo/Profaci problem was growing increasingly difficult and perhaps it would be best if Joseph Profaci were to step down as Family boss. A vote was taken and Lucchese sided with Gambino. On the other hand, Joseph Bonanno strongly disagreed with the motion and, so it is said, saved Profaci from early retirement (although he died later the same year from cancer). Gambino may have lost out on that occasion, but the whole episode only proved that he would not think twice before flexing his muscles either in his own Family affairs or in those of others.

During the 1960s Gambino enjoyed almost total control of New York's waterfront, in addition to which he had also begun sanctioning several of his crews' (including one captained by Carmine Fatico in which a young John Gotti operated) hijacking activities at John F. Kennedy International Airport. 'Gotti and others under Fatico's control,' wrote Gene Mustain and Jerry Capeci in their book on the future Gambino boss, 'began to treat JFK like a giant candy jar, using as many devious means as they could contrive to take away goodies. Sometimes it was easy, but not always productive.'[6] Gambino made good profits from these activities on top of which, with the death of Lucky Luciano from a heart attack early in 1962, he was made head of the Commission. When Tommy Lucchese died from a brain tumor on

This 1976 photograph of a frail and aged Carlo Gambino (far right) was taken only a few weeks before his death and shows some of his associates enjoying the company of Francis Albert Sinatra (second left).

July 13, 1967, Gambino was said to have inherited not only control over Teamsters Local 295 – a union operating the trucking of over 70 per cent of the garment industry's stock in America – but also of the entire Lucchese Family. After Tommy Lucchese's death, Carmine Tramunti was appointed acting Family head, but played a very minor role in the proceedings, preferring instead to let Carlo Gambino run the whole show. Now ostensibly in charge of two Families, Gambino was at the height of his power. As if to underline this, a US Justice Department report entitled 'La Cosa Nostra: The Commission', sited him as controlling Mafia enterprises in New York, Connecticut, Maryland, New Jersey and Florida. The report also remarked that as well as controlling twenty-seven crew captains, Gambino also had two union bosses, Anthony Scotto and Joseph Colozzo, on his payroll.

Despite his evident power, however, in 1969 Carlo Gambino was charged with masterminding an armed robbery – a truck hijacking – although the case itself was delayed over and over again due to Gambino suffering a heart attack followed by the death of his wife, Catherine. Desperate to find some other means of bringing Gambino down, the government switched tactics and attempted to have him deported back to Sicily as an illegal immigrant. Once again, Carlo suffered another heart attack and it is believed that while he was in hospital his associates bought off two US Senators (whose identities have never been discovered) by promising them $25,000 per annum for life in exchange for stopping the deportation order.

Having narrowly avoided deportation, Gambino was soon to face yet another ordeal. In May 1972, one of his nephews – Emanuel 'Manny' Gambino – was kidnapped. The assailants demanded a $350,000 ransom and, according to an FBI agent called Anthony Villano, who later wrote a book on the subject, the Family asked the authorities to become involved. Villano went to the drop along with Manny's brother, Tommy Gambino, but although the ransom was delivered, Manny never materialized. Villano then went on to describe how, over the following few weeks, he investigated Manny's life in an attempt to discover who might have captured him:

> Manny had fallen in love with a show-biz blonde. He wanted to leave his family because the girl refused to have anything more to do with him unless he gave up his wife and went full-time with her. Manny was advised by his betters in the clan to grow up and forget the blonde. In his circles it was okay to have a mistress but it was bad form to leave your wife, particularly if you were a nephew of Carlo Gambino.[7]

Villano also discovered that Manny's financial situation wasn't too healthy – probably because he was trying to run two households, as well as the fact that several gamblers owed him large sums of money.

Eventually, on January 26, 1973, Manny Gambino's body was discovered near Newark Airport at the Earle Naval Ammunition Depot. He had been buried in a sitting position and had a bullet through his head. In their book *Mob Star*, Gene Mustain and Jerry Capeci describe in detail how, as a consequence of this discovery, Carlo Gambino set John Gotti on the trail of one of Manny's supposed kidnappers, a man named James McBratney. On May 22, 1973 Gotti, together with two other associates, Angelo 'Quack Quack' Ruggiero and Ralph Galione, entered a tavern called Snoope's Bar & Grill. 'The barmaid, Miriam Arnold, age twenty-six, a part-time student, later said Snoope's was so well-lit that it was possible to read a book and so she recognized the trio instantly. She remembered that they were in the bar a month earlier, and that they looked around, acted suspiciously, and left without having a drink, although the one she later learned was John used the men's room.'[8] The three men then surrounded James McBratney as he sat drinking at the bar, pulled him up and pretended to arrest him as if they were the police. McBratney, however, resisted. Galione then fired a shot into the ceiling, after which all hell broke loose. McBratney managed to free himself from the threesome, but not for long. Galione hunted him down and shot his prey three times in full view of everyone in the bar. Later Ruggiero, Gotti and Galione were all arrested for the murder.

But this is only one version of the events that followed Manny Gambino's killing. Other sources allege that a man by the name of Robert Sentner – a small-time gambler who owed Manny a large amount of money – was responsible for the kidnapping. He was picked up by police and charged with Manny's murder along with another man by the name of John Kilcullen.

Whatever the truth, following Manny's death, Carlo Gambino's health, which over the past couple of years had not been good, took a turn for the worse. Weak and increasingly unable to cope with the pressures of being boss of such a large empire, Gambino decided to name a successor while he was still alive so that he could be sure the transition ran smoothly. To this end, he summoned several of his senior advisors to his bedside, including Joe Gallo, Anthony Gaggi, Jimmy Failla and both his brothers Paul and Joseph Gambino. Against their advice, instead of choosing Aniello Dellacroce, who was at the top of the list of prospective candidates, having served as Gambino's underboss for many years and been part of the Family as a whole for many more, Carlo named his cousin and brother-in-law Paul Castellano. No doubt he believed that Castellano would make a better job of developing the Family's interests in legitimate businesses, such as the construction and hospitality industries, while still being bank-rolled by the less salubrious side of the empire. Whatever the case, the decision to give the top job to Castellano came as a shock to many of the Gambino crews. Even though Dellacroce was in prison for tax evasion, he was still seen as Gambino's natural successor. Nevertheless, Gambino wouldn't be swayed and when Dellacroce was eventually released from prison, it seemed he was quite content to resume his role as underboss.

Having named the next-in-line to the throne, Carlo Gambino was now happy to

Gambino died while watching the New York Yankees on TV at his summer home in Massapequa, Long Island. Following a two-day wake, hundreds of mourners accompanied the coffin to the cemetery from Our Lady of Grace Roman Catholic Church in Brooklyn.

relinquish control of the Family. By this time he had suffered three heart attacks and, with the loss of his wife, had little companionship in his latter years. Ill health dogged him until the last, which finally came on October 15, 1976 when he died at his second home in Massapequa, on Long Island, following heart complications.

A two-day wake was held at the Cusimano & Russo Funeral Home, after which there was a service conducted by the Reverend Dominic A. Sclafani at Our Lady of Grace Roman Catholic Church in Brooklyn. Later still, hundreds of mourners carrying thousands of floral tributes followed the coffin through the streets to Saint John's Cemetery in Middle Village, Queens, where Lucky Luciano, Joe Colombo, Vito Genovese, Joseph Profaci and Salvatore Maranzano were already interred.

The obituary columns overflowed with facts and figures, some of which were true, while others were definitely wide of the mark. Whatever was written, the underlying theme was the same; Carlo Gambino had been an incredibly powerful force both as a legitimate businessman with interests in construction firms and manufacturing companies, and a criminal with illegitimate concerns, including the stranglehold he held over the unions. Almost as a tribute to his notoriety, Gambino was later listed in the book *Timetables of History* as one of three world-famous people who had died during 1976, the other two being John Paul Getty and Howard Hughes.

1   *A Man of Honor: The Autobiography of Joseph Bonanno*, Simon & Schuster, 1983.
2   Ibid.
3   Ibid.
4   Anastasio was the original spelling of their surname.
5   *Underboss: Sammy 'The Bull' Gravano's Story of Life in the Mafia*, Peter Maas, Harper Collins Publishers, Inc., 1997.
6   *Mob Star: The Story of John Gotti*, Gene Mustain and Jerry Capeci, Alpha Books and Pearson Education, Inc., 1988.
7   *Brick Agent: Inside the Mafia for the FBI*, Anthony Villano, Quadrangle/New York Times Book Co., 1977
8   *Mob Star: The Story of John Gotti*, Gene Mustain and Jerry Capeci, Alpha Books and Pearson Education, Inc., 1988.

VITO GENOVESE

Don Vitone

'If you went to him and told him about some guy doing wrong he
would have that guy whacked . . . and then he would have you
whacked for telling on the guy.'

Joseph Valachi

Born in Naples, Italy on November 2, 1897, Vito Genovese along with his
mother and father first set foot on American soil in 1913, quickly settling into
the Queens district of New York. Vito's father ran a small contracting
company while Vito himself was enrolled in school. As with so many immigrant boys
of that generation, however, life on the streets seemed much more exciting than a life
of study and soon Vincent was skipping school in preference for hanging around
street corners. By age sixteen he had been caught stealing vegetables from a market
trader but, or so the story goes, the trader soon let Vito go when the young boy
threatened to kill him if he called the police. In an attempt to stop their son sliding
into a life of crime, Vito's parents decided to send him to Little Italy to live with
relatives, but the stratagem was doomed to failure and shortly afterwards it is thought
Vito met up with a young thug by the name of Lucky Luciano. Though never
destined to be best buddies, Genovese quickly fell under Lucky's spell and for his
part Lucky soon felt a begrudging respect for the Neapolitan, whom he found to be
an extremely effective enforcer.

First arrested at the age of seventeen for carrying a gun, Vito Genovese was sent to
jail for sixty days; a term that seemed to do him no good, for when he was released he
returned to a life of crime almost immediately. With prohibition on the horizon,
Luciano, along with Bugsy Siegel and Meyer Lansky, was involved in bootlegging
operations, and the young Genovese threw himself into similar work. By the early 1930s
he had been charged with two counts of homicide, although neither case saw the light
of day as there was not enough evidence on which to convict him. Instead, Vito ducked
and dived, side-stepping the law while at the same time gaining control of the Italian
Lottery, which made him a very rich man. Always one to believe that money makes
money, Genovese then ploughed his fortune into buying up various nightclubs
(including the Savannah Club, the 181 Club and the Groton Village Club) in the
Greenwich Village section of New York. By this point, Vito was a married man but when
his first wife Anna Ragone died in 1931 (the details of her death are hazy) he almost
immediately fell in love with a woman by the name of Anna Petillo Vernotico – one of
his distant cousins. Unfortunately, Anna was already married but, never one to let the
small matter of a husband stand in the way of his happiness, it is believed Genovese
lured the poor man to the top of a New York high rise from where he threw the

unfortunate gent to his death. Two weeks later Vito and Anna were wed.

It was also in the early 1930s that Genovese, again with Luciano and company, went to work for Joe 'The Boss' Masseria – one of the most feared bosses in New York at that time. Shortly afterwards the Castellammarese War broke out, (see chapter on Joseph Bonanno) between Masseria and another crime family boss Salvatore Maranzano. The line-up on both sides was impressive with Vito Genovese, Lucky Luciano, Joe Adonis, Albert Anastasia and Willie Moretti behind Masseria, while Salvatore Maranzano relied upon such heavyweights as Joseph Bonanno, Thomas 'Three Finger Brown' Lucchese, Joseph Profaci (boss of the Profaci Family) and Joseph Magliocco. These were dark days for New York's crime Families – especially when Luciano double-crossed Masseria and came to an agreement with Maranzano to assassinate Joe 'The Boss.' Whether or not Genovese was involved in the plotting is unknown, but what is generally accepted is that he was one of the gunmen who, on April 15, 1931, shot Masseria to death in the Nuova Villa Tammaro restaurant on Coney Island. Luciano then went on to slay Maranzano. The assassination took place in Maranzano's Park Avenue offices on September 10, 1931 and, although no one knows for sure who the gunmen were, it is more than likely Genovese was one of their number.

Yet things did not always run so smoothly in Genovese's life. In 1937, under increasing pressure from the New York District Attorney's Office regarding the unsolved murder of one Ferdinand 'The Shadow' Boccia that dated back to 1934, Vito fled America (in possession, so people believe, of $750,000) and returned to his native Italy where he soon became a close friend of the Fascist dictator, Benito Mussolini.

The murder of Boccia was a typical tale of mob heavy-handedness and double-dealing – one that revolved around a rigged card game. Boccia had an uncle who was friendly with a wealthy Italian businessman whom he introduced to Genovese and Mike Miranda (one of Lucky Luciano's soldiers). The two mobsters conned a large amount of money out of this man in a card game, afterwards offering him a way of recouping his losses by purchasing a printing press which would print money. After the man bought the machine for a large sum, Boccia was outraged that his uncle's friend had been ripped off in this fashion – especially as he had seen none of the profits. He wanted Genovese to give him $35,000 for setting up the whole deal. Vito Genovese is said to have agreed, but privately it is thought he had already decided to have Boccia killed.

A week later Boccia was gunned down outside his uncle's coffee shop. The three gunmen were apparently identified as Georgie 'Blah Blah' Smurra, Gus Frasca and Solly Palmeri – while the hit itself had been organized by Pete LaTempa and Willie Gallo (who was Boccia's former business partner). After Boccia was murdered, however, it is thought that Genovese, not satisfied with killing just one man, then ordered a hit on Gallo, requesting that Ernest 'The Hawk' Rupolo carry out the shooting. Rupolo, following orders, took Gallo out for a meal on the night of the intended murder and afterwards drove him to an out-of-the-way spot where he proceeded to draw a gun and fire at his victim. But the gun failed to go off. The same

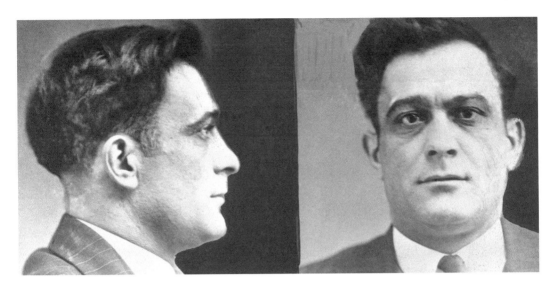

These mugshots of Vito Genovese were taken in 1937 shortly before he fled from the United States while under investigation for murder. His record then showed that he had been arrested ten times in the last twenty years, three of those arrests having been for murder.

thing happened when Rupolo tried firing it a second time. Luckily for him, Gallo thought the whole episode a huge joke. Eventually, Rupolo gave up and drove himself and Gallo to a nearby friend's house where he fixed the gun before taking Gallo for a walk and shooting him seven times. Miraculously, Gallo survived, identifying Rupolo to the police as his would-be assassin. Genovese and Miranda were also arrested, but there was little or no evidence on which to hold them. Eventually they were released. Nevertheless, the New York District Attorney's Office didn't give up trying to pin Boccia's murder on Genovese. Finally, Vito made the decision that it was safer to leave the country than remain to be hounded.

Settling down first in Naples and then in Sicily, Genovese soon became involved in the Italian narcotics rackets although later on, when the Allies invaded Sicily in 1944, Genovese was said to have helped them out as a translator and general facilitator.

Vito Genovese helped make life more pleasant for the officers of the occupying forces. He seemed to have an uncanny knack for coming up with a case of precious Scotch or scarce two-inch steaks . . . In their reports these officers described Vito Genovese in glowing terms. 'He would accept no pay; paid his own expenses; worked day and night and rendered most valuable assistance to the Allied Military Government,' wrote a major for whom Genovese worked.[1]

Helpful he may have been, but on August 22 of the same year he was arrested by the Military Police and held in a Naples jail – not only for the crimes he had committed on Italian soil, but also for the murder of Boccia back in America. As soon as the war came to a close, Vito Genovese was shipped back to the USA to stand trial. But luck (or the long arm of the Mafia) was on his side, for the prosecution's main witness against Genovese, Peter LaTempa, (who had decided to confess to his part in the murder) was at that time sitting in the Raymond Street jail in Manhattan. LaTempa had long suffered from stomach ulcers and was also awaiting an operation to remove a gallstone. On January 14, 1945, prison officers supplied him with his nightly dose of medication only to discover on the following morning that LaTempa had died. A post mortem examination revealed that LaTempa had huge amounts of poison in his body. Naturally, without their main witness, the authorities were not in a strong position to proceed with the case. Brooklyn District Attorney Julius Helfland knew of at least ten other bystanders to Boccia's murder but none of these were willing to give evidence. Finally, Helfland had to admit defeat and admit that he had nothing with which to hold Genovese. Vito was released.

Vito Genovese now set up a US arm of the narcotics business he had started back in Italy, but one thing had changed radically since he was last in the States, namely the incarceration and later the deportation of Lucky Luciano (see Luciano chapter). In fact, Luciano was sent back to Italy early in 1946, after which there was a vacancy at the head of the Family. The two main contenders for the role of boss were Frank Costello and Vito Genovese but it was the more guarded, less fractious of the two – Costello – who eventually won the day.

Naturally, Vito felt slighted – added to which he could see that his several years in exile hadn't served him too well in America. He could no longer rely on a close coterie of friends, unlike Costello who had forged strong allegiances within the underworld and whose financial status was all the time going from strength to strength. Nevertheless, when, late in 1946, Lucky Luciano made a return trip across the Atlantic to Havana in Cuba in order to meet up with all his old cronies, Genovese was in attendance. Also at the conference were Thomas Lucchese, Frank Costello, Joseph Bonanno, Albert Anastasia, Joe Adonis and Meyer Lansky. The meetings, for there were several, were chaired by Luciano and in the main concerned banning narcotics (Luciano thought it unwise to meddle in this area) and the question of Bugsy Siegel, who was losing the mob hundreds of thousands of dollars in building his dream hotel, The Flamingo, in Las Vegas. But the Havana conference, which was held at the Hotel Nacional, wasn't all about business. Frank Sinatra was flown down to provide the entertainment, although later in life Sinatra denied ever having known Luciano. But if Luciano thought he would be able to set up a power base in Cuba equal to that which he had run in the US, then he was sorely mistaken. The American government, by putting immense pressure on the Cubans, saw to it that Lucky was ordered to leave the country. Luciano set sail once again for Italy, only this time he is said to have been convinced that Vito Genovese had set him up by notifying the US authorities of his presence in Cuba – in order that there would be absolutely no question of him staging a comeback or muscling in on Genovese's hard-won territory.

With Luciano now out of the picture, the 1950s proved a lucrative if not an entirely settled decade for Genovese. Together with Frank Costello, he now ruled a well-armed empire of between 500–700 soldiers with between 20–30 capos (crew bosses) amongst them. Raking in money from all quarters of New York, including the unions, betting, the waterfront, the docks, construction companies, hijacking, nightclubs, sanitation companies, catering industries, garment industries, liquor and cigarettes, there was hardly a business in New York which wasn't touched by the Family.

Up to this time, Costello and Genovese had operated in relative secrecy but on March 13, 1951, all that was to change when a special Senate committee investigating organized crime began its work in New York. The 'Kefauver Committee' (named after the Democratic Senator Estes Kefauver) had initially been set up in 1950, but it wasn't until 13 March the following year that Frank Costello appeared before the board to begin his testimony. An estimated 13 million Americans sat down to watch him on their television sets. Waiving his right to take the Fifth Amendment and refuse to say anything that might incriminate himself, Costello was instead at pains to try to prove that he was a legitimate businessman. The questioning, however, was very aggressive. The committee requested a financial statement concerning Costello's assets. Only then did Costello take the Fifth, but by that point it was too late. All the time Frank had been on camera, the nation, glued to their sets, had been witness to a bizarre dance played out by his hands, which twisted and fluttered and tapped and rubbed while he was being questioned. Costello's testimony came to a close on March 21, and although other underworld bosses, such as Meyer Lansky and Joe Adonis, were also dragged in front of the committee, it was Costello whom everyone remembered as being the foremost racketeer. The Justice Department and the FBI quickly launched a major investigation into his business activities.

If this wasn't awful enough for Costello, by the autumn of 1951 Vito Genovese had also decided that he wanted to bring down Costello. He set about eliminating one of Frank's closest friends since childhood, Willie Moretti.

As one of those responsible for the death of Joe 'the Boss' and Salvatore Maranzano, he [Genovese] knew perfectly what dangers such ambition faces, but the Byzantine complexity of his mind was perfectly suited for the endless plotting and slow building of alliances for such a project.[2]

Moretti, who ran a number of successful gambling operations in New Jersey, had been known in the recent past to have acted quite strangely under pressure (in particular when being questioned by the Kefauver Committee), which gave Genovese the idea of spreading a rumor to the effect that Willie had started to turn a bit crazy. Moretti did himself no favors, either, because during this period he was prone to giving off-the-cuff news conferences to anyone who would listen, thus lending Genovese's story even more credibility. Vito subsequently called a meeting of all his capos to discuss the 'problem' during which he put forward the motion that Moretti be taken out. In fact, he softened his proposal by using the term 'mercy killing', to which no one disagreed except Costello, who was outnumbered. On October 4, 1951 Willie Moretti was shot (most people believe by Albert Anastasia – the then boss of the Mangano Family) in a restaurant called Joe's Elbow Room on Palisades Avenue, New Jersey.

With Moretti out of the picture, Vito Genovese now had a clear run at Costello but ironically, despite all his plotting and planning, it was the government that made the first move on Costello. Following the Kefauver hearings, Costello was brought to book on charges of contempt of the Senate and was eventually sentenced to eighteen months in prison. While he was in prison, the IRS began gathering enough evidence to put him away for a much longer term, on charges of tax evasion. At the same time, the government also decided to bring denaturalization proceedings against Costello. However, despite all of the above being thrown at him, and his lengthy periods behind bars, it was Vito Genovese who put the final nail in Frank Costello's coffin.

On May 2, 1957, while returning home to his apartment in the Majestic building on Central Park West, Frank Costello was shot at point blank range, once, in the head. Miraculously the .32 caliber bullet didn't kill him. Instead of entering his brain it tore the skin behind his right ear and lodged itself in the wall behind him. Costello was rushed to the Roosevelt Hospital where he was treated in the Emergency Department and later released. He said nothing to the police about the identity of his assailant or whom he thought might have wanted him dead, but privately he knew that Vito Genovese was the only suspect.

A little less than a week previously, Genovese had sat down with several of his most trusted lieutenants, including Joe Valachi and Vinnie Mauro, to hold a strategy meeting. He told them that Costello had turned government informer, a story the others believed. As a result, a hit was sanctioned and three men chosen for the job, Vincent 'The Chin' Gigante, Tommy Eboli and Dominick DeQuatro.

Vincent Gigante was later identified by the Majestic's doorman as being the gunman and immediately went into hiding (although he later turned himself in to police). Vito Genovese, on the other hand, was now even more determined to rid himself of Costello. Immediately after the attempted coup, Genovese and approximately thirty of his most trusted soldiers and bodyguards decamped to a house he owned in Atlantic Highlands from where he called a meeting of all his capos together with several Family bosses. Everyone was said to have showed up except for Anthony 'Little Augie' Carfano – a long time friend of Costello's – who was obviously still loyal to his old boss. The only other face missing from the meeting was Albert 'The Mad Hat' Anastasia who was also unhappy with Genovese's 'government informer' accusation against Costello. Anastasia, a powerful boss in his own right, was succinctly described by the author Robert Lacey as a 'Bugsy Siegel without the charm'.[3]

Genovese made it clear to anyone who would listen that he thought Costello an ineffectual boss who was only interested in lining his own pockets. Furthermore, Genovese stated that anyone caught siding with Costello would immediately be assumed an enemy and, therefore, fair game. But Vito's most extravagant gesture was to name himself the official boss of the Family and appoint Jerry Catena as his underboss. Costello, meanwhile, tried to find a peaceful resolution to the situation.

After all, not only had he amassed great personal wealth from his various gambling operations – and he had no children to whom he could pass on his title – but it had always been Costello's way to try to find peaceful resolutions to potentially violent situations. During his reign as Family boss, which had stretched from 1937 to the attempt on his life in 1957, New York's five major crime families had all enjoyed relative peace. Not so any longer. Genovese wanted Costello deposed and was willing to do almost anything to achieve his goal. The only realistic opposition to Genovese's plans was Albert Anastasia. Early on in his life Anastasia had earned a reputation as a ruthless killer. When aged twenty he beat and strangled a fellow longshoreman to death. Subsequently, he was given the death sentence and was due to be executed in the electric chair in Sing Sing prison, but was reprieved at the last moment and granted a second trial when several previous prosecution witnesses conveniently changed their stories. Anastasia was also one of those who set up the infamous Murder Inc., along with Lucky Luciano, Meyer Lansky and Bugsy Siegel, and it was during this time that he attained his second soubriquet of Lord High Executioner. Never one to shun a killing, Anastasia is thought to be responsible for countless murders, but by backing Costello when Vito Genovese was adamant Costello be removed, Anastasia put his own life on the line.

When he and Costello began conducting secret meetings, therefore, Genovese was naturally suspicious. He contacted a young Anastasia capo by the name of Carlo Gambino and convinced him that by ridding themselves of Anastasia they would both reap enormous benefits. It is then thought that Gambino sub-contracted the killing to Joseph 'Joe Bandy' Biondo.

On October 25, 1957, Albert Anastasia was shot dead in front of seven Italian barbers while he sat in a chair in the barbershop of the Park-Sheraton Hotel on Fifty-fifth Street in Manhattan. None of the barbers could later recall anything that would be of significant use to the police. In fact, all that the authorities could establish was that two gunmen had shot at Albert Anastasia. The word on the street, however, was that Vito Genovese was behind the hit. The underworld was in chaos and, as Joseph Bonanno states in his autobiography, this wasn't simply because one of their own had been killed; it was because of the imbalance now disturbing what had been a relatively calm period in mob history. 'Whoever killed Anastasia,' wrote Bonanno, ' – and the indications were that it was men within his own Family – was not really my concern, but the concern of his Family. The identity of Albert's slayers was of interest to those who wanted to avenge his death. My main preoccupation was with the effects of Albert's death. On the Commission, Anastasia's demise benefited both Genovese and Lucchese, whose animosity toward Albert was well known.'[4]

Three weeks after the hit, the mob then organized a huge get-together on the estate of one Joseph Barbara in Apalachin, northern New York, a meeting that Vito Genovese attended as unrivalled head of his Family. Nearly 120 other mobsters also showed up and some commentators have speculated that the attempt on Frank Costello's life, together with the grisly slaying of Albert Anastasia, must have been one of the main

Pictured here in police custody in New York in 1945, Genovese was extradited from Italy to face a murder charge for a killing that had taken place in 1934. When the prosecution's only witness was mysteriously poisoned while also in police custody, the case collapsed.

reasons behind the convention. After all, in as small a world as the one the mob inhabits, events such as this did not pass lightly. In his testimony before the McClellan committee in 1963, Attorney General Robert F. Kennedy stated that:

We know now that the meeting at Apalachin was called by a leading racketeer in an effort to resolve the problem created by the murder of Albert Anastasia. The racketeer was concerned that Anastasia had brought too many individuals not worthy of membership into the organization. To insure the security of the organization, the racketeer wanted these men removed. Of particular concern to this racketeer was that he had violated commission rules in causing the assault, the attempted assassination of Frank Costello, deposed New York rackets boss, and the murder of Albert Anastasia.[5]

Of course, Kennedy was referring to Vito Genovese, but no sooner had Apalachin begun than the conference came to an abrupt halt thanks to the observations of one Sergeant Edgar L. Crosswell of the New York State Police (see Paul Castellano chapter) who raided the grounds of the estate, scattering Mafia bosses left, right and centre. Over sixty men were arrested, including such figures as Carlo Gambino, Joe Profaci and the big fish himself, Vito Genovese. When asked why the meeting had been convened, everyone repeated an identical story; that Barbara had been ill and that they were paying him a visit to wish him well again – no matter that over a hundred of them had arrived on the same day! Frustratingly for the police, they had little or no evidence on which to hold anyone and eventually the detainees were all released.

But if Apalachin had ended badly it was nothing in comparison to the fate of Anthony 'Little Augie' Carfano, who had so blatantly turned his back on Genovese in favor of Costello. Two years after the attempt on Costello's life, Little Augie was still fuming over Costello's treatment at the hands of Genovese. Then, on September 25, 1959, Little Augie, together with a woman by the name of Janice Drake, went out on the town. No one is certain what the precise relationship between Mrs Drake and Augie was, but in all likelihood it was platonic – especially given that Augie was in his sixties while she was a lot younger and a former beauty queen – Miss New Jersey.

At first, the couple visited the Copacabana club where they had drinks and danced, but later that evening, having bumped into some mobster friends, they went to dinner at a restaurant called Marino's. During the meal, Little Augie took two phone calls, the second of which obviously spooked him enough for him to make his excuses and leave with Janice. Only a few hours later, both bodies were discovered sitting upright in Augie's black Cadillac on a street in Queens. Both had been shot in the head and police surmised from the angle of the bullet wounds that the assassins must have been crouched in the back of Augie's car.

Frank Costello, thanks in the main to some heavy duty work on the part of his lawyers, escaped several jail terms and deportation, but eventually succumbed to the law in 1958 when he returned to prison to serve out the rest of his tax evasion sentence. On his release in 1961 he chose to live out his days in peaceful retirement. Before he could really settle down and enjoy life outside the mob, however, Frank

It is believed that Vito Genovese was set up by his arch-enemy Frank Costello when he was eventually convicted of drugs trafficking. Pictured here in 1959 as he is led away to begin a fifteen year sentence, Genovese was 63 years old and destined to die in prison.

Costello laid plans to see his arch-enemy either dead or, at the very least, behind bars. Together with Lucky Luciano, who was still in Italy, Meyer Lansky, Sam Giancana and Carlo Gambino (who by this time was boss of the Mangano Family, having taken over from Albert Anastasia) it is thought Costello plotted to see Genovese caught while trafficking narcotics. He employed the services of Nelson 'The Melon' Cantellops, who was of Puerto Rican extraction and who, in 1958, was serving a five-year sentence in Sing Sing Prison for drug dealing. Nelson was approached while still inside with a deal; he was to call in the Bureau of Narcotics for a meeting at the prison and tell them that he had evidence of Genovese dealing in drugs. In exchange, Cantellops would be given a large sum of money (in the region of $100,000) and the mob would see what they could do to get him an early release.

For the setup of Genovese, Mooney [Sam Giancana] called on Willie Potatoes, who, in turn, brought in one of his soldiers, a low-level dope peddler, Nelson Cantellops. Mooney didn't have any idea who the guy was – and didn't care.

Cantellops was just a sap, he said, but a smart sap – tailor-made for their plot against Genovese [6]

The plan worked like magic. The Narcotics Bureau lapped up Cantellops' story and acted upon it almost immediately by dragging Genovese before a Grand Jury in Manhattan in July 1958. Vito and twenty-three others were indicted for conspiracy to traffic in drugs – a major coup not only on the part of Costello, but for all those who had begun to despise Genovese. On April 17, 1959 he was convicted and sentenced to pay a $20,000 fine and serve fifteen years in prison. Nelson Cantellops was released from Sing Sing and, as far as is known, lived a life of relative obscurity until 1965, when he was killed during a fight in a bar. On the other hand, Vito Genovese was now on his way to prison, although before he was carted off to begin his sentence he called all his Family members together and announced that he would fight his conviction tooth and nail. He knew it for what it was – a set-up – and was furious that of all the things he had done, the government had managed to convict him of something of which he was innocent.

Also discussed at the meeting was that Tommy Eboli would now be the temporary representative of the Family, with Jerry Catena acting as underboss and Mike Miranda as consigliere (advisor). For the next few years this is precisely how the Family was run, with Genovese taking on an advisory role from his prison cell. But being behind bars took its toll on Vito who had, during the past few years, suffered from various health problems, including a heart condition. Eventually, on February 14, 1969 Vito Genovese died of a heart attack in the Federal Prison medical centre at Springfield Penitentiary in Missouri. Few people mourned his passing.

[1] *Uncle Frank The Biography of Frank Costello*, Leonard Katz, W. H. Allen & Co, 1974.

[2] Ibid.

[3] *Little Man: Meyer Lansky and the Gangster Life*, Robert Lacey, Little Brown Inc, 1991.

[4] *A Man of Honor: The Autobiography of Joseph Bonanno*, Simon & Schuster, 1983.

[5] *Uncle Frank The Biography of Frank Costello*, Leonard Katz, W. H. Allen & Co, 1974.

[6] *Double Cross: The Story of the Man who Controlled America*, Sam and Chuck Giancana, Macdonald & Co (Publishers) Ltd, 1992.

SAM 'MOMO' GIANCANA
The Butcher of Chicago

'I want that dago, Sam Giancana, put away for good.'

Robert Kennedy

Perhaps more than any other mobster in history, Sam Giancana is worthy of the title 'psychopath'. His story is littered with murderous acts, which are said to have included not only the St Valentine's Day Massacre, but also the assassinations of both John and Bobby Kennedy, together with the murder of Marilyn Monroe. Whether or not there is any truth to these claims, one thing is certain, Sam 'Momo' Giancana enjoyed nothing better than causing murder and mayhem and was, as such, the personification of the anti-American dream.

Born on May 24, 1908 to Antonio and Antonia Giancana (who were originally from the Sicilian village of Castelvetrano) in Chicago's Little Italy, the boy was christened Momo 'Jimmy' Salvatore Giancana. The area in which he grew up was particularly impoverished, housing as it did mainly Sicilian immigrants, but with one more mouth to feed (the Giancanas already had a daughter, Lena) Antonio felt even more pressed for money. Ultimately, he took out his frustrations on his young son. Every misdemeanour was met with severe punishment and everything that went wrong within the family was blamed on Momo, including the death of his mother from a miscarriage in 1910, when the boy was just two years old. One can only speculate how this legacy of violence affected the young Giancana, but given his later predilection for murdering any and every opponent, it is probably safe to say his early experiences weren't helpful. By the age of ten, Momo's teachers had labelled him a delinquent and, not knowing what else to do with the young thug, sent him to the St Charles Reformatory for six months. Sadly, on his return his behaviour was not greatly improved, which led to him being thrown out of the family home (by this time his father had remarried). Momo bummed around the streets, slept in cars and shop doorways, stole what food he could, but eventually found a 'home from home' within a Chicago streetgang called the 42s.

Within the gang Salvatore/Sam was often referred to either as Momo or as 'Mooney' (an early twentieth century word for 'crazy'). The gang stole anything they could lay their hands on, but in particular cars, which could be stripped down and the parts sold on. In time, the 42s became a notorious gang, known throughout the area for their robberies and violence. Their only role models were gangsters like Johnny Torrio, Diamond Joe Esposito, Big Jim Colosimo and, last but not least, Al Capone.

In fact, it was Diamond Joe Esposito to whom the young Giancana eventually turned in search of work, aged just fifteen. Esposito ran one of the oldest Black Hand (extortionist) gangs in the whole of Chicago and utilized the services of the six Genna brothers (otherwise known as the 'Terrible Gennas') to run the bootlegging side of his business. When Giancana was little more than seventeen years old, he was spotted by Al Capone, who is said to have hired out Momo from Esposito in order to murder six of Esposito's own men – the Genna brothers. First to go was Angelo Genna, quickly followed by Mike and Tony. Subsequently, the remaining three Genna brothers fled Chicago in fear for their lives (although they would later return to run a legitimate food outlet).

Momo's reputation went from strength to strength and, despite a brief spell in prison for auto-theft, he knew he was on his way up. Even when he was indicted for the murder of a shopkeeper during a bungled robbery, Momo wasn't overly concerned. Instead, he had the only witness to the shooting, Alex Burba, killed. The case was dropped due to lack of evidence. Then, in 1928, Al Capone asked Momo (along with a handful of other young thugs) to carry out the biggest job of his career to date – the murder of Diamond Joe Esposito, the man who had given Momo his first big break. Seeing this request as an ideal opportunity to move up through the ranks, Momo was only too happy to oblige. On March 21, 1928, Diamond Joe, having first received death threats over the telephone, was gunned down outside his home by three assailants as they drove past in a car. Although no one was arrested (let alone convicted) for Esposito's murder, in their book *Double Cross* Giancana's brother and godson, Sam and Chuck, both imply that Momo was involved.

> Besides, with Diamond Joe out of the picture and with Capone building a
> bigger and bigger empire, Momo was a success story in the making. ' . . .
> Mooney Giancana was twenty years old, and every man, woman, and child in
> the neighborhood not only feared him but revered him, as well. His recent
> scrapes with the law, the murders he was known to have committed, his brutal
> intimidation tactics – all became legendary. Rather than diminish his stature,
> the stories the immigrants whispered among themselves only served to make
> the swaggering Mooney a larger-than-life figure. To the Italians, hoods like
> Mooney who'd roamed the streets as youths and were now pulling themselves
> up by the bootstraps to achieve financial success were simply symbols of a
> dream come true.'[1]

No wonder, then, that after the St Valentine's Day Massacre on February 14, 1929, Momo was dragged down to the police station for questioning. After all, he had already been in and out of jail charged with an assortment of crimes ranging from gang rape to burglary and suspicion of murder, not to mention the fact that he was a close associate of Jack McGurn – the supposed mastermind behind the St Valentine's Day murders. According to Sam and Chuck Giancana, Momo was hired to serve as both driver and assassin during the hit but with little evidence, the police couldn't hold Momo down at the station for long. His luck, however, wasn't destined to hold out, for in March of that same year he was again taken down to the police station for questioning. This time the crime was burglary and when the case came to trial, Momo was duly convicted and sent to Joliet State Penitentiary for between three to five years.

Momo was released on Christmas Eve 1932 and immediately returned to his old ways, falling in with Capone's crew. But a lot had changed in the intervening years. For a start, the whole of America was suffering from the Depression. A huge percentage of the working population had no work and families were finding it hard to make ends meet. Farmers were being evicted from land they had worked for generations and many once-successful businesses had gone bust. Although many gangster Families were still operating, Al Capone had finally been indicted by the Justice Department on charges of tax evasion and it was only a matter of time before he was on his way to prison. Paul 'The Waiter' Ricca had taken over where Capone had left off. Ten times more publicity shy than Scarface, Ricca left all the up-front jobs to his associates, men like Frank Nitti, Jake Guzik and a Welshman by the name of Murray Humphreys, who ran the 'protection' side of the business. Eager to welcome Momo back into the fold, Ricca gave him control of several of his South Side concessions, including some that involved the production of bootlegged whisky (although Prohibition was on the verge of being phased out). Momo's services were also occasionally required to help 'persuade' business people that paying for protection was the sensible thing to do.

It was also around this period that Momo began dating a Sicilian girl by the name of Angeline De Tolve. The two were wed on September 23, 1933. But marriage did nothing to soften Momo's character or to persuade him to go legitimate and in early 1939 he was arrested once again. Officials had uncovered one of his illegal bootlegging stills. The trial took place in May of that year and, although the judge went easy on several of the men who provided the premises and materials to make the whisky, Momo received over $3,000 in fines and was sent to Leavenworth prison, Kansas for four years.

By the time he came out in 1942, (as a result of early parole) once again the lay of the land had changed. Ricca had engineered a new racketeering business by taking over the International Alliance of Theatrical Stage Employees and Motion Picture Operators. He had put Frank Nitti in charge of intimidating members into handing over protection money. In turn, Nitti had farmed out the muscle work to Willie Bioff and George Brown, but when these two men were arrested and charged with racketeering offences, Ricca told Nitti that he was wholly responsible for anything that Bioff and Brown told the police. Frightened of his boss and scared of a prison sentence, Nitti went home and shot himself in the head. The knock-on effect was devastating. Without Nitti to stop them blabbing, both Bioff and Brown spilled everything they knew to the authorities who then arrested Ricca and had him thrown in jail for ten years.

By the time Momo came out of prison, therefore, he had a new boss, Anthony

Sam Giancana can claim a unique reputation as he has been associated with some of the most famous killings of all time, including the St Valentine's Day Massacre as well as the murders of Marilyn Monroe, John F. Kennedy and Bobby Kennedy.

Accardo (whom, it was suspected, had also been involved in the St Valentine's Day Massacre). Momo quickly ingratiated himself with Accardo and further enhanced his position within the mob by telling Accardo of a new scam that he had learned from a black prison inmate, Eddie Jones.

It's a kind of lottery. You pick some numbers and bet on 'em. With a nickel bet, you could win five bucks ... as much as two thousand dollars on a two-dollar bet ... But the real beauty is anybody can play. Everybody's got a nickel to spare. And there isn't a soul on the south side who doesn't play ... They all do. It's not the big-buck, heavy gambler shit ... pennies make nickels, nickels make dimes, and goddamn it ... dimes make dollars. Millions of dollars.[2]

After Jones was released from prison, Accardo gave Momo the go-ahead to set up the new 'policy' or 'numbers' racket and so Jones and Momo went into business, initially setting up in a predominately black area of Chicago. It wasn't long, however, before Momo wanted rid of his partner. After only a few months' partnership, Jones was kidnapped and held for a $250,000 ransom. It was also threatened that if he didn't hand over the entire operation to Momo and afterwards leave Chicago, he would be killed. Jones naturally complied. He didn't just leave Chicago, he left America altogether and headed for Mexico.

With the entire business now under his control, Momo began reaping rich financial rewards. Not only that, he was made Tony Accardo's underboss, a prestigious position which saw him traveling to New York, Florida, Cuba and California, in search of new business opportunities that included pinball machines, narcotics, nightclubs and jukeboxes. Momo also joined forces with the New York boss Frank Costello, in a gem-smuggling operation which saw him taking gems stolen in the Midwest to one of Costello's numerous fences, after which he would return with further stolen gems, which would be distributed back on Momo's home turf. Not only was this highly lucrative, but joining forces with Costello gave Momo a huge amount of credibility back in Chicago.

Riding on a wave of success, in 1946 Momo decided to open up a club that he called the Boogie Woogie, and which he boasted would be as good or better than the Cotton Club. He also bought a palatial mansion in the suburb of Oak Park for him and his growing family – by now Momo and his wife had three children.

But none of this could satisfy Momo's need to have his fingers in bigger and better pies. Together with Accardo, Guzik and Humphreys, Momo set his eyes on the Continental Press, which was a country-wide telegraph service serving bookies not only with racing forms and results, but also with track conditions, jockey changes and up-to-the-minute betting odds. Each bookie would pay the Continental Press $100 per day as a fee, but at the time Momo wanted to acquire Continental, it was owned by James Ragen. With a little help from his east coast Syndicate friends, however, (together with Bugsy Siegel who was now living in California) Momo and the others managed to 'persuade' Ragen that it would be in his best interests to pass Continental over to them.

Effectively, this gave Momo, Accardo, Humphreys and Guzik a connection with every gambling operation in the country. Momo was then convinced by Accardo that he should take his gambling operation overseas. Like Meyer Lansky, he set up clubs in partnership with Fulgencio Batista's government in Cuba, but also established concessions in Egypt and across South America. The most interesting element of these foreign operations was that, in order for the businesses to be established, Momo and friends had to gain the backing of politicians and ambassadors. And this 'backing' – which in effect meant buying off politicians – went, according to Sam and Chuck Giancana, right to the very top, including both Presidents Roosevelt and Truman. In the book *Double Cross*, Momo's brother recalls what Momo said about Truman's 1948 presidential win over Thomas Dewey.

> 'So, fact is, Truman owes everything he's got to us. Pendergast made him a judge and then, with the Italian muscle behind him, got him to the Senate. When the forty-four election came up . . . Kelly here in Chicago got him on

the ticket with Roosevelt. Shit, Chicago got Roosevelt and Truman nominated and elected. We were good to Roosevelt; he was good to us. He died and Truman's been our man in the White House ever since. It's smooth sailing with him there.'

Yet there was one area of Momo's life that was not plain sailing, an area he had no power to influence, for in 1954 both his father and his wife died. Angeline was in Florida when, on April 10, she suffered a cerebral embolism. Momo's father died suddenly on July 27. Both funerals, in a display of just how far Momo had risen from his poverty-stricken childhood, were attended by the rich and the infamous, mob leaders, businessmen, congressmen and senators.

By 1955 Tony Accardo and Paul Ricca were being investigated by the Internal Revenue Service for tax evasion and by the FBI. It was a blessing in disguise for Momo, for with these two names out of the picture he could assume overall control of the Chicago Syndicate, a position he had coveted all of his life. Momo's powers now extended far and wide, but they were about to reach their zenith with the appearance of one Joseph Kennedy on the scene.

Joseph Kennedy, apart from fathering two prospective presidential candidates, was himself a very wealthy Wall Street financier and all-round businessman. Back in the days of Prohibition, it is said that he partnered Diamond Joe Esposito in his booze running business, building up a small personal fortune. It was also Momo's belief that Kennedy, along with several other powerful businessmen, had manipulated the Wall Street crash and, by association, the Depression, cashing in when others were losing their livelihoods. Whatever the truth behind this last allegation, Joseph Kennedy was a powerful man, a man who had set his sights on his son Jack running for the White House. Early on in Jack's life, Momo had done Joseph Kennedy a huge favor by persuading 'the powers that be' to annul a career-threatening marriage of Jack's and, further to this, to dispose of all the paperwork documenting the union as though it had never existed. Then, in May 1956, Joseph Kennedy showed up in Chicago wanting another, larger favor from Momo. Somehow, he had aggrieved New York boss Frank Costello, snubbing him to the extent that Costello had put out a contract on the old man. Now Joseph Kennedy wanted Momo to persuade Costello to call the contract off.

According to legend, Momo made Kennedy sweat until the old man, at breaking point, swore that if his son were elected President of the United States, he'd forever be in Momo's debt, that there would be no favor the President would refuse. The deal was struck and within a week Momo had persuaded Frank Costello to call off the hit.

Nevertheless, despite all of Joseph Kennedy's promises, a short while later, in January 1957, Bobby Kennedy helped set up the McClellan Committee which (like the Kefauver Committee in the early part of the decade) was specifically created to investigate mob activity. To begin with, Momo believed, as Joseph Kennedy had persuaded him, that the Committee was just for show – a good way to illustrate how Jack Kennedy was a whiter than white, good guy. After all, Joseph Kennedy was in

Momo's debt. But when the Committee began its work proper it soon became clear that Bobby Kennedy was planning a full-scale attack on the underworld. Senator McClellan began dragging in mob men and their bosses to testify in front of television cameras. The nature of the inquiry fell into three phases. The first phase concerned the theft of union funds; the second phase examined the history of the unions with reference to racketeering; and the third phase – improper labor practices with direct reference to the leaders of organized crime.

Suddenly, the entire nation was glued to their wirelesses and television sets, learning words such as Mafia, Camorra and La Cosa Nostra. Joseph Amato from the Bureau of Narcotics also stated on November 13, 1957 that: 'We believe there does exist . . . a society, loosely organized, for the specific purpose of smuggling narcotics and committing other crimes . . . It has its core in Italy and it is nationwide. In fact, international.' This statement was well-timed for a month previously, on October 25, 1957, New Yorkers had been treated to one of the Mafia's most famous hits when Albert Anastasia was gunned down as he sat in a barber's chair. Numerous theories surrounded his execution, some thought Meyer Lansky was behind the killing because Anastasia had wanted to set up casinos in Cuba, while others speculated that Vito Genovese ordered the hit because Anastasia was supporting Genovese's rival, Frank Costello. Whoever was responsible, it was all grist to the mill for McClennan who, much to Momo's annoyance and disgust, now called him to testify before the Committee.

Joseph Kennedy assured Momo that the investigation was simply a show-trial, a masquerade to help Jack win the Presidency. In fact, Jack was about to announce his candidacy for the 1960 Democratic Party Race, but Momo was less than convinced that Joseph was telling the truth. When he appeared on television before the Committee, his performance was far from relaxed, especially as Bobby Kennedy, who was Chief Counsel, seemed to take great pleasure in making fun of Momo who answered every question – thirty-four times in total – with the stolid response, 'I refuse to answer on the grounds it may incriminate me.'[3]

But if Momo was being ridiculed in front of the cameras, behind the scenes he was working flat out to dig up as much dirt as he could on Jack Kennedy. Nor did it take long to discover JFK's great weakness; women (including Marilyn Monroe), or to build up a large arsenal of tape recordings and photographs of the President-to-be in compromising situations. At the same time Momo was, of course, backing JFK for the White House. He and his union men were out in the field promoting him for all they were worth. Finally, on 8 November 1960, John F. Kennedy beat Richard Nixon to become the thirty-fifth President of the United States. It had been a close run thing and Momo was in no doubt that he and his men were the ones who had eventually won it for their candidate.

Always one to enjoy the high life, Momo did not restrict himself to rubbing shoulders with the politicos; he also enjoyed the bright lights of Hollywood. He mixed with the likes of Sammy Davis Jnr, Peter Lawford, Natalie Wood and Frank Sinatra. But there were even stranger bedfellows to come for, with the ousting of Batista in

Cuba by Fidel Castro, Momo had begun working with the CIA to topple the new anti-democratic, anti-American dictatorship that now sat on America's back doorstep. It has been alleged that Momo's job was to assassinate Castro, for which he would be paid handsomely, and after which he could resume his gambling rackets with a percentage to be turned over to the CIA. A number of authors who have researched and written about this period maintain that JFK knew of this deal and had sanctioned it, as had the director of the FBI, J. Edgar Hoover. Batista loyalists were also involved in the plan and began liaising with US gun runners. One of these was Jack Ruby, who owned a Texas strip-joint and who would later become renowned for a much more public event.

But, as the history books show us, all did not go well. Having tried various unsuccessful attempts on Castro's life (including slipping poison into one of his drinks) the CIA ordered an invasion of Cuba in April 1961 by approximately 1,500 exiles (consisting of Cuban ex-soldiers, mercenaries and secret agents), the success of which not only relied on resident Cubans rising up to overthrow Castro, but also on the US President supporting the operation. After the first attack at the Bay of Pigs failed, however, Kennedy backtracked on his promise and refused to send in air support. Suddenly, the invading 1,500 Cubans were overwhelmed by Castro's 200,000-strong army, leaving many dead and the rest as prisoners of the new regime.

Naturally, the event was broadcast worldwide. In public, at least, Kennedy was forced to take responsibility for the entire fiasco, but in private he blamed the CIA for allowing the plan to get as far as an invasion. No one was spared his wrath, not the director of the CIA, Allen Dulles, or the director of covert operations, Richard Bissell. In fact, Kennedy is thought to have vowed to splinter the CIA into a million-and-one pieces. But if Kennedy was incandescent, so too were the CIA, who began to think of him as a very real threat to their autonomy. In turn, Sam 'Momo' Giancana, who had been assured of Kennedy's staunch support for the Cuban project and who now looked like a fool, was also furious.

As if to fire his anger even more, shortly afterwards Bobby Kennedy ordered full-time surveillance of Momo by the FBI. Wherever he went, whatever he did, Momo was followed and watched to the extent that he became so paranoid that he ordered the murder of a man by the name of William 'Action' Jackson, whom he thought was a stool pigeon.

Jackson's murder was one of the most gruesome in mob history – forcibly taken to a meat-rendering plant in downtown Chicago, he was hung up, while still alive, on a meat hook while Momo's henchmen set about torturing him with razors, knives, ice picks and even a blowtorch. Jackson was also shot in the knee and had an electric cattle prod jammed into his rectum on to which water was poured.

Meanwhile the Kennedys, now that they were in power, were trying to distance themselves from their mobster connections as fast as was humanly possible. This included informing Frank Sinatra that he was now persona non grata at The White House, as well as making it clear to Momo that he no longer had the President's ear.

Sam Giancana appeared before a Senate Rackets Committee in Washington in 1959
where he invoked the Fifth Amendment, refusing to answer any questions linking him with
a pinball, pizza and prostitution ring.

Enraged at these snubs, Momo determined to destroy the Kennedys and the image
they had created of a Camelot-like government. Momo put together some
information on a girl both Jack and Bobby Kennedy had been associating with –
Marilyn Monroe. Through his Hollywood connections, Momo had come to know
Monroe personally (it is alleged that he had had an affair with her early on in her
career). According to his brother, Monroe confessed to Momo that she had fallen in
love with Bobby Kennedy. This confession, (or so Sam and Chuck Giancana
theorized) sealed Monroe's fate. When the CIA, who were increasingly anxious about
revelations that the actress might make concerning themselves and the President,
ordered Momo to assassinate her, Momo also saw a chance to even the score between
himself and the Kennedys:

> According to guys in the Outfit, it was at this time that the CIA, fearful of
> exposure by a vengeful, drug-addicted Monroe, requested that Mooney have

her eliminated. And Mooney, smelling blood, seized on the CIA contract as a way to achieve another objective, as well. By murdering Monroe, it might be possible to depose the rulers of Camelot.

Having learnt through his connections that Bobby Kennedy was to visit California on August 4, 1962 and that he had arranged a secret tryst with Monroe, Momo set his plan in motion.[4]

All it needed was a little forward planning. When Bobby Kennedy visited California on August 4 and met up with Monroe, Momo is said to have sent 'Needles' Gianola and 'Mugsy' Tortorella to execute her after Bobby Kennedy had left her house, but to make it look like a suicide. Later, at her inquest, Momo was in no doubt that the Attorney General would have to mention a cache of love letters sent to Monroe by Bobby, which she kept in the house and which the police would naturally discover. But Momo was to be disappointed, for when the news broke of Marilyn's death, the Kennedys made absolutely certain that their name was kept out of the papers. Their whiter than white image remained intact.

Whether or not this story is to be believed, what is beyond question is the fact that, after Monroe's death, Momo was put under even more severe scrutiny by the FBI. His home, his offices, even the hotels he stayed in, were bugged. When he took the government to court on the grounds of invasion of privacy, the case was thrown out.

Shortly afterwards, on November 22, 1963, the unthinkable happened; John F. Kennedy was assassinated while riding in an open-car cavalcade through the streets of Dallas. There are countless theories as to whom was behind the hit, but once again in Chuck and Sam Giancana's memoir of Momo, they pose a predictable theory – that Momo himself was behind the world's most famous assassination. According to them, Momo '. . . fixed Chuck in a steely, impenetrable gaze. "We [the CIA and the Mob] took care of Kennedy . . . together." He lifted his cigar to his lips and a cruel smile curled like an embrace around it.'[5]

To add weight to this theory, Chuck Giancana states that it wasn't until he heard it was Jack Ruby who had shot and killed Lee Harvey Oswald that he was 100 per cent certain his brother had been involved in Kennedy's death. After all, Ruby had been Momo's 'man in Chicago,' running all kinds of illegal businesses as well as running guns for the CIA. And, in addition to Sam and Chuck's memories of the occasion, Seymour Hersh in his book *The Dark Side of Camelot* states, 'One immediate suspect was Sam Giancana, who had been overheard by the FBI since early 1961 claiming again and again that he had been double crossed by Jack Kennedy.'[6]

With the arrest and subsequent killing of Lee Harvey Oswald, the case was, at least officially, closed. Even four-and-a-half years later, in 1969, when Bobby Kennedy was also shot dead, this time in a mob-owned hotel, no one thought to investigate Momo even though, according to Chuck Giancana, it was well known in underworld circles that Momo had ordered the hit.

Momo was now in his early sixties and while he had no plans to retire, a brief spell

This 1974 photograph was taken about a year before Giancana was murdered. Shot in the head, the mouth and five times under the chin, detectives presumed his body was sending the message that he had been shot to stop him from talking to the authorities.

in prison during 1965-66 for not responding to a Justice Department subpoena had taken its toll. On his release Momo decided to move to a luxurious villa in Mexico, from where he could run his South American businesses as well as being able to pop over to Europe.

Despite him being out of the country, the FBI weren't finished with Momo. From the late 1960s into the early part of the 1970s, they tried several ploys to lure him back over the border. Eventually, under immense pressure from the US Government, Mexico had him extradited to the States where, after a brief illness, he was scheduled to appear in Washington, DC before a Senate Select Subcommittee on Intelligence. Before this could happen, however, on June 19, 1975 Sam 'Momo' Giancana was gunned down in the basement kitchen of his home by a person or persons unknown. In fact, he had been hit once in the head, once in the mouth and five times under the chin, leading detectives to surmise that he had been shot to keep him from talking. Detectives also concluded that Momo must have known his assailant as there was no sign of forced entry into the house. Whoever brought Momo down (and theories range from the CIA to other Mafia bosses who feared Momo's high profile), the fact remains that it was a fitting end to a violent career. Throughout his life Momo had lived by the sword, surely it was only right and fitting that he now died by it as well.

[1] *Double Cross: The Story of the Man who Controlled America*, Sam and Chuck Giancana, Macdonald & Co (Publishers) Ltd, 1992.
[2] Ibid.
[3] The consquences of the McClellan Committee were very low-key – in fact not one underworld associate was sent to jail as a result of anything divulged during the inquiry.
[4] *Double Cross: The Story of the Man who Controlled America*, Sam and Chuck Giancana, Macdonald & Co (Publishers) Ltd, 1992.
[5] Ibid.
[6] *The Dark Side of Camelot*, Seymour Hersh, Little, Brown and Co, 1997.

JOHN GOTTI

The Teflon Don

'Gotti is street. Gotti is flash. Gotti is publicity. Gotti is everything
Castellano doesn't want.'
Boss of Bosses: The Fall of the Godfather, Joseph F. O'Brien & Andris Kurins

When one imagines the Mafia, most people picture films such as *The Godfather*, *Goodfellas*, *Made in America*; films that depict violence as an everyday occurrence; films that are purely fiction – aren't they? In December 1985 fiction exploded into fact when Paul Castellano, boss of the Gambino Family (along with his underboss, Thomas Bilotti) was gunned down a week before Christmas in central New York. The scene was bloody and shocked all those who had witnessed it, but it was to be almost seven years before anyone was convicted of the murders. By that time John Gotti – the main defendant – had built up such a reputation as a fast-talking man-about-town, running a hegemonic empire of which Caligula would have proud, that he had become part of modern-day popular culture.

John Joseph Gotti Jnr was born on October 27, 1940 in the Bronx, New York. His parents Fannie and John Joseph Snr had in total thirteen children, (two of whom died while still infants) of which John Jnr was the fifth. Growing up in the South Bronx, there was plenty for a young boy to see and do. There were numerous street markets, cafes and social clubs, there was the Harlem River to play beside, the Yankee Stadium to dream about and a short trip across the water was the largest population of Italian-Americans in the whole of the USA, all living in Italian Harlem.

By the time he was eleven, the young Gotti, although poor, enjoyed his surroundings and, while probably unaware of the term 'Mafia,' would have felt its ubiquitous presence. To the wider public, however, in 1951 the hot topic of conversation was the Kefauver Committee hearing, which was being televised nationwide and which, in summing up its findings, concluded that:

> There is a sinister criminal organization known as the Mafia operating throughout the country with ties in other nations …The power of the Mafia is based on a ruthless enforcement of its edicts and its own law of vengeance to which have been credibly attributed literally hundreds of murders throughout the country.[1]

Oblivious to this and other rumblings concerning organized crime, the young Gotti was instead mixing it up with his local street gangs. By this time his family had moved to the Brownsville-East area of Brooklyn, a sector mainly made up of poor southern Italian immigrants and eastern European Jews. The street gangs were a way of life, a means of comradeship bestowing a sense of belonging on their members.

John Jnr joined a gang that called themselves the Fulton-Rockaway Boys (named after a street intersection in Brooklyn). One of his elder brothers was already a member and several of his younger brothers later joined up, too. Two other gang members also became life-long friends; Angelo 'Quack-Quack' Ruggiero and Wilfred 'Willie Boy' Johnson, who was of American Indian descent.

'Johnny Boy,' as Gotti was known by those to whom he was closest, was great with his fists, but perhaps his most lethal weapon in those early gang years was his growing resentment at being born poor. He wanted to be like the wiseguys who dressed in smart suits, drove large cars and who always seemed to have plenty of ready cash. A habitual truant from school, at age sixteen Johnny Boy quit education and became a fully-fledged member of the Rockaways – first getting arrested for 'disorderly conduct' on May 15, 1957 after being involved in a gang fight (although the judge later threw the case out). Gotti was also arrested for burglary for which he was given probation and later still for 'unlawful assembly.' All these arrests, together with his tough, streetwise attitude, meant that Gotti soon developed a reputation as a fearless thug, thief and all-round hustler; a reputation which was to stand him in good stead with one of the largest Mafia families in New York.

Before his Mafia career began, however, Gotti actually secured himself a legitimate job as a coat presser in a large Brooklyn clothes factory. Also during this period he met and fell in love with a young girl called Victoria L. DiGiorgio who was two years his junior. The couple were married on March 6, 1962 and within three years they had produced three children.

Giving up his job as a coat presser soon after he was married, Gotti became a truck driver's assistant for the Barnes Express Company which taught him all he needed to know (especially in his later career) about the way warehouses and shipping operated. While earning a legitimate wage, Gotti did not entirely relinquish his illegal activities and in 1963 he was jailed for the theft of a car. He was also, in subsequent years, arrested for breaking and entry, possession of bookmaking records and petty larceny. Getting caught must simply have seemed a professional hazard to Johnny Boy, as it wasn't long before he gave up his legitimate job to earn his living from crime.

Having earned himself a reputation as something of a hard man, Gotti came to the attention of Carmine and Daniel Fatico, who were members of a more adult type of gang than the Rockaways. The Faticos' gang was connected to Albert Anastasia, boss of the Mangano crime Family. As fate would have it, however, not long after Gotti joined the Fatico brothers, they all got a new boss when Anastasia was gunned down in a barbershop in what was then the Park-Sheraton Hotel in Manhattan. To this day, no one is certain who ordered the hit, but in its wake Carlo Gambino took over Anastasia's mantle and the Family became known as the Gambino Family.

Firmly entrenched now within the organized crime circuit, Gotti began his underworld activities as a 'hijacker' at John F. Kennedy International Airport. Unlike today, where the term 'hijack' has terrorist connotations of a quite different nature, back in the mid-sixties a hijacker was someone who stole whole shipments of goods as they were being transported from one destination to another. The airport made for rich pickings and anything and everything was up for grabs, including shipments of women's clothing, fur coats and cigarettes. Gotti enjoyed his new employment, although he was twice caught and imprisoned for theft during these first few years. His second sentence was served at the United States Penitentiary in Lewisburg, Pennsylvania.

Lewisburg was unlike any jail in which Gotti had previously been incarcerated. The inmates were mainly hardcore criminals, amongst whom was Carmine Galante, the then boss of the Bonanno Family, who had been convicted on drugs charges. In fact, there were so many inmates connected to underworld organizations within Lewisburg's walls that one part of the prison was referred to solely as 'Mafia Row.' It was the perfect training ground for would-be criminals and during his three-year stay, Gotti no doubt made good use of these contacts.

Gotti was released from Lewisburg in January 1972 and in order to satisfy his parole officer took a job with his father-in-law at the Century Construction Company. It wasn't long before he was once again involved in a life of crime. In May of that year Carmine Fatico, who was the leader of Gotti's particular crew, was charged with loan-sharking activities. Already up on a 'conspiracy to commit murder' charge that dated from 1968, Fatico decided to take a back seat for a while and, with the consent of the Gambino underboss Aniello (Neil) Dellacroce, nominated Gotti to take over his role as crew leader. It was a privileged position and one that meant Gotti was moving up rapidly through the ranks of his underworld family. But even Gotti couldn't have predicted that not long after this promotion, Dellacroce would be convicted on charges of tax evasion, so with both his immediate bosses behind bars, he began reporting directly to the Family boss himself: Carlo Gambino.

These were exciting times for John Gotti; he was making good money, mixing with the 'right' people and would soon be made a fully-fledged member of the Family. But first there was the small matter of his credentials for, in order to be made an associate of a Family, it is said that you need to at least participate in, if not actually commit, a murder.

In 1972, Carlo Gambino's nephew, Emanuel 'Manny' Gambino, had been kidnapped and held for a $350,000 ransom. His wife had duly gathered together as much cash as she could and made the relevant drop, but Emanuel never came home and a few months later his body was discovered in New Jersey. He had been shot through the head (see Carlo Gambino chapter). Move forward a few months and on May 22, 1973 three men by the names of Angelo Ruggiero, Ralph Galione and John Gotti arrive on Staten Island at Snoope's Bar & Grill. On entering the bar they head straight towards a large man, James McBratney, whom they surround and attempt to frog-march outside. But McBratney resists and in the ensuing mayhem Galione shoots him three times at close range in the chest.

It wasn't the cleverest of hits. It was carried out in the middle of a crowded bar

Flanked by his bodyguards, John Gotti Jr., son of the Mafia Don, takes a stroll in Howard Beach, Queens, in 1994. John Jr. took over from his father as Family boss but soon joined his father behind bars, convicted on charges of racketeering and extortion.

and not long afterwards both Ruggiero and Galione were picked out of a police photo spread by at least two witnesses. Gotti, on the other hand, might have walked away from the murder, as no one seemed able to pinpoint who the third man had been, but then he began boasting to his friends that he'd been involved in taking out the scum who had murdered Gambino's nephew. Picking up on this rumor, the NYPD had one of the Snoope Bar waitresses identify a picture of Gotti. On October 17, 1973 Johnny Boy was indicted by a state jury on a charge of first-degree murder. Frightened at the thought of being sent back to prison, Gotti immediately went into hiding.

The search was now on, but it took the police nearly a year to capture their prey. The FBI had an informer, known only at the time as Source BQ5558-TE or 'Wahoo', (but later uncovered as Willie Boy Johnson – Gotti's childhood friend) and eventually it was this source that led FBI agents to the Nevermore Social Club in New York where they placed Gotti under arrest – although he was later bailed for $150,000. Arrogant to the last, Gotti was determined not to go to prison again and he had more reason than most for, with Carlo Gambino growing increasingly old, Neil Dellacroce still in jail and Carmine Fatico facing yet another sentence for loan-sharking, Gotti was beginning to hold out hope of progressing even further up the Family ladder. In the meantime he also had several businesses to attend to – Gotti had acquired stakes in a motel, a restaurant and a disco; he also ran an illegal crap game in Brooklyn. However, on August 8, 1975, Judge John A. Garbarino sentenced Gotti to four years in jail. It was a short sentence considering both the charges and the fact that he would probably serve only two years inside, but still it meant time in one of New York's worst penitentiaries, Green Haven Correctional Facility. Even more galling for Gotti was the fact that on October 15, 1976 Carlo Gambino, having previously suffered three heart attacks, died. With Dellacroce still in prison, Paul Castellano was nominated for Gambino's job. Gotti could do nothing except watch from the sidelines, something he wasn't used to doing and which left him exceedingly frustrated.

Despite the changes to the Family landscape by the time he was released, Gotti was still made an associate member. He also – for the sake of his parole – took a job at the Arc Plumbing and Heating Corporation. This, of course, was only ever a cover job, the main part of his income still being derived from his illegal businesses. Gotti also had his crew to attend to and would regularly meet up with them at Carmine Fatico's club, the Bergin Hunt and Fish Club. In their book *Mob Star*, the authors Gene Mustain and Jerry Capeci have noted that the FBI had linked over a hundred mob 'names' with this venue, all of whom seemed to have an appropriate nickname: 'There was Willie Boy and Tony Roach of course, but also: Frankie the Beard, Frankie the Caterer, Frankie Dep, Frankie the Hat, and Frankie Pickles; Mike the Milkman, Brooklyn Mike, Mickey Gal, and Mikey Boy; Tommie Tea Balls and Tommy Sneakers; Johnny Cabbage and Joe Pineapples; Little Pete, Skinny Dom, and Fat Andy; Joe the Cat and Buddy the Cat; Jimmy Irish, Joe Butch, and Tony Pep; Joey Piney, Joe Dogs, Donny Shacks, Eddie Dolls, Philly Broadway, Nicky Nose, Anthony Tits, and Jackie the Actor; Old Man Zoo, Redbird, Steve the Cleaner, and Captain Nemo.'[2]

Not only were these nicknames colorful ways of announcing one's underworld credentials, they were also a marvelous way of confusing the FBI who were most probably bugging the meetings.

As the months passed by, Gotti grew more and more accustomed to running his crew with a rod of iron and more and more people would come to him for advice as well as for back-up in business pursuits. But it was in 1980 that Gotti was presented with his biggest challenge to date.

At this point in his life, he and his wife Victoria had five children, one of whom was a young boy called Frank. On March 18, Frank Gotti borrowed a motorized mini-bike from a neighborhood friend and went for a ride around the local area in which the Gotti family now lived – Howard Beach – when he was accidentally knocked down and killed by a passing motorist, John Favara. Victoria Gotti was inconsolable and unsurprisingly, given who it was that had been knocked down, not everybody thought Frank's death accidental. Not long after the boy's funeral Favara began to receive death threats, culminating in a funeral card and photograph of Frank pushed into his mailbox. The word 'murderer' was also spray-painted across the front of his car. On one occasion, Victoria Gotti attacked Favara with a baseball bat and hurt him so badly that he had to go to hospital for treatment, although he didn't press any charges against her. Instead, he put the family home up for sale.

Sadly for the Favara family, this wasn't the end of the matter. A few weeks later, while the Gottis were conveniently in Fort Lauderdale, Florida, enjoying a holiday, Favara was abducted from his place of work. Witnesses saw Favara walking towards his car when a large man hit him over the head with what appeared to be a piece of wood, and then dragged Favara into the back of a van. Favara was never seen again and despite several attempts on the part of the police to discover where his body might have been buried, no one in the underworld was willing to talk. It has been speculated that both Favara and his car were driven to a wrecking-yard operated by a Mafia Family member and that Favara's body was then set in cement and thrown into the ocean while his car was crushed.

By 1981 John Gotti was gambling heavily and was also heavily in debt. He had opened a private gambling room of his own, strictly for Family members, above the Bergin Club, but even in his own establishment he couldn't hit a winning streak. Another set-back came in the form of a woman called Diane Giacalone, an Assistant US Attorney who around this time began an investigation into both Neil Dellacroce and John Gotti in an attempt to link them to a couple of armored-car robberies. At the same time, the FBI were also investigating several Gambino Family crews for loan-sharking and illegal gambling. They had also begun to suspect that Gene Gotti (John's brother), Angelo 'Quack Quack' Ruggiero and John Carneglia were involved in dealing drugs. This went strictly against the clear instructions of Gambino boss Paul Castellano, who stated that no members of the Family should involve themselves with narcotics. Whether John Gotti was a participant, the FBI couldn't be one hundred per cent certain, though there was little doubt in their minds that he would have been taking a cut of the profits. In the early 1980s, the FBI began to bug Angelo Ruggiero's home telephone. The Bureau already knew that Angelo's brother, Salvatore, was heavily involved in dealing drugs, so Angelo seemed the most likely 'in' to the Gambino crew's operations. Salvatore had, in fact, been a fugitive from the law for almost six years but, on May 6, 1982, having chartered a private plane to fly him and his wife to Florida, the plane crashed killing everyone on board. Angelo employed the services of an attorney called Michael Coiro to tidy up Salvatore's estate and this was when the FBI struck gold for, in several taped conversations, the two men – together with Gene Gotti – talked about unloading heroin and other incriminating material. The FBI held out for a mention of John Gotti's involvement in the deals but none was forthcoming and eventually they had to make their move without his name on the list.

On August 8, 1983 Angelo Ruggiero, Gene Gotti, John Carneglia, Michael Coiro and Mark Reiter were all arrested on drugs charges (although it would take almost six years to see them convicted). The FBI had hours of taped conversations. As well as the mention of heroin dealing, it was also discovered that the group had made countless disparaging remarks about the Gambino Family boss, Paul Castellano, who, on hearing the news, demanded that copies of the tapes be sent to him as soon as the prosecutors handed them over to Ruggiero's defense team. There was no love lost between Paul Castellano and John Gotti and, following the above arrests, it is thought that Castellano blamed Gotti for the whole fiasco:

> 'John Gotti is on the carpet with Big Paul Castellano over the drug bust,' Agent Abbott wrote after Wahoo reported in, 'as Paul feels John was either involved himself and if he was not, then he should have known his crew was involved and therefore he cannot control his crew.'[3]

Castellano, however, wasn't above the law either, for early in 1984 he, too, was indicted, this time on charges of car-theft, prostitution, racketeering and twenty-five counts of murder. John Gotti was said to be delighted at the prospect of the Gambino boss spending the last years of his life behind bars. At the same time, Neil Dellacroce – now suffering from cancer – was indicted on tax evasion charges.

Gotti wasn't a stupid man, he knew it was only a matter of time before the FBI or Diane Giacalone charged him with something and on March 25, 1985 his prediction came true. John Gotti, along with several others, was charged with murder, racketeering and conspiracy indictments in what became known as the RICO (Racketeer-Influenced and Corrupt Organizations) trial. The charges came with forty-year prison sentences if convicted, but before this latest Gambino Family case came to court, something far more important in terms of the Family hierarchy occurred.

On December 2, 1985 (ironically the day his trial was scheduled to start) Neil Dellacroce died. It had only been a matter of time before this happened, but when it finally did, Paul Castellano surprised everyone by not attending Dellacroce's funeral. It was an insult unlike any other. Loyal Gambino Family associates of long standing took this as a great affront to the memory of Dellacroce. As though to rub salt in the wound, Castellano subsequently announced that his bodyguard, Thomas Bilotti, would assume Dellacroce's role as underboss, cutting out any others within the organization who may have ranked high enough to expect to be offered the job. One of these, of course, was John Gotti. For Gotti, however, there was even worse to come. Castellano also declared his intention to disband John Gotti's gang and reassign them to other crews.

Gotti's reaction to this news can only be imagined, but two weeks later both Bilotti and Castellano were dead.

On December 16, 1985 Paul Castellano was due to meet up with several associates at one of his favorite restaurants in the city, Sparks Steak House, at 210 East Forty-Sixth Street in midtown Manhattan. Castellano was picked up from his house by Thomas Bilotti and driven to his first meeting of the day in Bilotti's black Lincoln. It wasn't until later in the afternoon that the two men approached the Steak

Pictured arriving for one of his many court appearances, John Gotti, 'The Teflon Don,' earned his nickname from the way that no charges against him would ever stick. The charges did finally stick, however, in 1992 when he was jailed for life for murder.

House by which time a group of less than appreciative Gambino men were already hanging around outside, some in cars, some on the street. At approximately 5.30 p.m. Bilotti's black Lincoln drew up outside the restaurant and as both men stepped out of the car, they were gunned down at point blank range. Later, Sammy 'The Bull' Gravano – one of the hit men – recalled the following:

> We concluded that nine days before Christmas, around five to six o'clock at night, in the middle of Manhattan, in the middle of the rush hour, in the middle of the crush of all them shoppers buying presents, there would be literally thousands of people on the street, hurrying this way and that. The hit would only take a few seconds, and the confusion would be in our favor. Nobody would be expecting anything like this, least of all Paul. And being able to disappear afterwards in the crowds would be in our favor. So we decide this is when and where its going to happen.[4]

With Bilotti and Castellano safely out of the picture, the way lay clear for John Gotti to take over as head of the Gambino Family. Unfortunately for him, his temporary triumph was to be tempered by another spell behind bars. By May 1986 Gotti found himself in the Metropolitan Correctional Center on charges of assault. Back in September 1984, well over a year before Castellano was murdered, a refrigerator repair man by the name of Romual Piecyk had been driving through Queens when he found his car blocked in by another car that was double parked. Piecyk sat on his horn until the owner, Frank Colletta, showed up. Colletta was a Gambino man and he punched Piecyk in the face then took a wad of money from Piecyk's coat pocket. Piecyk began fighting back at which point John Gotti entered the fray and, according to Piecyk, took something that looked very much like a gun from his waistband. Gotti warned the repairman, 'You better get the fuck out of here,' a warning that Piecyk heeded. He went straight to the police. They in turn promptly arrested Colletta and Gotti who were subsequently indicted with felony assault and theft. It would take twelve long months before the case came to trial, during which time the Castellano/Bilotti double murder hit the news and John Gotti's face was splashed all over the newspapers and daily TV news bulletins. If Piecyk wasn't intimidated before, he certainly was now. On the day he was due to give evidence, Piecyk didn't show up in court. Rather than believe he had been the victim of foul play, the court decided he had simply been too frightened to testify. They couldn't have been more right. Piecyk was eventually tracked down to Long Island and the trial resumed, but when he was asked if the two men who had attacked him were in the courtroom, Piecyk claimed they were not. Asked to describe the men, Piecyk then answered that it was all so long ago he couldn't remember. Following this, the judge named Piecyk a hostile witness after which the case crumbled. Gotti had beaten the charges, but he still wasn't free from the courtrooms. Just two weeks after this trial, Gotti was in court again, this time in the RICO trial brought about by the painstaking work of Diane Giacalone. Gotti wasn't the only one being prosecuted, of course, alongside him in the dock were his brother Gene Gotti as well as John Carneglia,

Willie Boy Johnson, Armond Dellacroce (Neil Dellacroce's son) and several others. Unlike the rest, Armond Dellacroce pleaded guilty to the charges against him, a move that upset Gotti as he was convinced it would reflect badly on his own case. However, none of this discouraged Gotti from attempting to intimidate government witnesses, and court proceedings were further disrupted when on April 9 a bomb threat was telephoned through to the courthouse, although this later turned out to be the work of a mental patient. A real bomb would, however, add to the drama of the trial when, on April 13, the new underboss of the Gambino Family, Frank DeCicco, was blown up by a car bomb. It is believed that he was killed by the rival Genovese Family, who were angered that Gotti hadn't asked their permission before murdering Paul Castellano. Gotti had sought the approval of all the other Families, but had somehow by-passed the Genoveses.

America had never experienced a trial quite like it; nor did the press help, turning the whole case into a carnival-like spectacle. On April 28, Judge Nickerson decided to postpone the trial for four months until things settled down. No one was surprised, but Gotti did appear shocked when the judge revoked his bail on the grounds that he would possibly try to intimidate further witnesses or, worse still, jurors.

Four months later the trial reconvened and on September 25, opening statements were delivered during which Giacalone stated that Gotti had been involved in the murder of James McBratney for the sole reason of trying to ingratiate himself with Carlo Gambino. She then asked what kind of an organization was it, where the only means of advancement were murder. In response Gotti's defense lawyers claimed that the only family Gotti knew was that of his wife, children and grandchildren. In fact, the prosecution's case had many set-backs during the course of the trial with witnesses being delayed or, in the case of one Edward Maloney, due to testify about the motive for the James McBratney murder, disallowed on the grounds that the evidence was nothing but hearsay. The defendants constantly made disparaging remarks about the prosecution team (in particular about Giacalone); remarks which, though whispered, were still audible to the jury. Time and again the judge directed Gotti to be silent, but this only seemed to spur him on. Gotti was irrepressible, he appeared to be loving every moment of his time in the media spotlight and to everyone who observed him, he seemed entirely confident that he would eventually win and be declared a free man. In fact, he would be cleared, but only because Gotti had bought one of the jurors for $60,000.

George Pape, who has been described as a 'middle-aged suburbanite with a drinking problem'[5], had, on being selected for the jury, almost immediately contacted someone with underworld connections to inform them that he was up for sale. No sooner was the word out than a deal was struck. Whatever the circumstances, whatever the evidence, Pape would vote 'not guilty' so that the worst that could happen to Gotti was a hung jury.

The trial dragged on through October, November and December until finally, in mid-January, the prosecution concluded its case. But the fireworks were far from over.

Gotti chats to his attorneys during his trial for ordering the 1986 assault on John F. O'Connor who was badly beaten as well being shot in the leg and hip as punishment for trashing a restaurant that was being built using non-union labor.

The defense now began throwing accusations at the prosecution to the effect that witnesses had been approached with bribes of drugs, and even that on one occasion, Giacalone had offered her underwear so that one witness could 'facilitate' himself, after informing Giacalone that he wanted to get laid. It was farcical, it was sordid, but the press lapped up every last detail and splashed it all over the newspapers. Finally, after almost seven months of evidence the case came to a close. Now it was the jury's turn to deliberate, which it did for seven long days, although right from the start George Pape told his fellow members that he thought all the defendants not guilty.

On March 13, 1987 John Gotti was declared a free man and the courtroom erupted with applause. Gotti, so it seemed, was untouchable – and the myth of the Teflon Don, to whom no charges would stick, was born. Yet it was still not plain sailing for the newly-crowned King of New York. Having been linked to the murder of Castellano and Bilotti, there were those in the underworld none too happy with Gotti. These included members of Castellano and Bilotti's blood family, as well as

members of the Genovese clan who hadn't been informed of the hit. Soon Gotti
heard rumors that reprisals were afoot and in turn this led to the murder of a man by
the name of Jeffrey Ciccone. Gotti had just left the Bergin Hunt and Fish Club when
a car backfired causing him to duck down in fear that someone was trying to shoot
him. Across the road stood Ciccone whom Gotti's bodyguards presumed to be the
assassin. They chased after Ciccone, shot and wounded him then loaded him (in full
view of witnesses) into the boot of a car. Later, Ciccone was executed with six bullets
to the head.

A few months later, Gotti decided to rid himself of Willie Boy Johnson with whom
he had grown up, but whom Gotti had discovered was the FBI's top informer. He
engaged Sammy Gravano and Eddie Lino to arrange the hit and on August 29, 1988,
as Johnson walked out from his home in Brooklyn towards his car, he was fired on,
once in each thigh and six times in the head.

In the autumn of 1987 the case against Gene Gotti, Angelo Ruggiero and John
Carneglia eventually came to court. By this time Ruggiero had been diagnosed with
lung cancer and was consequently released, leaving Gotti and Carnegia to fight on.
They managed to evade conviction twice due to 'mistrial', but on the third attempt
the prosecution came up trumps and both defendants were found guilty and given
lengthy prison sentences.

Nor had John Gotti seen the last of a courtroom. Back in 1986 a man by the name
of John F. O'Connor, angry that a new restaurant was being built using non-union
carpenters, trashed the premises causing thousands of dollars worth of damage. The
owner of the restaurant went straight to Gotti, who ordered that O'Connor be beaten
up. For this he assigned the 'Westies' – a gang of Irish thugs. Among the many injuries
they inflicted upon O'Connor, the Westies shot their victim in the leg and hip.
O'Connor survived the attack and nearly two years later Gotti was indicted for first-
degree assault. In the meantime, the FBI had begun tapping Gotti's new place of
'business,' the Ravenite Social Club in Little Italy, as well as the apartment of Nettie
Cirelli which was located above the Ravenite. It was here that they believed Gotti
would feel relaxed and safe enough to speak openly and freely. As a result, the FBI
had mountains of incriminating tapes together with two main informants, Vincent
'Fish' Cafaro and James Patrick McElroy, the latter of whom informed a packed
courtroom that it was Gotti who had ordered O'Connor to be 'whacked.' The
defense challenged the authenticity of the tapes saying that they had been tampered
with and finally, the jury, (who had been sequestered so that they couldn't be
intimidated) found Gotti not guilty. The *New York Times* commented:

> However fearless the jurors themselves sounded afterward, some defense
> lawyers hypothesize that subliminal fear of the 'Dapper Don,' a man who
> appears to thumb his nose at the authorities with impunity, may have affected
> their deliberations. And that fear, they say, can only be exaggerated by three
> weeks sequestration.

After this latest acquittal, the FBI were even more determined that they would be the ones to have Gotti convicted. They began compiling further evidence linking Gotti to the murder of Paul Castellano and Thomas Bilotti. On December 11, 1990 Gotti was arrested along with Sammy Gravano, Frank Locascio and Thomas Gambino. The trial was to be Gotti's last, not only because of the FBI's tapes and the weight of evidence these brought to the trial, but more sensationally because Sammy 'The Bull' Gravano suddenly, on November 8, 1991, decided to defect and give evidence against his former boss. On April 2, 1992 John Gotti, the Teflon Don, was found guilty of murder and sentenced to life imprisonment, leading the assistant director of the FBI's New York branch, James M. Fox, to gloat, 'The Don is covered with Velcro, and every charge stuck.'

Gotti began his prison sentence in the United States Penitentiary in Marion, Illinois, a broken man, but worse was yet to come. Ten years later he was diagnosed as suffering from throat cancer. This was to be his last fight and one that, like the last court case, he lost. John Gotti died on June 10, 2002. His body was buried in a crypt alongside the grave of his son, Frank, in Queens cemetery. Although his other son, John Jr, took over as Family boss, he too is now behind bars, having been convicted on charges of racketeering and extortion. At long last it seems that the reign of the Gottis is over.

[1] Kefauver, Third Interim Report.

[2] *Mob Star: The Story of John Gotti*, Gene Mustain and Jerry Capeci, Alpha Books and Pearson Education, Inc., 1988.

[3] Ibid.

[4] *Underboss: Sammy The Bull Gravano's Story of Life in the Mafia*, Peter Maas, Harper Collins, 1997.

[5] *Mob Star: The Story of John Gotti*, Gene Mustain and Jerry Capeci, Alpha Books and Pearson Education, Inc., 1988

SAMMY 'THE BULL' GRAVANO

The Underboss

'The car was a mess. Back in the neighborhood, we washed down
the inside real good. We were all scared, not like afraid, but
excited. I can't really describe it. But then I felt a surge of power. I
realized that I had taken a human life, that I had the power over
life and death. I was a predator. I was an animal.
I was Cosa Nostra.'

Sammy Gravano on murdering Joseph Colucci, from *Underboss: Sammy 'The Bull'
Gravano's Story of Life in the Mafia*, Peter Maas, Harper Collins Inc., 1997.

When Sammy 'The Bull' Gravano broke the Omerta (the Mafia's sacred code of silence) and gave evidence against his former employer, John Gotti, boss of the all-powerful Gambino family, it sent shock waves through the whole of the Mafia. No one who had enjoyed such a respected and privileged position within the underworld had ever before defected to the other side. No one of such stature had informed on those closest to him, and no one with so much detailed inside information had described what went on within Cosa Nostra's most secret inner sanctum. Implicated in the murders of nineteen people, including that of his own brother-in-law, Sammy 'The Bull' Gravano has to be one of the most notorious members of the Mafia, from whichever side of the law you view him.

Born on March 12, 1945 to Caterina and Giorlando Gravano, who were both Sicilian by birth, Salvatore Gravano was the youngest of three children. His parents lived in a neighborhood called Bensonhurst in south-west Brooklyn, an area that was best known for one of the grandest Mafia funerals ever seen, that of Frankie Yale, allegedly murdered by Al Capone. Naturally, given the fact that Bensonhurst was Mafia-dominated, the young Salvatore Gravano knew of this secret organization's existence from a tender age and, despite his parents trying to steer him clear of trouble, the odds were stacked against him. Nor did it help that Sammy, as his family nicknamed him, was severely dyslexic. This was a condition about which little was known in the 1950s, other than that those who suffered from it were regarded as slow learners. Thus, at the age of ten, when children most like to be judged equal, Sammy was singled out at school and held back a grade. Humiliated, he would hit out at anyone who teased him and later he was to admit that it was at school that he first began to hate all forms of authority.

It was this single-mindedness, (some might say bloody-mindedness) combined with his aggressive nature that first earned him the nickname, 'The Bull.' On his tenth birthday, Sammy was given a bicycle by his parents, a gift he treasured. When it was stolen a few weeks later, it can only be imagined how aggrieved he felt. Before long, he discovered that two older, bigger boys had taken his present and, without giving it a second thought, Sammy marched right up to them and began beating them up. The fight took place outside a neighborhood bar and a couple of men who knew Sammy came out to watch. It was one of them who eventually called Sammy 'a little bull.' The soubriquet stuck and ever afterwards everyone, including the police, referred to him as Sammy 'The Bull.'

This was not the only childhood incident to influence the young boy adversely. One day while he was working in his parents' shop, two men entered the premises and told Sammy's father that he would have to start making payouts if he wanted to continue in business. The episode shocked Sammy and made him angry, but his father said he would talk to a Mr Zuvito and he would sort the whole matter out. Sammy wasn't impressed. Mr Zuvito was an elderly, frail man. How could he be of any use? But the next time the two thugs showed up at Gravano Senior's shop, they were full of apologies. Mr Zuvito, Sammy concluded, must be a very powerful man. The young boy was duly impressed.

Sammy's schooling continued on a downward slope over the next few years and there were at least two recorded incidents of him hitting out at school officials. He also began skipping classes, preferring instead to hang around with the local wise guys, who always seemed to have a steady supply of cash. Even when Sammy moved up to High School at New Utrecht, he couldn't contain his contempt for education and eventually found himself moved to a school for 'incorrigibles.'

Sammy now joined a street gang called The Rampers, a group of young thugs who were feared by all the other gangs in the neighborhood. Slowly but surely he transferred his hatred of authority from his school teachers to the police. He was always on the wrong side of the law; he seemed to revel in it: "'We did mostly burglaries and stealing cars," he said. "We did cars for their parts or to be shipped out of the country. We never burglarized homes. That was against what we wanted to do. It was all commercial places. We'd break in at night, robbing clothing stores, hardware stores, stuff like that. We'd hold up jewelry stores, you know, with ski masks on. They all had insurance.'"[1]

It wasn't long before Gravano became adept at handling a gun. He and his fellow Rampers members became involved in a shoot-out with a gang led by 'Crazy Joe' Gallo. No one was killed, although two men were badly wounded, but it was an early indication of the road down which Sammy Gravano was headed. Shortly after this incident, Gravano, along with four other Rampers members, was arrested on charges of burglary. Gravano's lawyer did a deal with the judge, saying that his client would prefer a spell in the army rather than go to jail. The judge dismissed the case, but as luck would have it Gravano was drafted in 1964 anyway and shipped off to Fort Jackson in South Carolina.

Gravano's spell in the US Army might have been the making of him had it not been for the fact that it was here he first got a taste for gambling (not only participating, but running his own games) and for loan-sharking. At the end of his two year stint, he confessed that he'd have been happy to go to Vietnam, because out there you received medals for killing people, but he was quite content to return to civilian life.

His parents having retired to live on Long Island by now, Gravano rented an apartment in Bensonhurst and was soon back to his old ways, running with the Rampers and getting into trouble. He was almost killed one night when, having stolen a car, the owner gave chase and shot Gravano and his accomplice, seriously wounding them both. The two thieves escaped with their lives but no sooner had Gravano's wounds healed than he resumed his criminal career.

Having built up quite a reputation as a hardened criminal and all-round tough guy, Gravano was approached, through a friend of his in the Rampers, to meet Thomas 'Shorty' Spero, a mid-ranking member of the all-powerful Colombo crime Family. This was the opportunity Gravano had been waiting for and when he finally met up with Spero, he jumped at the opportunity to join the Family whose boss was Joseph Colombo. Gravano was immediately assigned to Shorty Spero's crew and not long afterwards he did his first job for the mob by robbing a clothes store. 'I go in first, I don't have a mask, I don't want to alert the guy. I put a gun in his face and Tommy and Lenny come in,'[2] is how Gravano described it to author Peter Maas. Afterwards, a witness identified Gravano as one of those involved, but this witness was soon persuaded to retract his statement and Gravano was released. Incidents such as this were commonplace. Not long after the clothes store heist, Gravano was involved in a bank robbery, identified, but later released when the witness developed selective amnesia.

Around this time Gravano was also building up his own business enterprises, buying into a bar on 17th Avenue and 62nd Street, as well as setting up a club in Bensonhurst and establishing a loan-sharking business, but it was his work with the Family that took up most of his energy.

Early in 1970 Sammy Gravano was assigned his first murder. 'Making your bones' (carrying out your first murder) was an important, if not an essential, part of belonging to Cosa Nostra, so when Shorty Spero called on Gravano to take out a fellow member of the Colombo family, Joseph Colucci, Sammy took the job very seriously. It was explained to him that Colucci wanted to see Gravano dead (later, Gravano discovered that Spero was having an affair with Colucci's wife and wanted the husband out of the picture) so to Gravano it was simply a matter of kill or be killed.

Tommy Spero and Sammy planned everything down to the last letter and, having enjoyed an evening of drinking and dancing together with Colucci, everyone piled into a car to drive home. A Beatles tune was on the radio:

As that Beatles song played, I became a killer. Joe Colucci was going to die. I was going to kill him because I had been ordered to do it and because he was plotting to kill me. I felt the rage inside me . . . I pointed the gun at the back

John Gotti's right-hand man, Sammy Gravano, seen here leaving the Ravenite Social Club with his boss, who would later rue the day he had ever set eyes on Gravano when 'The Bull' gave evidence against him in court.

of his head. Everything went into slow motion. I could almost feel the bullet leaving the gun and entering his skull. It was strange. I didn't hear the first shot. I didn't seem to see any blood. His head didn't seem to move, like it was a blank instead of a real bullet . . . I shot a second time in the same spot. This time everything was different. I saw the flash. I smelt the gunpowder. The noise was deafening. Now I saw his head jerk back, his body convulse and slip sideways. I saw the blood. Joe Colucci was dead.[3]

After the hit, the car was driven to a secluded spot where the body was dumped. Driving away, Gravano rolled down the window and fired three more bullets into the corpse. It was a job well done and Gravano was congratulated on his work by leading members of the Colombo family who were impressed not only at the swiftness of the hit, but also that Gravano hadn't been pulled in for questioning by the police. Gravano himself recognized this as being a seminal moment in his relationship with the mob.

On April 16, 1971, Sammy married a young girl by the name of Debra Scibetta, but romance always took second place to his life with Cosa Nostra and, after a brief honeymoon, Sammy quickly returned to work. He set up a store with Tommy Spero called the 'Hole in the Wall' selling damaged goods. Initially, it wasn't much of a success but when Spero suggested they tell people the goods were 'hot,' everything sold out almost immediately. Tommy Spero's father then decided he wanted in on the business, but shortly after he joined them, Gravano realized the older man was ripping them off. The ensuing tension was unbearable and led directly to Sammy being officially 'released' from the Colombo Family, although it had been prearranged that he would transfer directly to the Gambino Family. His new crew was headed up by Salvatore 'Toddo' Aurello, an old-time mobster who had once worked alongside Albert Anastasia. Gravano liked Aurello's company and the older man became a kind of father figure to the young gangster, teaching him all he knew.

Having become a father himself, (to a baby girl named Karen) Gravano suddenly decided that his priorities lay with his own family and against Aurello's advice tried to go straight. He moved to Long Island and began working for a construction business that was owned by his wife's family. Later, he was to say that he quite enjoyed the work and was contemplating setting up his own construction company, when a call came through that would change Gravano's life forever. Arrest warrants had been issued by Brooklyn D.A. Eugene Gold for Gravano and an associate of his, 'Alley Boy' Cuomo, for the 1969 murder of two brothers, Arthur and Joseph Dunn, who had owned a local automobile repair shop. Both Gravano and Cuomo denied any involvement in the hits, but an old associate of theirs, Michael Hardy, had named them in connection with the slayings in order to get himself off the same charge.

Initially, Sammy and Alley Boy took off for Florida, but finally they returned to New York to face the music and were immediately placed in the Brooklyn House of Detention. Also detained was Louis Milito, but Gold's real target was a Colombo Family associate by the name of Dominick 'Mimi' Scialo. Gold told Gravano that if he shopped Scialo he would be allowed to walk free, but Gravano had no intention of turning stool pigeon just yet. Besides, on making bail, Gravano discovered that Scialo had been killed by the Colombo Family for becoming involved with drugs. Sammy and Alley Boy were still facing trial for murder and, according to Gravano, finding it increasingly difficult to pay for good lawyers. Suddenly Gravano needed to earn large amounts of cash fast, and before he knew it, he'd gone back to his old ways, robbing everything in sight. Ironically, one week before the trial was due to begin all charges against the two defendants were dropped but, having returned to a life of crime, Sammy 'The Bull' Gravano had no more intentions of going straight. His fate was further sealed when Toddo Aurello, overjoyed to see his young pupil return to the fold, proposed Sammy for proper membership into the Gambino Family.

Being 'made' was a huge honor for any potential mobster and Gravano was no exception. Told to show up at Frankie the Wop's house in Bensonhurst, he did as instructed, arriving promptly. Gravano was led down to the basement where the Gambino Family boss, Paul Castellano, was seated alongside Neil Dellacroce and Joe Gallo. The rules of Cosa Nostra were explained to him, after which came the pricking of the index finger to draw blood, the burning of a saint's picture and the kissing on both cheeks by each Family member. Finally, Gravano was confirmed as a made member and Paul Castellano began telling him some of the local rules and regulations with which he would have to comply:

He told us that the man we answered to was our captain. He was our direct father. You do everything with him. You check with him, you put everything on record with him. You can't kill unless you get permission. You can't do anything, basically, until you get permission from the Family. You don't run to the boss. You go to your captain. That was the protocol. Your captain will go to the administration of the Family, which is the boss, the underboss and the consigliere. Paul said, 'You are born as of today. Any grievances you have, anybody you have disliked from before, don't bring it up. As of today, it's over with.' [4]

Sammy Gravano bought in to everything Castellano said; he was proud to be a made member of the Gambino Family and went about his business with a new confidence.

Nick Scibetta was the kid brother of Sammy Gravano's wife. He had been brought up well but, with the drug culture of the seventies reaching its zenith, had gone slightly astray. Scibetta had also begun drinking heavily and become involved in several brawls inside mob-owned clubs. He was getting into too much trouble, insulting people – including the daughter of Georgie DeCicco, the uncle of Gambino Family member Frank DeCicco. Something had to be done about him and eventually word came through from on high that Scibetta was to be hit. The order was directed at Frank DeCicco who was told not to inform Gravano, but eventually DeCicco (with Paul Castellano's permission) did let Gravano in on the details with the proviso that should he object, Gravano too should be killed. According to his memoirs, when Sammy first heard what was to happen to his brother-in-law he was furious, and shouted that he'd kill Castellano, but DeCicco talked him round, saying that if he attempted going up against Paul, Gravano would be killed and afterwards his brother-in-law, too. Whatever happened, Scibetta was going to die. Sammy had to choose sides. In the end, Gravano chose to hunt with the pack. Nick Scibetta disappeared, although some weeks later his hand was discovered by the police.

Shortly after this, Sammy opened a new club called The Bus Stop in Bensonhurst. Everything was going well until a group of bikers entered the premises, the leader of whom informed Sammy that he was going to take over the place. Naturally, Sammy was incandescent at the biker's nerve and a fight ensued during which Gravano broke his ankle. The bikers then escaped from the scene, but Gravano wouldn't let the incident go. The next day he went straight round to Paul Castellano's to get permission to kill the group, and in particular their leader. Tooled up, Gravano and a team of associates tracked down the bikers, killing one man and beating some of the others to a pulp. When Castellano heard that Gravano, despite his injury, had participated in the hit, he was amazed. Surely Gravano would have been better off taking a back seat? It was Toddo Aurello who pointed out that Sammy Gravano enjoyed violence, that there was nothing that scared him.

Gravano's businesses were now growing into real moneyspinners. He opened another after-hours club and took over the running of the Plaza Suite, a disco in Brooklyn. With his earnings he bought a large farm for himself and his family in New Jersey. Yet despite this new, rural existence Gravano was never far from violence.

In early 1980 he was directly involved in the murder of John 'Johnny Keys' Simone, who had been in the running to take over as boss of a Philadelphia Family. Having lost the contest, however, Castellano informed Gravano that he was to take out Simone. Sammy kidnapped his victim as he left a country club and stuffed him into the back of a van. Then, on the journey to a wooded area where the murder was to take place, Simone told Gravano that he wanted only two things before he was killed. He had promised his wife that he would die with his shoes off and that, if he was to be executed, he wanted to be killed by a 'made' man. Gravano obliged on both counts. When the van arrived at the designated area, he allowed Simone to remove his shoes then had a made man, Louie Milito, shoot him in the back of the head. This was not, by any means, the end of the bloodshed.

In 1982 a millionaire named Frank Fiala wanted to rent Gravano's discothèque, the Plaza Suite, for one night in order to give himself a surprise party. Officially, Fiala had earned his money as a manufacturer of marine parts; unofficially he was heavily involved in cocaine trafficking. This latter fact, however, was unknown to Gravano who, after Fiala had thrown a successful party in the disco, was offered one million dollars by Fiala to buy the place – $100,000 as a down payment, a further $650,000 under the table and $250,000 on closure of the deal. Gravano, knowing that the club was only worth in the region of $200,000, agreed. Then the troubles began. Fiala immediately began acting as if the disco were already his, bringing in his own bouncers, using Gravano's office and knocking down walls to redecorate. Sammy was furious and eventually confronted Fiala who drew out an Uzi machine pistol. Fiala's biggest mistake was not using the weapon immediately. As soon as Gravano realized he wasn't going to be shot, he began plotting Fiala's murder. He had his men guard the exit from the disco and when Fiala and his entourage emerged from the club, the millionaire was immediately gunned down, receiving a bullet in each eye. With the murder over, however, Gravano still had problems to face. Not only would he be confronted by a full police investigation, but he had also broken one of the Mafia's golden rules – he hadn't asked Paul Castellano's permission for the hit. Thinking on his feet, Sammy 'The Bull' quickly came up with a solution and the next time he met with Castellano he told him that he hadn't wanted the boss to know anything about the murder in case something went wrong and he was implicated. Thankfully, Castellano bought the story, otherwise Gravano is certain he would have been executed. The police also played into Sammy's hands as they were unable to pin the murder on Gravano. He didn't escape altogether, though, as the Internal Revenue Service also became involved in the investigation. Gravano had to sell his farm to finance his defense when he was indicted on charges of tax evasion, although a jury eventually acquitted him.

Gravano now decided to concentrate on building up his construction and plumbing business, which he had started a few years previously with another of his wife's brothers. This time he wanted to concentrate on paving and cement – an essential part of the building trade. It wasn't long before he was embroiled in yet another dispute, however, this time with one of his construction company partners, Louis DiBona – who was a member of another Gambino crew. Gravano accused DiBona of ripping him off to the tune of $200,000 and eventually it was left to Castellano's underboss, Neil Dellacroce, to settle the matter. He instructed the two that they should dissolve all business dealings with each other.

It was also around this time in August 1983 that members of another Gambino Family crew, this one run by John Gotti, were arrested. The three men involved were Angelo 'Quack Quack' Ruggiero, Johnny Carneglia and Gene Gotti, (John Gotti's brother) who were all indicted on charges of heroin smuggling by a special team of FBI officers led by Agent Bruce Mouw. Having tapped their phones and found himself an informant in the shape of Wilfred 'Willie Boy' Johnson, (known to agents by the codename Wahoo) Mouw seemed to have a pretty strong case. Not only that, but Paul Castellano, having learned that there were less than flattering things said about him by his own crew members on the tape recordings, was spitting blood. Castellano had always regarded John Gotti as a threat to his role as boss – now with these tapes he had the perfect excuse to throw his weight around, disband Gotti's crew and relegate him to the lowly status of foot soldier. But Castellano also had problems of his own with the law, for not only was he about to be indicted on various counts of murder, car theft, prostitution, racketeering and drug dealing, he was also caught up on RICO – Racketeer Influenced and Corrupt Organizations – charges[5] due to his having attended a Mafia Commission meeting in South Beach. The

Commission gathering had been photographed by an FBI surveillance team and the case was to be prosecuted by Manhattan District Attorney Rudolph Giuliani. Famously, this case later became known as the 'Commission Trial.'

With his back to the wall and in the certain knowledge that the FBI tapes contained recordings of his own people making disparaging remarks about him, Castellano was in no mood to act kindly towards John Gotti or his crew. Suddenly, everyone in the Gambino Family was taking sides, preparing for a civil war, and Sammy Gravano was no exception.

I don't think John really gave a fuck about Angelo – or the tapes. I think he was looking to create a situation to capitalize on our other grievances about Paul. I think John did give a fuck when Neil died[6], which we all knew would happen sooner or later. He's looking ahead, and he sees trouble. Even if he isn't killed

A troubled Sammy 'The Bull' in 2000, in court in Phoenix, Arizona, on drugs charges. Gravano had been running an Ecstasy operation that peddled up to 30,000 tablets a week to users in Arizona – while he was supposed to be in a witness protection program.

himself, all of John's sights on being Mr Big Shot are crippled. Paul is already talking about when Neil dies, he's going to close down the Ravenite. He's going to break John down to a soldier, stick him somewhere in a crew, maybe under Joe Butch, and treat him like a fucking hard-on. Without even being dead, he's finished.[7]

In September 1985 Gravano was summoned to meet up with John Gotti and Angelo Ruggiero in Queens. When he arrived for the meet, however, only Ruggiero was present. He told Gravano that he and Gotti were going to make a hit on Castellano – was Gravano in or out? Gravano explained that he wanted to know where Frank DeCicco stood on the matter and went to DeCicco's house to discuss the hit. According to DeCicco, Castellano believed he might be sent to prison after the forthcoming trial and had said he wanted Thomas Gambino to take over as boss of the Family, with Tommy Bilotti as underboss. Neither of these choices appealed to Gravano or DeCicco. Their minds were made up – they would run with John Gotti.

On December 2, 1985, Neil Dellacroce died of cancer and in a move guaranteed to fuel the intrigue and backbiting that was already running rife within the Gambino Family, Paul Castellano failed to turn up at the wake. If his stock had been running low before Dellacroce's death, it now hit rock bottom. Two weeks later, on December 16, Castellano was gunned down outside Sparks Steak House in Manhattan where he was due to hold a meeting with the Family captains. The hit was planned down to the last detail, the gunmen even wearing identical white trench coats and black Russian fur hats so that it was almost impossible to tell one from the other. Gravano was one of these men.

After the hit, John Gotti was duly elected the new boss of the Gambino Family with Frank DeCicco as his underboss. Toddo Aurello then announced his retirement and Sammy 'The Bull' Gravano was made up to capo.

If they thought the bloodshed was over, however, then they couldn't have been more wrong. On April 13, 1986, John Gotti called a meeting at the Veterans and Friends Club in Bensonhurst. As it transpired, Gotti couldn't show up for the meeting, but Frank DeCicco was there along with Sammy Gravano and several others. At one point, DeCicco had to go back to his car to pick up something he had forgotten. As he climbed into the vehicle to open the glove compartment, a bomb exploded. DeCicco was blown to pieces. Although Gravano was within meters of the car, there wasn't so much as a scratch on his body. The bomb had been intended not just for DeCicco, but for John Gotti as well. It had been arranged (according to Gravano's account) by Antony 'Gas Pipe' Casso and Vincent 'The Chin' Gigante of the Lucchese Family and Genovese Family respectively. They had been angered, so the story goes, that Gotti hadn't asked their permission for the Castellano hit, although he had gained it from all the other leading Families.

Gotti quickly shrugged off this threat on his life as he had other concerns on his mind. He was involved in a string of court cases, for not only were the FBI eager to prosecute him, but US attorney Diane Giacalone also wanted a piece of the action.

Gotti found himself behind bars pending trial, having been denied bail. It was from here that he gave Gravano his first orders to kill. The hit was a man by the name of Robert DiBernardo, who belonged to the Gambinos and who Gravano respected and liked. He was, so Gravano says, loathe to kill the man, but Gotti insisted, saying that DiBernardo had been talking behind his back. Gravano had DiBernardo shot twice in the back of the head.

Shortly after this Angelo Ruggiero, Gotti's new underboss, ended up behind bars too, having had his bail revoked pending trial. This left a gaping hole in the Gambino Family structure. There had to be someone running the organization on the outside and it was then that Gotti decided on Sammy Gravano. He would be the new underboss, taking charge until Gotti was released. That finally happened on March 13, 1987 after Diane Giacalone lost her case, Gotti being pronounced not guilty.

Gravano's rapid rise within the Gambino Family's ranks had not gone unnoticed by the FBI, and two agents, Frank Spero and Matty Tricorico, began to take a particular interest in him. They began staking out not only Gravano's offices and a restaurant that he owned (Tali's), but also a florist shop which belonged to Gravano's daughter, Karen. With Gotti's release, Gravano's position within the Family changed rapidly. Between 1986 and 1987 he was variously the underboss, then a co-underboss with Angelo Ruggiero, after which he became a co-consigliere with Joe Armone. When Armone was then convicted on charges of racketeering, Gravano was named the official consigliere. Then Angelo Ruggiero, who had narrowly escaped prison for his narcotics indictment due to a terminal illness (his fellow defendants, Gene Gotti and Johnny Carneglia were eventually both found guilty and sent to jail for fifty years), died on December 5, 1989. Gravano was named underboss.

The early years with John Gotti as boss were also very bloody ones where Gravano was concerned; he is said to have murdered eleven men in six years. The list included Nick Mormando, Robert DiBernardo, Mike DeBatt, Louis Milito, Francesco Oliverri, Wilfred Johnson, Thomas Spinelli, Eddie Garafolo and Louis DiBono. But according to Gravano in his book *Underboss*, perhaps the worst thing John Gotti did – and the one that eventually disillusioned Gravano to the point of no return – occurred when Angelo Ruggiero was dying. Gotti refused to visit Ruggiero. In fact, he wanted Ruggiero taken out because of the tapes on which he had bad-mouthed Castellano and which had brought the Family so much trouble. A friend since childhood, Ruggiero was now persona non grata and when he died, Gravano said he had practically had to drag Gotti to the funeral.

> If I didn't say a word and he don't go to the funeral, none of us would have gone. That's how John really wanted to send Angie out. With nobody. With no respect. Nothing. And I'm talking about a life-long thing, like from when they were five, six years old.[8]

Gravano was apparently disgusted, but as yet he didn't make his move, instead standing by Gotti to the extent that he made sure his boss would get the required 'not guilty' verdict in yet another court appearance by intimidating the victim (John

O'Connor) into retracting his statement. But the FBI net was now beginning to draw ever tighter around John Gotti, for Bruce Mouw had been keeping a constant tab on his target, bugging Gotti's offices and apartments at the Ravenite club and even setting up video cameras to record all the comings and goings. Suddenly, Mouw started amassing evidence that was rarer than gold dust. Gotti was caught on tape identifying himself as the head of an international racketeering enterprise as well as acknowledging that he had ordered the murders of Robert DiBernardo, Louie DiBono and Louie Milito. With this evidence and other material gathered over the years, a Grand Jury was ready to once again indict John Gotti, together with Sammy Gravano and another Gambino member, Frank Locascio. But then something untoward occurred – Sammy 'The Bull' disappeared.

According to Gravano, it was Gotti's idea that he should make himself scarce, for once Gotti was arrested and held in prison pending the trial, he required someone on the outside to run the business for him. Leaving New York, Sammy went to stay at a holiday home that belonged to his father-in-law in the Pocono Mountains in Pennsylvania. He then flew to Florida, then on to Atlantic City. But his life as a fugitive wasn't to last long for the moment John Gotti called him back to New York for a meeting, Gravano was arrested. He was furious, not at the FBI, but at John Gotti, who'd insisted they meet at the Ravenite club, which was under constant police surveillance. Gravano was taken to the FBI's New York headquarters and the next day was indicted along with John Gotti on charges that ranged from illegal gambling to loan-sharking (only Gotti was charged with the murders of Castellano and Bilotti).

It was at the bail hearings that the fireworks really began. During the proceedings, parts of the Ravenite tapes were played in court and for the first time Gravano heard John Gotti putting the burden of blame on his shoulders for several of the murders that Gotti himself had ordered. As if that wasn't humiliating enough, Gotti was also heard making disparaging comments about Gravano's various business enterprises.

> He [Gotti] ain't looking at me. Only his fingers on his right hand are drumming on the table. They say when I'm really mad, my eyes turn blank, kind of glassy. I guess some of the court officers, the marshals, whatever, caught what I was feeling because the media reported that afterwards I went at John in the hall back of the court, even grabbed him by the throat. I didn't do that at all. This is Cosa Nostra, and he's the boss. I am mad that there's a betrayal, but not to the point that I would raise my hands to him.[9]

In point of fact, Sammy 'The Bull' Gravano was about to do something much, much worse. On October 10, 1990, Frank Spero and Matty Tricorico received word from Sammy that he wanted to talk. Suddenly the prosecution had a star witness – a key member of the Gambino Family who was willing to talk in exchange for complete immunity. Swiftly thereafter, Gravano was moved from the detention center he was being held at to a US Marine base in Quantico, Virginia, and on February 12, 1991 the trial of Gotti and Locascio began. Less than two months later, on April 2, both men were found guilty of all the charges that had been laid against them and were

Sammy Gravano's son, Gerard, was indicted along with his father and over forty others involved in the Arizona Ecstasy ring. Among the forty was Gerard's mother, Debra. Sammy Gravano apparently believed in keeping business in the family.

committed to life imprisonment without parole. Gravano then proceeded to give evidence over the next few years which would see at least a dozen key Cosa Nostra members jailed on an assortment of charges ranging from racketeering to murder. But Gravano himself also had to face the music, although his sentence (five years in jail, followed by three years supervised release) was a drop in the ocean in comparison to the punishments of his former associates. On his release, Gravano went into a witness protection program. His wife refused to join him and later decided on a divorce.

Despite their separation, when Gravano was charged on January 2, 2000 with operating an Ecstasy drug ring from Arizona, his wife and his children (Debra and Gerard) were indicted along with him. While he was in prison in Colorado serving out his sentence for the Ecstasy conviction, Gravano was further charged on February 24,

2003 with arranging the 1980 murder of a New York police officer, Peter Calabro.

It can only be hoped that this time Sammy 'The Bull' Gravano, responsible for murdering a minimum of nineteen people, will remain behind bars.

1 *Underboss: Sammy The Bull Gravano's Story of Life in the Mafia*, Peter Maas, Harper Collins Publishers, Inc., 1997.
2 Ibid.
3 Ibid.
4 Ibid.
5 Indicted at the same time were Gerry Langella – the Colombo Family's acting boss, Anthony Corallo – the Luchese Family boss, Phil Rastelli – the Bonano Family boss, Athony Salerno the Genovese Family boss and Carmine Persico – the Colombo Family boss.
6 Neil Dellacroce was suffering from cancer at the time.
7 *Underboss: Sammy The Bull Gravano's Story of Life in the Mafia*, Peter Maas, Harper Collins Publishers, Inc., 1997.
8 Ibid.
9 Ibid.

MEYER 'LITTLE MAN' LANSKY

The Chairman of the Board

'For a man who, in all respects, will carry out only his profession
of good, will be apt to be ruined among so many who are evil. A
prince, therefore, who desires to maintain himself must learn to
be not always good, but to be so or not as necessity may require.'

The Prince, Machiavelli

If Al Capone represents all that is associated with traditional gangsters, that is to say with violence, with guns hidden in violin cases, extortion with menaces, speakeasies, bootlegging and profiteering, his near-contemporary Meyer Lansky stands for all that is clever, sophisticated and reserved within the mobster underworld. Lansky was the proverbial poor boy made good; not quite the all-American success story but as near to it as it was possible to get while still being Jewish and on the wrong side of the law. Believed to be the Mafia's banker, at the height of his powers Lansky was the target of law enforcement agencies across the board. The Internal Revenue Service was investigating his tax returns, the Immigration and Naturalization Service wanted to have him deported and the Federal Bureau of Investigation was trailing him in the hope of garnering enough evidence against him to take him to court. In short, Lansky was one of the U.S. Justice Department's foremost targets – one of the biggest criminals ever known in the United States of America.

Born Meyer Suchowljansky around 1902 (his precise date of birth remains unknown) in the Polish/Russian border-town of Grodno, Meyer was nine or ten years old when his parents, Max and Yetta, decided to emigrate to America. Max Suchowljansky went on ahead of his wife and children in 1909 and spent two years saving enough money to bring them all over, an event which finally occurred on April 8, 1911 when Yetta, Meyer and his younger brother Jacob all landed on Ellis Island.

The family moved straight away to the Brownsville area of Brooklyn where Max Suchowljansky had found work as a garment presser. Meyer was then immediately enrolled at Brooklyn Public School 84 where records show the family had already changed their name to Lansky. The young Meyer was a bright student, achieving mainly straight A's in his studies and, more surprisingly given his later notoriety, for conduct as well, which was judged to be exemplary. But if Meyer Lansky was achieving success at school, the same cannot be said of his father, whose fortunes sadly seemed to dwindle rather than grow in the new country. When Meyer was eleven the Lansky's moved house from Brownsville to an even less salubrious area of Manhattan

in New York's Lower East Side. Manhattan in this period was busy with the hustle and
bustle of illegal business ventures. 'On sunshiny days the whores sat on chairs along
the sidewalks,'[1] wrote one commentator while gambling parlors and saloons were ten
abreast. But the illegal activity which most caught the eye of Meyer Lansky and first
drew him away from his studies towards the more colorful world in which he was
living, was the street-corner crap game. With a gift for mental arithmetic and a sharp
eye for knowing when to place a bet, Lansky began to get a taste for earning 'easy'
money. It was also while pursuing this hobby that Lansky first met a boy who was later
to become one of his closest friends, Benjamin 'Bugsy' Siegel.

Followed by a police detective, Meyer Lansky strolls nonchalantly down the steps of Fifty-
Fourth Street Police Station in New York, having just been booked on a vagrancy charge in
1958. Such 'nuisance charge' tactics were used by the police to harass and pressurize mobsters.

Siegel was a wild, exuberant child while Lansky remained a quiet, studious boy, but they complimented each other perfectly. A third child then entered the mix, a young Sicilian gang leader by the name of Salvatore Lucania – later to become known by the soubriquet 'Lucky Luciano'. There were many ethnic neighborhoods in the Lower East Side, but the main three were, without doubt, the Jewish neighborhood, the Italian/Sicilian neighborhood and finally the Irish neighborhood. Each had its own gangs and its own rules, but when it came to making alliances, the Italians and Jews would nearly always gang together against the Irish. Thus, Lansky, Siegel and Luciano often ran as a threesome and formed a mutual respect for one another at an early age.

Meyer Lansky eventually left school shortly after his fifteenth birthday and went to work in a local tool-and-die shop, but this wasn't really suitable employment for a young man who harbored big ambitions and three years later, when the Volstead Act brought about Prohibition, Meyer downed tools and seized what he and so many others recognized as one of the best business opportunities the government could ever have handed them.

To begin with, Meyer (together with Siegel and Luciano) went to work for one of New York's foremost gangsters of the time, Arnold 'The Brain' Rothstein, as a bootlegger and speakeasy host. At the same time, he also set up several of his own gambling businesses and introduced his younger brother, Jake, to the trade. He was a fair boss, a clever man with a head for figures, but a distaste for violence. 'We were in business like the Ford Motor Company,' Meyer opined in later life of his bootlegging activities. 'Shooting and killing was an inefficient way of doing business. Ford salesmen didn't shoot Chevrolet salesmen. They tried to outbid them.'[2] Despite this measured, almost philosophical sound-bite, in March 1928 Lansky was arrested on charges of attempted homicide. According to police records, he and a group of friends, which included Benny Siegel, had taken a man by the name of John Barrett, whom they suspected of swindling them, on a journey out of town. Once they had reached a remote spot, they pushed Barrett out of the car and used him for target practice, wounding him four times. Barrett escaped being killed by the narrowest of margins and immediately afterwards named Lansky and company as his assailants, but later, with a trial pending, he withdrew his statement. In fact, between the years 1918 to 1931 Lansky appeared seven times as a defendant, but none of the cases amounted to much. The most the police ever managed to pin on him during this period was a $100 fine for a violation of the Volstead Act.

Some time in 1928, Meyer Lansky fell in love with a young woman by the name of Anne Citron. The couple were duly married in spring of the following year and nine months later Anne gave birth to the couple's first child, Bernard Irving Lansky, whom they nicknamed Buddy. Sadly Buddy, it was later discovered, suffered from some form of spine-damage and was never quite able to walk properly. In September 1932 Anne then gave birth to a second son whom the couple named Paul. But Buddy was always at the forefront of Meyer's mind and in 1933 the family decamped to Boston where specialist treatment could be given to the young boy.

The mainstay of Meyer Lansky's work, of course, remained in New York and even after Prohibition ended on December 5, 1933, Lansky continued to keep his businesses in the Big Apple. Deciding at least to look as if he were going legitimate, Lansky became a partner in the Molaska Corporation, Inc., but even with the end of Prohibition there was still money to be made from untaxed liquor. Lansky's new company was used to supply illegal brewing businesses with the raw materials of their trade. Never having relinquished his illegal[3] gambling businesses, Lansky also decided to give this area of his empire a lot more attention. Arnold Rothstein introduced Lansky to Saratoga Springs where the first of the great casinos had already been established by, amongst others, John Morrissey. Under Rothstein's guidance, Lansky began running franchises inside Rothstein's casinos (or 'carpet joints'[4] as they soon became known) and by the beginning of the Second World War he had moved on to being part-owner (along with Frank Costello and Joe Adonis) of the most successful casino, the Piping Rock, in the whole of Saratoga.

Perhaps it was because Lansky was so successful at setting up this and other business ventures, or perhaps it was because he had begun to enlist the help of several powerful government officials, that in 1938 Lansky attracted the attention of the Cuban dictator Fulgencio Batista who, so it seemed, wanted to boost his country's gambling revenues. Gambling was huge in Cuba, but Batista felt there was a problem as the large numbers of Americans who came to Cuba for a flutter, had begun to think the casinos and, in particular, the racetracks, were crooked. Suddenly the Americans were bypassing Cuba and taking their dollars to Puerto Rico. Batista wanted Lansky to clean up this mess.

Lansky went to Havana and brought a handful of his most loyal business friends and colleagues with him in order to help. At the Oriental Park racing track, he installed a man by the name of Lou Smith who introduced a mechanical starting gate and a photo finish at the track to ensure there was no further cheating. Smith also introduced drug testing for the horses. And as far as the gambling houses were concerned, Lansky transported his own crews down to take over from the Cubans.

It was all tremendously successful and later on, in 1955, he even succeeded in establishing a new casino in the Hotel Nacional with Eartha Kitt topping the bill on the opening night. While Lansky's businesses were going from strength to strength, some of his friends, in particular, Lucky Luciano, were far less fortunate.

In 1935 Thomas E. Dewey was appointed New York's Special Prosecutor with responsibility for the many racketeering businesses that had, in recent years, mushroomed out of all control. Dewey's first target was Dutch Schultz, but after Schultz was gunned down, Dewey turned his attention to Luciano and in June 1936 charged him with compulsory prostitution. The case went to court and subsequently Luciano was found guilty and sentenced to between thirty and fifty years in jail.

Meanwhile, despite his own illegal activities, Lansky's stock rose to the point where, not long after the bombing of Pearl Harbor, he was approached indirectly by a man called Red Haffenden, a naval reserve officer. Haffenden was in charge of documenting as much useful information as he could on those suspected of aiding and abetting German agents down on the waterfront. It was a complicated job and one for which he needed the help of powerful insiders – step forward Meyer Lansky.

Lansky's first piece of advice was that they needed to speak to Luciano, whose contacts among the Italian labor bosses, fishermen and dock workers were second to none. Luciano was moved from Dannemora prison on the Canadian border to Comstock prison, which was only two hours drive from Albany. A few days later, Commissioner of Corrections John A. Lyons, wrote to the warden at Comstock as follows:

> Dear Warden:
> This is to advise you that I have granted permission to Mr. Meyer Lansky to visit and interview Inmate Charles Luciano in your institution when accompanied by Mr. Polakoff, the inmate's attorney . . . You are authorized to waive the usual fingerprint requirements and to grant Mr. Lansky and Mr. Polakoff the opportunity of interviewing the inmate privately.[5]

The above is an extraordinary indictment of how the American criminal underworld often worked (and perhaps still works) hand-in-hand with the US government. But for Lansky, it was proof that he was a patriotic citizen and no doubt it also boosted his self-image as a man of incredible importance, one to whom the US government would turn in times of crisis. And the alliance seemed to pay dividends for, shortly after several meetings had taken place between Luciano and Lansky, eight German secret agents were arrested as they came ashore, four of them in Florida and four in Long Island. Subsequently, Luciano's lawyers petitioned for clemency for their client in exchange for his 'war work' and eventually this plea was granted, although at a cost, for instead of being able to remain in the States, Luciano was deported to Italy. Lansky visited him on Ellis Island one last time before he boarded his ship home. It was the last time the two friends ever saw one another on American soil.

On February 14, 1947, after seventeen relatively miserable years of marriage, Meyer and Anne Lansky divorced. Ann had suffered for years from mental instability, probably not helped by the fact that her husband had begun sleeping with other women. Ann kept custody of their three children (the two boys and a little girl called Sandra) but Meyer's alimony payments were hardly what one might call generous. Money worries must have added to her later inability to cope with life.

Meyer, on the other hand, pursued his business operations like never before. The war had ended; Americans were all for having some fun after years of austerity and the place to be seen in was Florida. Lansky already had carpet joints in that State, now he added to these by buying shares and going into partnership with other gambling outfits. But the profits didn't all end up in Lansky's pocket. Apart from his business partners, payments were made to several associates such as local government officials, the North Miami Police Department, the West Miami Police

Association and the local Hallandale police. On top of this, Lansky would always make certain that the IRS was also kept in the loop.

Like many a good taxpayer, however, Meyer Lansky and his partners did not quite present the whole story in the figures which they submitted to the IRS. At the end of every gambling shift, the 'drop' from each table in the casino would be brought into the counting room. There, Meyer and Jake Lansky would personally count the mounds of dollar bills until they reached the 'handle' – the amount of money they needed to meet their daily expenses. The handle, with the addition of a moderate sum for cash reserve and profit, would be passed on to be recorded in the credit column of the casino's ledger and, eventually, in the accounts that were presented to the IRS. Anything in excess of this went directly into the pockets of the Lansky brothers and of their partners.[6]

One of these partners was Lansky's old friend with whom he had set up the Piping Rock in Saratoga, Frank Costello. Together they opened a new club outside New Orleans called the Beverly Club. This was, like all of Lansky's ventures, very successful, but like any good businessman, Lansky was eager to continue expanding his empire. When his childhood buddy, Benny Siegel, asked for funding to set up a huge gambling arena (called the El Cortez) in the, at that time, relatively unheard of town of Las Vegas, Lansky obliged. The El Cortez was duly purchased and run very successfully; so successfully, in fact, that less than a year later, Siegel and his partners sold the complex for a huge profit then reinvested the money in a new hotel/casino, The Flamingo. Both of these establishments were Benny Siegel's babies. Lansky took a back seat, preferring to concentrate on his Florida businesses. Meanwhile, Benny had huge plans for The Flamingo, plans that eventually outran his funds. More money had to be borrowed and Siegel's partners began to grow restless. But even when The Flamingo finally opened in March 1947, the situation didn't improve. Nor did Siegel's temper. He was becoming increasingly unreasonable, given to bouts of anger and prone to serving threats on those who didn't comply with his demands. How much of this affected Meyer Lansky has never been established, but on June 20, 1947, while Siegel was in Los Angeles, he was gunned down and killed. Later in life, according to an interview given to Uri Dan (an Israeli journalist), Lansky denied any involvement in the hit, emphasizing that Siegel had been a childhood friend. That said, Lansky would certainly have known who did order the execution. Seldom one to bloody his own hands, Meyer Lansky was not the kind of man to let friendship stand in the way of business.

A little less than two years after he divorced Anne, Meyer Lansky met a woman by the name of Thelma 'Teddy' Schwartz and the two were married at the end of 1948 in Havana. It was to be a much happier union than that he had enjoyed with Anne, Thelma being a far stronger character than his previous spouse and in the summer of 1948 Lansky decided to take Thelma on a honeymoon to Europe. He booked passage on a liner, the *Italia*. Being who he was, this booking aroused the suspicion of the Bureau of Narcotics who always kept a close eye on the passenger

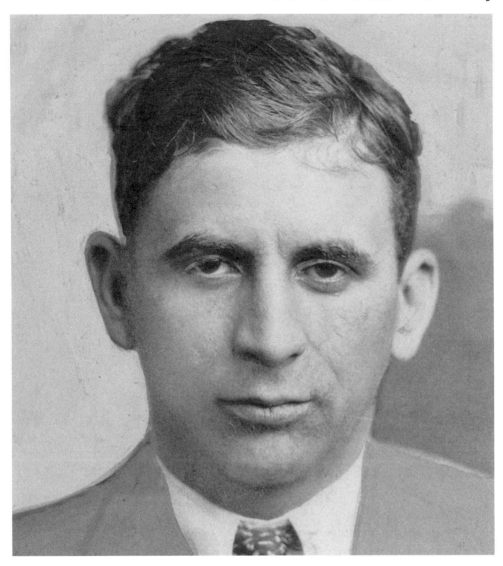

Lansky treasured his anonymity, shunning the limelight that attracted so many underworld figures, but when he took his second wife on a honeymoon to Italy, the press splashed his luxury cruise (billed as a trip to meet Lucky Luciano) all over the front pages.

lists of any ship either entering or exiting New York. In fact, so suspicious were they of Lansky's upcoming journey, especially as he was likely to meet up with his old friend Lucky Luciano, that two agents visited him at his apartment. Surprisingly, given that Lansky was normally such a secretive individual, he told the officers that yes, he would probably meet up with Luciano, but that he would never involve himself in drug trafficking. He also said, on being asked what exactly his profession was: 'Common gambler, I guess. I don't try to fool or impose on nobody. If I just met you casually, I would call myself a restaurant operator. If we warmed up to each other, I would tell you I was a common gambler.'[7]

But unlike any 'common gambler' Lansky's trip had not only created interest from the Bureau of Narcotics, but also from the newspapers. Lansky's photograph was splashed over the front page of the *New York Sun* as he entered the stateroom on board the *Italia* with the headline: 'Expected to Confer with Luciano. Underworld Big Shot and Wife in Regal Suite; Cost $2,600 One Way.' Suddenly the quiet man who had, (unlike Capone or Luciano or Siegel) shunned publicity, was thrust into the limelight, making him as big an underworld 'star' as any other mobster in history.

By the end of the 1940s the heyday of illegal gambling joints was drawing to a close for, after the euphoria experienced at the end of the Second World War, the government began to try to return law and order to the country. Suddenly, crime commissions began springing up in all the major cities including New York, Miami and Chicago. On September 19, 1950 Lansky found himself served with a subpoena to appear before the Kefauver Committee. But if Senator Estes Kefauver thought Lansky would furnish him with any incriminating evidence, he was wrong. Having agreed that he knew such underworld figures as Lucky Luciano, Joe Adonis, Frank Costello and Bugsy Siegel, Lansky took the Fifth Amendment and would answer no questions as to the nature of those friendships. He also took the Fifth when asked about his gambling ventures, especially those in Saratoga, Miami and New Orleans, instead preferring to talk about other business ventures which included part shares in a Wurlitzer company and a television company. The outcome of the Kefauver Committee investigation was that Lansky was named as one of the leading lights in America's organized crime syndicates which in turn spelt the beginning of the end for Lansky's illustrious underworld career.

In September 1952 Meyer Lansky, together with five others, was indicted by a grand jury on charges of conspiracy, gambling and fraud. Disinclined to be questioned in the witness box and run the risk of possibly incriminating others, and always one to fight shy of publicity, Lansky pleaded guilty and was sentenced not only to pay a fine of $2,500, but also to three months in Ballston Spa Jail. His stay in prison was uneventful. Indeed, he was let out one month early for good behavior, but during his time inside the Immigration and Naturalization Service (INS) had begun an investigation into whether Lansky had disclosed his criminal record at the time he applied for naturalization. Suddenly, Lansky's past came back to haunt him because, as the INS soon discovered, their suspect had been involved in an attack on John Barrett back in 1928. But while the INS's net was slowly closing around him, Lansky continued with 'business as usual.'

In 1952 Fulgencio Batista was elected president of Cuba for a second time and, as with his first term of office, one of Batista's priorities was to ensure that gambling within the country was seen to be straight. Once again, Meyer stepped into the fold, in fact this time he was paid an annual retainer by the Cuban government as an advisor on gambling reform. Meyer also went into partnership with the owners of the

Montmartre Club and it was during this period that he opened the casino at the Nacional Hotel with Eartha Kitt topping the bill. Lansky's business ventures in Cuba seemed to be going from strength to strength and when, in 1955, President Batista passed Hotel Law 2074 which granted tax exemptions to all hoteliers who provided tourist 'accommodations,' Lansky set about building his own luxurious hotel in Havana, called the Riviera. On opening night it was a huge success, with Ginger Rogers topping the bill, but if Lansky was riding high in Cuba, back in the United States things were far less sweet.

On October 25, 1957 Albert Anastasia was gunned down in the barber's shop of the Park Sheraton Hotel in New York. Rumor, together with a certain amount of evidence, suggested that Anastasia was about to buy shares in The Hilton, a new hotel to be constructed in Havana that would rival anything Lansky had built. Was Lansky, therefore, behind the hit?

As luck would have it, a few months after Anastasia's killing, Meyer Lansky was flying back from Havana to New York. On his arrival he was immediately arrested and booked on a charge of 'vagrancy' due to his refusal to answer any of the police's many questions. Despite a thorough search, the police could find no incriminating evidence on Lansky's person and, having spent a night in jail, Lansky was released on bail the following morning. Naturally, the police then put their number one suspect under surveillance, but soon realized that Anastasia's murder, far from being connected to gambling in Cuba, was more than likely linked to business dealings closer to home (Vito Genovese was rumored to have been behind the hit). As for the outstanding charge of vagrancy against Lansky, the case eventually came to court and was dismissed.

A free man again, Lansky began spending increasing amounts of time in Cuba looking after his business interests there. Although he was aware that Batista's dictatorial reign might not last forever, he didn't realize just how close it was to an end. In fact, on New Year's Eve 1958, while Lansky sat in the Riviera Hotel listening to the celebrations, Batista decided to flee the country, leaving the opposition (in the form of Fidel Castro) in charge.

In terms of bloodletting, the Cuban revolution was relatively peaceful but in its immediate aftermath, Havana's casino businesses were slaughtered by Castro who hated the idea of any kind of American influence besmirching his country. Nonetheless, only a few months after he had taken over as president, economic realities (in the form of the countless men and women whose livelihoods depended on the American-owned hotels) forced Castro to rethink his strategy and allow the hotels to reopen. It was an uneasy compromise and Lansky was soon to discover that his old habit of trying to bribe officials didn't wash with the new, politically ideological Cuban officials. Lansky was also suffering from ill health, with stomach ulcers and swelling in his joints. Then, on May 7, 1960, Cuba openly began political negotiations/relations with the Soviet Union. Suddenly, Lansky was aware that he might lose that which was closest to his heart, that which he had spent millions of dollars in building and which garnered him huge revenues – the Riviera Hotel. On 24 October 1960 the nightmare came true; the Riviera was effectively confiscated and nationalized along with 165 other American businesses.

After this tremendous blow (which decimated Lansky's personal fortune), his health unsurprisingly continued in a downwards spiral until eventually he suffered a heart attack and was twice hospitalized. Despite these setbacks, he managed to rally himself and, though by no means a well man, did continue to lead a relatively normal life. Meanwhile, the INS was continuing its research into Lansky's past with a view to having him deported while the IRS was keeping a close eye on his tax returns. The FBI had put him under close surveillance, even bugging his apartment.

It was this last move that eventually spawned the now famous Lansky quote, 'We're bigger than US Steel'. On May 27, 1962, while watching a TV documentary on organized crime, one of the contributors to the program stated that organized crime was second only in size to the government itself. In response, Lansky is supposed to have turned to his wife and said that 'organized crime was bigger than US Steel.'[8]

But if Lansky was formerly one of the most influential men in America, during these last years he seemed to be leading a quiet life, spending most of his time in a modest house in the northern suburbs of Miami. Health permitting, he played golf or joined friends at the racetrack but, much to the FBI's chagrin, didn't seem to be interested in anything remotely illegal. That was until the FBI, who appeared to be tapping every crime syndicate boss in the country, began garnering information that Lansky was involved in a 'skimming' business in Las Vegas that was earning him approximately $1 million per annum. But the FBI were out of luck when it came to prosecuting Lansky for, just as they thought they had him cornered, a man by the name of Edie Levinson (formerly the manager of the Riviera) who now ran the Freemont Hotel in Las Vegas, discovered an illegal tap in his offices and took the FBI to court for 'illegal entry, invasion of privacy and violation of constitutional rights.'[8] Naturally, this case had a knock-on effect and although Lansky immediately brought his 'skimming' business to a close, the Levinson case provided him with a means to avoid prosecution. At the same time, neither the INS nor the IRS could come up with enough evidence to either prosecute or deport Lansky despite the IRS having good reason to believe that he had begun a money laundering business.

The Bahamas was the site of this offshore activity with money being transferred out there to the Bank of World Commerce and from this point further dispatched to any destination in the world. At that time, if you wanted to bring your untaxed (and occasionally 'dirty') money back into the US from abroad, you might try to do so through fake loans or dummy companies. This activity became known as 'laundering' and Meyer Lansky, either rightly or wrongly, was reputed to be the genius that had dreamed up the whole scam. Nevertheless, although the IRS followed this paper trail as closely as possible and knew of Lansky sending money out to a Swiss bank account, they never once found him bringing the cash back into the States. Once again they were foiled as far as prosecuting him was concerned.

To add insult to injury, all the time that the FBI were trying to find enough evidence with which to bring Lansky down, the press were building Lansky up into a mathematical genius, a mastermind of accountancy, worth in the region of three hundred million dollars. Undoubtedly the sum mentioned was way beyond what Lansky was actually worth, but the fact remained that this shadowy, secretive little man seemed capable of anything he set his mind to – including giving the FBI the slip. Yet the authorities kept on battling and in 1970, returning to Miami from a trip to Acapulco, Lansky was found by customs' officials to be in possession of a phial of pills for which he had no prescription. Suddenly, Lansky was up in court, this time on a drugs' charge but as with his 'vagrancy' court appearance, the judge threw the case out. 'If the Defendant were John Smith instead of Meyer Lansky,' said Lansky's lawyer, Joseph Varon, 'there would never have been a prosecution.'9

Lansky was now feeling persecuted to the point where he no longer wished to live in the United States and in July 1970 he and his wife, Teddy, flew to Israel (Lansky had been here briefly once before on a two week holiday), where he applied for citizenship. He engaged the services of a young lawyer and constitutional expert, Yoram Alroy, to whom he gave several newspaper cuttings outlining his 'supposed' criminal activities. Back in the United States, meanwhile, the Justice Department issued a subpoena for Lansky to appear before a grand jury on charges of money 'skimming.' Within two months of this subpoena being issued, the US Embassy in Tel Aviv was then instructed to inform Lansky to hand over his passport and return to the United States. Having long wished to deport Meyer Lansky, the US government had done a complete 180-degree turn and now wanted him extradited back into the country! The Israeli press suddenly caught on to the fact that Lansky, the crime boss of America, was in their midst and splashed this news all over the front pages. Lansky sued, but the damage was already done and in September 1971 he was denied Israeli citizenship. Never one to take anything lying down, Lansky's lawyer demanded a hearing before the Israeli Supreme Court, but this also proved a failure and on 11 September 1972 he was once again denied citizenship.

There now followed an attempted escape from Israel worthy of a Hollywood film, with Lansky and a friend by the name of Yoskeh Sheiner (Teddy remained for the meantime in Israel) trying to fly first to Switzerland, then to Rio, then from Rio to Buenos Aires and finally from Buenos Aires to Paraguay. But the couple only got as far as Buenos Aires before they were detained by the local FBI and from there Lansky was flown back to the United States.

Meyer Lansky arrived in Miami on November 7, 1972 and, save for a short appearance in court where bail was granted, he headed immediately to Mount Sinai Hospital. Three days later Teddy joined her husband only to be informed that whilst on the flight to South America he had suffered a heart attack.

The IRS continued to try to prosecute Lansky on charges of 'skimming' while at the same time another charge was added to the list. A character by the name of

Meyer Lansky was a canny survivor. He was in his eighties when he died of lung cancer in Mount Sinai Hospital in New York, having enjoyed a final few years of peaceful retirement.

Vincent 'Fat Vinnie' Teresa had implicated Lansky in a 'failure to declare income' offence. Between these two charges and a third on contempt of court for not appearing when issued with a subpoena whilst he was in Israel, Lansky faced spending the rest of his life in jail.

The first case to be heard was the one of 'contempt' which Lansky lost and for which he was sentenced to one year and one day in prison (albeit in a medical wing.) The second case to be heard was that which Fat Vinnie's testimony had brought about. This time Lansky was luckier and his lawyers pulled Vinnie's evidence to shreds. The jury returned for the Defendant.

Lansky was jubilant. Now there was only one outstanding case to be heard but, owing to Lansky's ill health, it had to be repeatedly postponed until, on November 3, 1976, the Justice Department announced it would be dropping the case.

Meyer Lansky was now reaching his seventy-fifth birthday, tired and ill yet in the last years of his life he vigorously pursued the right to return to Israel, even writing a letter to Israel's new prime minister, Menachem Begin, begging him to overturn the court's decision. When his request was turned down, Lansky put his faith in a young Israeli lawyer, Yoram Sheftel, who managed to acquire what no one else had – an entry visa for Meyer Lansky. But the good news was short-lived when Lansky discovered he would have to put up a $100,000 bond. This he refused to do, baulking at the suggestion that his visit should come with conditions. Some people have now speculated that, in addition to being insulted at having to pay a bond to enter Israel, Lansky might not actually have had this kind of money. Certainly, he had nowhere near the millions of dollars that the press speculated he possessed.

The last years of Meyer Lansky's life were peaceful, although he continued to suffer from ill health and was diagnosed as having lung cancer. He died on January 15, 1983 in Mount Sinai Hospital. His funeral was a small, family affair as far removed from the large gangster send-offs as it was possible to get. Nevertheless, his obituaries appeared worldwide, but perhaps *The New York Times* best summed Lansky up when it wrote that 'He would have been chairman of the board of General Motors if he'd gone into legitimate business.'[10] As it was, Lansky did it his own way, much preferring to stay on the wrong side of the law.

[1] From *Jews without Money* by Michael Gold, New York: Carroll and Graf, 1984.

[2] *Meyer Lansky; Mogul of the Mob* by Dennis Eisenburg, Uri Dan and Eli Landau. New York: Paddington Press, 1979.

[3] In 1933, in every state except Nevada, gambling (save for horse racing and in some instances dog racing) was illegal.

[4] Carpet joints were so named because they were one step up from the sawdust strewn gaming houses of old and demonstrated a certain luxurious atmosphere.

[5] Statement of Vernon A. Morhous. Dewey Papers, Series 13, Box 13.

[6] *Little Man: Meyer Lansky and the Gangster Life* by Robert Lacey, Little Brown Inc, 1991.

[7] Bureau of Narcotics, Report of Agent John H. Hanly, 28 June, 1949.

[8] To SAC Miami, from Director, March 23, 1960. FBI.

[8] *Little Man: Meyer Lansky and the Gangster Life* by Robert Lacey, Little Brown Inc, 1991.

[9] *Miami Herald*, 19 June 1970.

[10] *New York Times*, 16 January 1983.

CHARLES 'LUCKY' LUCIANO
The Father of Organized Crime

'I'd do it legal. I learned too late that you need just as good a
brain to make a crooked million as an honest million. These days,
you apply for a license to steal from the public. If I had my time
again, I'd make sure I got that license first.'

Interview given by Charlie Luciano to the
New York Herald Tribune, 27 January 1962.

On February 8, 1962, a plane landed at New York International Airport having flown in from Naples. On touchdown, a coffin was unloaded from the hold and placed in a waiting hearse which then drove on to Saint Johns Cemetery in Queens County. There, the coffin was taken to the Lucania vault and in the presence of FBI agents, reporters, detectives and officers – together with two mourners – the body was officially laid to rest. Less than two weeks earlier, the man in the coffin had died of a heart attack at Naples Capodichino Airport while under surveillance by both Italian and American agents who wanted to question him as head of an international drugs cartel. The man's name was Charles 'Lucky' Luciano (the name by which Salvatore Lucania was best known throughout his life), one-time thug, thief, murderer and, according to the FBI, the first modern-day Mafia overlord.

Born in 1897 in Lercara Friddi, Sicily, Lucky Luciano suffered a childhood of poverty. His parents could barely scrape a living together, and in 1906, in the hope of finding a better life, they set sail for America, arriving in New York harbor some time in November of the same year. Initially, the Lucanias (Lucky also had two brothers and a sister) found an apartment on First Avenue and Lucky was enrolled at school from where he more often than not played truant. By age fourteen he had quit school and taken a job in a hat factory, but, like many of his contemporaries, he took little interest in his work and the job didn't last long. The young boy found it more interesting and certainly more profitable hanging around New York's street corner crap games. 'Never, I am sure,' wrote newspaperman Hickman Powell in his book on Luciano, 'has there been such a city, such a conglomeration of vice, of virtue, of plain human energy, as that huddled mass of stinking tenements, that maze of crowded streets, roaring with elevated trains, jammed with pushcarts, bedraggled with washing on the line. We say very easily that the congested areas breed criminals. They also breed strong men to conquer, idealists to preach.'[1]

Sadly, Luciano wasn't one of the latter, instead taking to a life of crime like the proverbial duck to water. Always one to be drawn towards trouble, the young Luciano was soon arrested on charges of shoplifting and also began his first racket – preying on young Jewish kids, extorting money from them with the threat that if they didn't pay up, they'd be beaten. It was in this manner that Lucky befriended the young Meyer Lansky. Refusing to pay Lucky any protection money, the plucky Polish boy immediately made an impression on Luciano and the two soon became firm friends. They found that they had in common a mutual distrust of the Irish. 'Whenever there was a fight between Irish and Italians,' Meyer Lansky later recalled, 'or an incident involving Irish with Jews, the cops would always take the side of the Irish.'[2] Resenting this blatant prejudice, the two boys decided to bring their respective gangs together to fight off any and all Irish youths. The collaboration worked well and the two remained allies throughout their public and private lives.

By 1916, when Luciano was nineteen years old, he was already a leading member of the notorious Five Points Gang and had also built up a reputation with the police, mainly for narcotics offences (aged eighteen he had spent a short spell in prison for dealing in heroin.) Lucky also set himself up with Lansky and Bugsy Siegel in the bootlegging business. It was undoubtedly this latter activity that eventually caught the eye of Mafia supremo Joe 'The Boss' Masseria. During the 1920s, Masseria, together with another Mafia boss Salvatore Maranzano, was a leading light in the criminal underworld. Better known as 'Mustache Petes' for their old-world, conservative ways, they saw little need for change and often resented the new breed of up-and-coming young thugs who numbered amongst them, Lucky Luciano. Nevertheless, Luciano worked for Masseria for a short while before growing disillusioned with the older man's narrow-mindedness. Luciano grew frustrated with Masseria's refusal to do business or join forces with non Italian/Sicilians whom he always regarded as beneath him. Luciano, it would transpire, was something of a visionary when it came to observing that dividing criminal activities up along ethnic lines meant that everyone lost out and that it would be better for all concerned if the different nationalities could settle their differences and work together. Masseria also blotted his copy book with Luciano in one other way for, early in 1929, Luciano found himself being forced at gunpoint into the back of a black limousine. His mouth was taped over and he was repeatedly punched and stabbed in the face and stomach until he lost consciousness. The next thing Luciano recalled was waking up on a beach in lower New York. He was bleeding profusely, but managed to crawl and stagger to a police booth from where he was rushed to hospital. Luciano survived the attack, but it left him with a scar down his right cheek and his right eye drooping slightly, giving him an incredibly evil demeanor. On being discharged from hospital, Luciano was understandably eager to discover who had ordered the attack. According to legend, it was Meyer Lansky who informed Lucky that Masseria was responsible. Lucky's boss had grown tired of his underling's constant pressure to move business in a different direction. This was a fatal move on Masseria's part. Salvatore Maranzano, who had long been at loggerheads with Masseria in what is best known as the 'Castellammarese War,' persuaded Luciano to change sides and join him on the proviso that Lucky organized a hit on his rival. Joseph Bonanno, who was also a Maranzano man, remembers meeting Lucky for the first time during this period.

> This meeting gave me my first opportunity to meet Charlie Luciano. He was a thin man with a full head of black hair and a scarred and pockmarked face. He walked obliquely, lurching slightly to the side. His Sicilian was scant, but what words he knew he spoke well. He usually expressed himself in American street slang. But he was not a big talker; he liked to get to the point without any flourishes. Luciano had an ardent, intelligent look about him.[3]

Maranzano, according to Bonanno, was at pains to point out that he wanted Luciano, and not one of his associates, to organize and carry out the hit, a request with which Luciano happily complied. On April 15, 1931, Luciano, Masseria and two others, Ciro Terranova and Vito Genovese, whom Lucky had known since childhood, drove to the Nuova Villa Tammaro Restaurant on Coney Island. Everyone enjoyed a sumptuous meal after which Masseria's dining companions excused themselves, leaving Masseria alone with Luciano. The two then began playing a card game during which Luciano retired to the men's room. Seconds later, four men burst into the restaurant and gunned Masseria down (also see chapter on Bugsy Siegel).

With the job done, Luciano was able to step in to Masseria's shoes and take over Little Italy's lottery rackets, while Maranzano was free of his old-time enemy for good. The celebrations, however, were short-lived for not long afterwards, Luciano began to suspect that Maranzano, who had now named himself *capo di tutti capi* – the 'boss of all bosses,' wanted him dead. Once again, Joseph Bonanno provides us with a fascinating insight into the minds of these killers, specifically highlighting Maranzano's delusions of grandeur. Shortly after Masseria was gunned down, Maranzano organized a meeting of New York's main crime bosses near Wappingers Falls in the Catskills at which he hired a plane to circle the hotel:

> 'The plane is circling the grounds,' Maranzano said when heads turned to him for an explanation. 'The plane is armed with machine guns and bombs. Please remain in your seats. We're about to start.' Maranzano had hired the pilot, the son of someone in our Family, to circle overhead and be on the lookout for police cars. But the guests, who didn't know that, probably thought the airplane might be used against them. It was precisely to impress these people – the uncommitted and the undecided – that Maranzano was being theatrical.[4]

Whether suffering from delusions of grandeur or whether he truly was just trying to intimidate his guests on this occasion, the fact was that Maranzano's actions did little to make Luciano feel any less threatened. Luciano decided that Maranzano had to die before he himself was killed. He hired four of Meyer Lansky's and Bugsy Siegel's best gunmen and on September 10, 1931, while pretending to be IRS officers raiding Maranzano's Park Avenue office, shot and stabbed Maranzano to death. No one was arrested for the murder, although at a much later date Abe 'Bo' Weinburg (Dutch Schultz's right-hand man) and Red Levine both said they were part of the hit squad.

At the same time as Maranzano was killed, it is also widely believed that there

The young Lucky Luciano was the victim of a beating ordered by his Mafia boss, Joe Massena, which left him with facial scars and a forever drooping eye.

began a nation-wide purge of other old-time Italian/Sicilian Mafia bosses by teams of younger gangsters, a theory backed up by this piece of FBI testimony:

> Following the death of Salvatore Maranzano, a wave of gangland slayings, known as the 'Sicilian Vespers,' swept the country.[5]

> In fact, many commentators have noted that these slayings marked a turning point in the history of organized crime in America.

For Lucky Luciano, the murders also marked a personal turning point. They gave him respect among his contemporaries and free range when it came to business. But to build up a nationwide crime network, Luciano needed his friends. He couldn't work alone and no one was as trustworthy or more skilled an entrepreneur than Meyer Lansky. They made a good partnership and later in life Luciano commented that Meyer must have been 'wet-nursed by a Sicilian,' as the two got along so well.

On December 5, 1933, Prohibition was repealed, but this didn't mean bootlegging altogether drew to a halt as stiff taxes were now levied on the production of alcohol. Nevertheless, Lansky, Luciano and their counterparts all saw the need to diversify and both Lucky and Meyer took the opportunity of running franchises in Arnold Rothstein's (one of America's first underworld bosses) casinos and 'lake houses'[6] in Saratoga Springs. Luciano also concentrated on bookmaking, prostitution, narcotics smuggling – heroin being part and parcel of the prostitution scene at this time. The profits were good, allowing Luciano to take permanent suites at both the Waldorf-Astoria Hotel and the Barbizon Plaza. Lucky was also something of a celebrity by this point, being seen in the company of baseball star and one-time husband of Marilyn Monroe, Joe Dimaggio.

Another area where Luciano and Lansky (together with Bugsy Siegel) worked well was in the establishment of the notorious Murder, Inc. The mob had never had any qualms when it came to executing their own, but Luciano and the others decided it would be more efficient if they were to organize a group of armed killers who could be called on to do the business. Thus, Murder Inc., was born. Probably its most famous hit was Dutch Schultz, who was gunned down in October 1935. Albert Anastasia – nicknamed the 'Lord High Executioner' – is often referred to as the group's leading light, although it has also been speculated that Louis Lepke, a leading racketeer of that time, was in overall command. However, Lucky Luciano, Meyer Lansky, and to some extent Frank Costello, were nearly always consulted when a judgment was required. They were never personally involved in the actual killings, of course.

Although participating with Meyer Lansky in his gambling ventures and with Murder Inc., Lucky Luciano's real forte was in prostitution and pimping – areas Lansky studiously steered clear of. Luciano set up several brothels and organized a team of bookers to look after the girls and bring in work, while at the same time often sampling the goods himself. This led, or so it is said, to at least seven bouts of gonorrhea and one bout of syphilis. It has also been said that Luciano wasn't particularly pleasant in his treatment of 'girlfriends'. This account of Lucky came from a friend of one of his partners, Betty Cook:

> She [Nancy Presser] was eating with Betty one evening at the Tip Toe Inn at Eighty-sixth Street and Broadway when Charlie [Luciano] came in and joined them. Right away he and Betty got in an argument. As Nancy sat and listened, anger boiled up in her. She had never heard a man talk to a girl like that, and there was nothing shrinking about Nancy . . . She spoke up sharply to Luciano. She told him to quit talking to Betty that way. That was no way to treat a girl. Luciano turned to her slowly, stared at her steadily, coolly for a while without speaking. She will never forget the icy black anger in his eyes. His eyes held hers as if by force. Now she knew why Betty Cook feared him like death. This man Luciano was full of pent-up force, and serpentine malevolence seemed to strike from his stone-like face.[7]

It was this serpentine malevolence that no doubt helped Luciano syndicate just about every brothel in New York and, further, to put all the madams who ran the establishments on a fixed salary. Those who wouldn't comply with his wishes more often than not either ended up in hospital or disappeared entirely. It was a tough game, but one that reaped the man at the top huge profits, profits which soon saw Luciano being investigated by the new, thirty-three-year-old Special Prosecutor of New York, Thomas E. Dewey. Dewey had already made his mark as an Assistant United States Attorney, successfully prosecuting Waxey Gordon – a big-time mobster – for income tax evasion, and there is no doubt that had Dutch Schultz not been murdered days before his trial on similar charges, he too would have become one of Dewey's victims.

Together with a handpicked team of approximately twenty agents, the newly appointed Special Prosecutor organized raids on eighty New York brothels. Hundreds of madams, girls and bookers were arrested and taken in for questioning. Lucky Luciano's entire world began to fall apart. Those who had been arrested began talking to the police, divulging the secrets of Lucky's numerous brothels to the point where Dewey (who had initially wanted to prosecute Luciano on charges of tax evasion or narcotics trafficking) had enough material to put out a warrant for Lucky's arrest.

Luciano, meanwhile, had not been seen in New York for several months. In fact, since Dutch Schultz's murder he had been lying low, first in Miami, and subsequently in Arkansas at the winter resort of choice for top gangsters, Hot Springs, where he was supposedly 'taking the waters.'

A detective was sent out to Arkansas and Lucky was finally arrested while sitting on Bath House Row with a group of his friends. Amazingly, the judge then set his bail at a mere $5,000 – a figure Lucky could immediately pay. He walked free, but not for long. When Dewey heard of his release it is said that he almost suffered a coronary, screaming down the phone that they had just freed America's Public Enemy No.1. Lucky was dragged into court again, but this time the judge set bail at $200,000. Suddenly, Lucky Luciano was fighting for his life. He began by employing the finest Arkansas lawyers that money could buy. Dewey, only too aware that his prey would do anything to escape conviction, sent twenty state troopers to return Lucky to New York where he could keep a close eye on the prisoner. This whole episode was hugely humiliating for Luciano, not least because of all the rackets in which he was involved, prostitution was the most sordid, the least glamorous. He denied that he had any hand in running brothels, stating that he was a 'bigger man than that,' but no one was listening. Lucky was brought back to New York where Justice McCook immediately held him on $350,000 bail.

On May 11, 1936, the trial of Charles 'Lucky' Luciano began. The main prosecution witness was a streetwalker and part-time madam by the name of Cokey Flo Brown. Unfortunately, her testimony was vulnerable as her witness statements were given while in withdrawal from heroin, and thus were open to the accusation that she would have said anything in exchange for drugs. Luciano's defense team made much of this point, but Cokey Flo stood up well to their accusations. She claimed she was present at a conversation where Luciano had expressed a desire to organize New York's prostitutes and madams into a proper syndicated business on which he could levy a tax.

> Another time she [Cokey Flo] saw Charlie Lucky, said Flo, was about four o'clock in the morning when she and Jimmy went down to a restaurant in a basement in Chinatown. She couldn't remember the address but she remembered the big figure 21 outside the entrance . . . So far as Flo could remember, this was in the summer of 1935. She and Jimmy found Lucky, Little Davie, and Tommy Bull sitting there eating, and again they talked mostly in Italian. But there was some talk in English about bonding. It was a discussion, Flo recalled, about making the madams pay up and getting more places.

'They were speaking of bonding and madams being stubborn and not paying, and Charlie said to Jimmy: "I told you just talking won't do any good – that you have got to put the screws on them a little bit."'8

Cokey Flo's evidence was damning enough, but the prosecution also elaborated about Luciano's dissolute lifestyle, the fact that he had taken suites at the Waldorf-Astoria and Barbizon Plaza hotels and that he often enjoyed the company of prostitutes – several of whom were giving evidence at the trial. Jospeh Bonanno went so far as to say that Dewey's case against Luciano was not so much against the man and what he had done, but against his 'name', and that in mixing with undesirables such as prostitutes, pimps and brothel owners he was an unsavory character who deserved to be sent down.

Nor did Luciano help his case much when he took the stand himself. He denied ever knowing any of the witnesses, including Cokey Flo Brown, and he denied that he had ever had anything to do with the prostitution business other than to use their services privately. 'I always gave,' said Lucky. 'I never took.'

Dewey, however, wasn't giving up easily. Knowing that Luciano wouldn't give an inch on the question of running a prostitution racket, he questioned Lucky on his past convictions, thus illustrating to the jury that the defendant was a career criminal and that anything he said was not to be trusted. The ploy worked. Lucky kept getting trapped by Dewey in half-truths and lies; he looked foolish, he looked like a man trying to hide something and when the jury retired it was really only a matter of time before they returned with a verdict of guilty on all sixty-one charges. In an interview (the authenticity of which several people have questioned) included in a book entitled *The Last Testament of Lucky Luciano* by Martin A. Gosch and Richard Hammer, Luciano is alleged to have said of the verdict:

After sittin' in court and listening to myself being plastered to the wall and tarred and feathered by a bunch of whores who sold themselves for a quarter and hearin' that no good judge McCook hand me what added up to a life term, I still get madder at Dewey's crap than anythin' else.9

Lucky Luciano was sent down for between thirty to fifty years. It appeared that he was a broken man who would never see freedom again.

In stark contrast, the trial was the making of Thomas E. Dewey. Known nationwide as the man who had successfully prosecuted the Mob, whenever his picture appeared on newsreels a cheer would erupt. It was also the beginning of a hugely successful political career. In 1937, Dewey won the election as New York District Attorney and thereafter he thrice became governor of New York. Not only that, but he twice secured the Republican nomination for President, only missing out on the job itself when pipped at the post by Harry Truman in 1948. Nor was Dewey the only one to achieve stardom after the trial, for several of the prostitutes who had testified, including Cokey Flo Brown and Mildred Harris, were approached by Warner Brothers' who were interested in making a film based on the trial. *Liberty* magazine interviewed the girls and subsequently printed a series of ghost-written stories entitled 'Underworld Nights.'

Meanwhile, within only a few hours of the guilty verdict being read out, Luciano had been given an assessment by Dr L. E. Kienholz, an assistant psychiatrist in the classification unit at Sing Sing Prison. Kienholz swiftly concluded that Luciano was of limited intelligence and rather optimistically suggested that he should learn a trade while in jail. Kienholz also recommended that because of Luciano's drug addiction he should be moved to Dannemora Prison (otherwise known as the Siberia of all US penitentiaries) in upstate New York where it was less likely he could get hold of any illegal substances. At Dannemora, when not confined to his cell – which could be for up to sixteen hours a day – Lucky was put to work in the prison laundry. It was an ignominious existence, particularly for a man who had commanded so much respect – at least, from his employees and fellow mobsters – on the outside. Nevertheless, always optimistic, Lucky had his lawyers put together an appeal on the grounds that several key witnesses (in particular prostitutes such as Cokey Flo, Nancy Presser and Mildred Harris) now wished to repudiate their testimonies. Naturally, the prosecuting team could only speculate that Luciano's men had somehow threatened the girls with violence to make them retract their statements, but despite these threats and the motion that Luciano be re-tried, five judges from the Appellate Division of the Supreme Court ruled that the initial trial was sound and that Luciano's conviction should stand.

This news was a huge blow to Luciano. All he could realistically now expect of the future was years and years spent in a cold, dank prison cell with little or no creature comforts. He might even die in prison. Then something he could never have predicted occurred. Japanese planes bombed Pearl Harbor in 1941 and the United States was propelled into World War Two. Bizarrely, this was to result in Lucky's eventual release.

Immediately after Pearl Harbor, the United States began losing ships off the American coast due, for the most part, to their being torpedoed by German U-boats. To add insult to injury, no German U-boat had ever been sunk in return, leading the Americans to believe that the enemy was receiving information from German spies inside their own ranks. Further to these suspicions, in 1942 a ship called the *Normandie*, which was being fitted out as a troop vessel on the Hudson River, was set alight and destroyed. Something had to be done; everyone was under suspicion of being a Nazi sympathizer or a saboteur, including dock workers and longshoremen as well as US Navy staff. Step into the limelight – Meyer Lansky.

Lansky suggested to Red Haffenden – who led the US Naval Intelligence Unit – that with his dockland connections, numerous labor rackets and the respect he still commanded within New York's underworld community, Lucky Luciano would be the best man with whom to liaise in order to uncover the spies. First, of course, Luciano would need to be moved from Dannemora. Sing Sing was suggested, but eventually it was decided to relocate Luciano to Great Meadow Prison in Comstock. On May 12, 1942 this was arranged.

Luciano could be absolutely charming with ladies, as seen here in this 1949 picture of him socializing at a party, but he could be despicably abusive to his girlfriends, too, and suffered several bouts of gonorrhea as well as contracting syphilis from the prostitutes he used.

For his part, Luciano knew nothing of the reasons behind his transfer; not until Meyer Lansky showed up requesting that Lucky help the US Navy, and in particular Red Haffenden, with its war work. At this point in his life, Luciano still had at least twenty-four years to serve of his sentence and wouldn't even be eligible to apply for parole for a further fourteen years. It was a bleak outlook. Striking a deal seemed the better option.

But this was sticky territory for Luciano, who knew that there was a deportation order attached to his sentence, meaning that on his release he would be forced to return to Italy. If Luciano agreed to help the US Navy and anyone in Italy found this out, he was scared he'd be killed. Red Haffenden promised the collaboration would remain top secret, but they needed Luciano's help. Despite never having been in charge of the New York waterfront, Luciano had done several deals with the men who were, deals involving drug running and bookmaking, so he knew the right people and which strings to pull.

Finally, Luciano agreed, and in the weeks that followed, a procession of dockland bosses made their way to Comstock for secret talks, which resulted in the arrest of several German spies and men intent on sabotaging US assets.

By the early months of 1943 cargoes were flowing rapidly and freely through the port of New York, the largest single supply point for the war in Europe. New convoy arrangements out in the Atlantic had significantly cut down the sinkings of merchantmen by the U-boats, and Navy intelligence again turned to the underworld for help with a new mission. With the recent conquest of North Africa, the Allies were planning an invasion of Italy, which would almost certainly commence at Italy's southernmost tip – a naval-supported landing by US forces on the island of Sicily. Red Haffenden turned to Meyer Lansky, who raised the subject with Charlie on his next visit to Comstock.[10]

Although there is very little hard evidence to suggest Luciano helped the US when it came to invading his homeland, it is generally believed that without his information and contacts the mission would not have been the success that it was. On VE Day, May 8, 1945, Luciano's lawyer, Moses Polakoff, drew up a petition for clemency on behalf of his client stating that it was a trade off for all Luciano's help with the war effort. Initially, the Navy denied any knowledge of Luciano having helped them. Both Polakoff and Lansky persisted in their efforts to secure Luciano's freedom and on January 4, 1946, inmate number 15684, Charles Lucky Luciano finally walked away from Great Meadow Prison – straight into custody of the US Immigration and Naturalization Service. Thomas E. Dewey knew only too well that Luciano had never actually applied to be a naturalized citizen of America and his presence in the country was, therefore, illegal.

On February 10, 1946, Lucky Luciano was transferred to Ellis Island to begin his long voyage home. Meyer Lansky, Moses Polakoff and Frank Costello all visited him several times to say their farewells, after which Luciano boarded the SS *Laura Keene*, which was sailing to Genoa. Frank Costello was the last of this threesome to see Luciano in America for on the night before he sailed, Costello visited him on board ship together with a group of union longshoremen for a meal of spaghetti, lobsters and wine.

On his return to Italy, the Italian government stressed several rules that Luciano had to follow in relation to his livelihood. He was only allowed to travel a few miles outside Naples, where he had established himself, and he had to inform them if he was going to receive foreign visitors. Neither of these rules seemed to matter to Luciano, who, thanks to old friends such as Lansky and Bugsy Siegel, soon set up new gambling businesses in both Havana and Las Vegas. But friendships and business ventures do not always make good bedfellows, as Meyer Lansky was about to find out. It is thought that, having lent Bugsy Siegel a substantial amount of money to continue building his Flamingo hotel project and not seeing any imminent return of the loan, Lansky was one of the men behind Bugsy's murder in 1946. Siegel died in a slew of bullets while sitting reading a newspaper in his girlfriend's Beverly Hills home.

Lucky's own end was a little less spectacular. At the age of sixty-five, while waiting to meet a scriptwriter off a plane at Naples airport, he suffered a massive coronary. At long last, Luciano could return to America, albeit in a coffin. There have been several 'trials of the century' in America since Thomas Dewey's success story, but very few have matched Lucky Luciano's for colorful language, interesting characters, shock revelations and downright hard-nosed determination. Ironically, it is this, if for little else, that Luciano will best be remembered.

1 *Lucky Luciano: The Man who Organized Crime in America*, Hickman Powell, Barricade Books Inc, 2000.

2 *Meyer Lansky: Mogul of the Mob*, Dennis Eisenberg, Uri Dan, Eli Landau, New York: Paddington Press, 1979.

3 *A Man of Honour: The Autobiography of Joseph Bonanno*, Simon & Schuster 1983.

4 Ibid.

5 'Chronological History of La Cosa Nostra', FBI Criminal Investigative Division.

6 The lakehouses were part casino, part gentlemen's club.

7 *Lucky Luciano: The Man who Organized Crime in America*, Hickman Powell, Barricade Books Inc., 2000

8 Ibid.

9 *The Last Testament of Lucky Luciano*, Martin A. Gosch & Richard Gosch, (publisher unknown), 1975.

10 *Little Man: Meyer Lansky and the Gangster Life*, Robert Lacey, Random Century Ltd, 1991

GEORGE MORAN
The Bug

'Judge, that's a beautiful diamond ring you're wearing.
If it's snatched some night, promise me you won't go hunting me.
I'm telling you now I'm innocent.'

Bugs Moran to Judge John H. Lyle

If Al Capone is known as the instigator of the St Valentine's Day Massacre, then George 'Bugs' Moran is best remembered as one of massacre's victims. Born to Julius and Diana Moran on August 21, 1893 in St Paul, near Minneapolis in Minnesota, George Clarence Moran was not a Chicagoan by birth, but was resident there throughout the city's most tempestuous years when bootlegging ran rife and gang warfare tore the underworld apart. During the Roaring Twenties, Moran's name appeared almost weekly in newspaper columns outlining his various misdeeds and alcohol-related crimes. Yet for all his notoriety, and for all the money he made during Prohibition, Moran was to die an ignominious death; his body disposed of in a pauper's grave.

George Bugs Moran enjoyed a relatively normal first few years in St Paul although, as some authors have pointed out, the town was not the most wholesome place to bring up a young family. In his autobiography, *Public Enemy Number One*, the bank robber, Alvin Karpis, gives a fairly unflattering description of the town – albeit a few years after Moran grew up there:

It was a crook's haven. Every criminal of any importance in the 1930s made his home in St Paul. If you were looking for a guy you hadn't seen in a few months, you usually thought of two places; prison or St Paul.[1]

Nevertheless, Moran's parents (his father was of Irish stock, and his mother hailed from Poland) were hard-working, honest people who only wanted the best for their children. With this in mind they decided to move from the Minneapolis area to Chicago around 1899, when little George was six years old. According to those who were acquainted with the family, the young boy resembled his mother closely, inheriting her large, studious brown eyes.

Newly arrived from out of town, the Morans chose to live north of the Chicago River, in the Irish enclave of Kilgubbin. When it was first established in the middle of the nineteenth century, Kilgubbin was a fairly respectable suburb of the city, but over the years it had fallen into decline and, when the Morans moved there was little more than a thieves' den which was aptly nicknamed either 'Hell's Kitchen' or 'Little Hell.' Billiard halls jostled for space between saloons, brothels and street markets and as the author Rose Keefe comments, 'For every family scrambling to remain decent, there were dozens of thieves, prostitutes, and tramps. Regular moral precepts and common decency went by the wayside.'[2]

Unsurprisingly, all of this had an effect on the young Bugs Moran and soon he was spending time on the streets rather than attending school. From an early age, the youngster also learned an extremely valuable lesson; that for all his hard work, his father rarely earned enough money to put enough food on the table to feed his family. In an attempt to help out his father, Bugs began earning nickels and dimes by stealing dray horses and holding them to ransom until their owners paid up. It was a risky enterprise, but one that earned him a reputation for being a young Jesse James and helped him gain entry into some of Kilgubbin's toughest street gangs. There was very little that these youths wouldn't do; they ran protection rackets, pick-pocketed, broke into houses and shops, tried their hand at safe-cracking and some even had shootouts with the police. The most feared (or revered) street thug of all was a cock-sure youth by the name of Charles Dean O'Banion, a highly regarded member of the Reiser Gang. Moran joined forces with O'Banion and by 1917, when he was little more than twenty-four years of age, Bugs had notched up a crime sheet which included a prison term in 1910 for robbery, a second prison term in 1913 for robbery and larceny and a third case in 1917 for forfeiting bonds, although this indictment was subsequently dropped. Of course, Bugs Moran was not the only teenager to fall under Dean O'Banion's spell; others who joined the Reiser Gang included Hymie Weiss and Vincent 'The Schemer' Drucci. It was Bugs Moran, however, who was caught during a warehouse robbery in 1912. He was sent to Joliet State Prison in south Chicago to serve a two year sentence.

No prison is a palace, but Joliet was exceptionally low-grade. The living conditions were filthy, the work tedious and the guards vicious. Moran kept his head down, served his time and when he was released went straight back to the gang, who received him with open arms. O'Banion in particular was impressed with Moran for not having 'grassed' the rest of them and when, shortly afterwards, he and Hymie Weiss set up their own band of thugs called the North Siders, Moran joined their ranks.

The North Siders weren't interested in small-time operations. O'Banion and Weiss wanted to make good money and concentrated their efforts on stealing top-quality goods such as women's furs, on which they could make substantial profits. There was another money-making venture with which they were also involved, working as enforcers for the newspaper business. At that time in Chicago there were two main dailies, William Randolph Hearst's *American* and Medill McCormick's *Chicago Tribune*. In order to increase their circulations, each paper employed men to intimidate the opposing side's news dealers – the newspaper vendors and paperboys. O'Banion and his gang sided with Hearst and roamed the streets armed to the hilt in search of targets to beat up. Sometimes they would burn down the vendor's stall, other times it would simply be a matter of suggestion before the vendor crumbled. Through all of this, Moran was right by O'Banion's side. Never someone who could hide his temper, Bugs exploded like a volcano when he was angry – hence his nickname 'Bugs', which in street slang means 'crazy.' At first, Moran hated the soubriquet and threatened anyone who dared call him by it, but later he was said to have enjoyed the reputation that came with the label.

Bugs and O'Banion, along with Weiss and Drucci, used to hang around McGovern's Saloon and Cabaret on North Clark Street. O'Banion even did a stint there as a bartender. But McGovern's, as well as being a good place to meet and relax with friends, also numbered among its customers politicians, civil servants, industry captains, judges, businessmen and union bosses, whose friendships were to become very important to the North Siders. When elections were held, O'Banion and cronies like Bugs Moran were paid to disrupt voting in every way possible. In his book *Bloodletters and Badmen* Jay Robert Nash writes that: 'Deanie's boys swarmed through polling places, stuffing ballot boxes, herding floaters and repeaters through the lines, and bribing officials to dump votes for the opposition.'[3] In return, the politicos saw to it that the North Siders rarely if ever went to jail. It was a match made in heaven

Bugs Moran was thirty-four years old by the time he met and married a showgirl of Sioux Indian blood called Alice Roberts, but domestic bliss did little to calm his appetite for violence as he had just taken over the North Siders gang and was waging war with Al Capone.

and one that Bugs Moran was to enjoy for many years to come.

By 1923, Bugs was Dean O'Banion's right-hand man and was feared by almost everyone who came into contact with him. He was also a relatively wealthy individual, thanks in the main to Prohibition, which had become law early in 1920 (see chapter on Al Capone). Despite such associations as the 'Anti-Saloon League' backing the new belief that society would be better off sober, the majority of Americans didn't agree with Prohibition and flouted the law whenever they had the chance. Nor was the average American too picky about the quality of alcohol they drank, or from where it originated. This meant that Dean O'Banion and the other bootleggers grew rich in a very short period of time. Prohibition was the making of hundreds, if not thousands, of gangsters. Thieves, murderers, smugglers and hijackers – everyone made a killing including Dean O'Banion and Bugs Moran, who not only imported whisky and beer from Canada, but also started brewing it on their home territory. During Prohibition, bootleggers were seen more as local heroes than dastardly villains. They were providing the average man and woman with a commodity they craved and they were doing everyone a favor. So what if every now and again a fight erupted or someone was shot? Across America, hoodlums like Lucky Luciano, Jack 'Legs' Diamond, Arnold Rothstein and Dutch Schultz stepped up to the mark and made themselves and their companions rich, thanks to Prohibition. Naturally, the government attempted to fight back. The production, sale and consumption of liquor was illegal, after all, but although the Treasury Department had several units of federal agents, they were either outnumbered by the mob, or were on the mob's payroll.

Moran, O'Banion and company were now in total command of Kilgubbin – politicians and policemen were in their pockets, their territory was ever increasing and their influence likewise. If you were on the North Siders' territory then the speakeasies you attended and the whisky or beer that you drank were all owned or supplied by Moran, O'Banion, Weiss, Drucci and company. But no one owned the whole of Chicago and there were other areas ruled over by other gangs. In Chicago's south side Johnny Torrio and his new sidekick, Al Capone, were in charge.

Torrio was an astute businessman who had already put his own uncle in an early grave because the latter didn't see fit to go into the bootlegging business. Never one to drag his feet himself, Torrio had sewn up the south side of Chicago and he was, as John Kobler describes in his book on Al Capone, 'in his heyday . . . the nearest equivalent to a true mastermind criminal outside the pages of detective fiction.'[4]

In 1921, realizing that the best way for everyone in the bootlegging industry to make money was to settle their differences, Torrio called a conference at which boundary lines were drawn up and partnerships agreed upon. Bugs Moran, together with Dean O'Banion and his pals, was in charge of the North Side; Torrio and Al Capone took a large part of the South Side; Frankie McErlane and Joe Saltis were handed the Stockyards area; Klondike O'Donnell was in charge of the West Side, and Spike O'Donnell was given the Auburn Highlands area. But, as with most attempts to share, the peace did not last long. Encroachments were made by certain parties into their neighbors' territories. Moran, more perhaps even than O'Banion, was certain that when the North Siders' goods were looted, the culprit was almost certainly Johnny Torrio. Moran and O'Banion also nursed a particular hatred for Al Capone. Referring to him variously as 'the Behemoth' or 'Scarface,' Moran blamed him for nearly everything that went wrong on the North Side. In retaliation, O'Banion set Capone's boss up for a big fall. In May 1924 he informed Torrio that he was going to retire from the brewery business, and would Torrio like to buy out his share of the Sieben Brewery for $500,000? Torrio agreed, at which point O'Banion told him to come to Siebens on May 19 to conclude the deal. However, unknown to Torrio, Dean O'Banion had had word that the brewery was to be raided by police on that date. When Torrio showed up, he was duly arrested and because it was his second liquor-related offence, he was given a nine-month jail term. O'Banion, on the other hand was let off with paying a paltry fine. This and other apparent betrayals and slights, set the scene for a massive show down.

On November 10, 1924, Dean O'Banion was executed by three unidentified gunmen who burst in on him while he was at work in his beloved florist shop (see Dean O'Banion chapter). His funeral was one of the largest that gangland had ever seen. Thousands upon thousands of people lined the streets to watch the funeral cortége as it passed by and onlookers reported that O'Banion's wife appeared inconsolable. Also devastated were Dean's closest friends, Hymie Weiss, Schemer Drucci and, last but not least, Bugs Moran. Once O'Banion had been laid to rest, the trio took out an advertisement in Chicago's major newspapers saying that, as a group, they would be taking over O'Banion's business enterprises. They signed the article from the 'Board of Governors.' Another close friend, Louis Alterie, also made a public announcement, though his was far less measured. He said he wanted to fight it out with whomever had killed O'Banion:

'If I go, I'll go with a smile because I know that two or three of them will go with me. If I knew who killed Dean, I would shoot it out with the gang of killers before the sun rose in the morning, and some of us, maybe all of us, would be lying on slabs in the undertaker's place.'[5]

Perhaps ruffled by this announcement, or simply because he wanted to get out of town, Johnny Torrio left Chicago with his wife, Ann. Capone, on the other hand, stayed put – a move he would come to regret.

On the evening of January 12, 1925, with Chicago under several inches of snow, a black sedan slowed down outside a restaurant on State and Fifty-Fifth Streets, and from which stepped Al Capone. Capone walked up to the restaurant's door, but just as he was about to enter, three men, Bugs Moran, Hymie Weiss and Schemer Drucci, cruised past in a car of their own. Each man was carrying an automatic and without further ado let rip at Capone's car, wounding his chauffeur, Sylvester Barton. Having left the car, Capone was unhurt, but the close call must have shaken him considerably.

Johnny Torrio returned to Chicago in mid-January. On January 24, he and his wife returned to their home from a shopping trip when Torrio was set upon by two gunmen – Bugs Moran and Hymie Weiss. Weiss fired first, wounding Torrio in the chest and jawbone, after which Moran moved in for the kill. Holding his automatic to his victim's temple he is supposed to have muttered the words 'Coup de grace,

Photographed as he left court having been acquitted of vagrancy charges in 1930, Bugs Moran may look as though he hasn't a care in the world but his business enterprises were still struggling to recover from the deaths of six of his most trusted men in the St Valentine's Day Massacre the previous year.

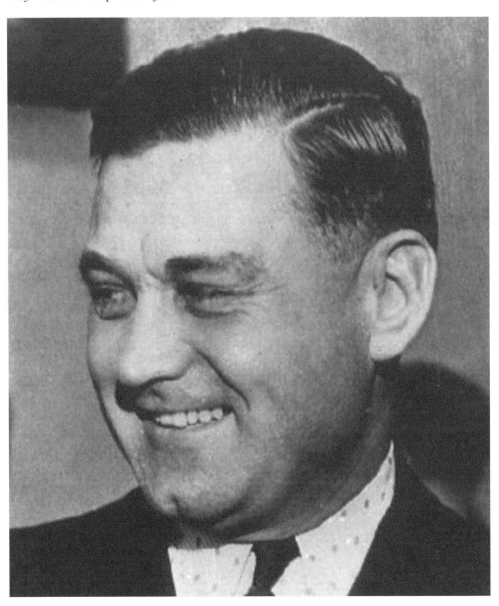

compliments of Deanie,' although this is probably apocryphal. What happened next, however, is undisputed. Moran pulled the trigger only to realize that the chambers of his weapon were empty. Hollow click followed hollow click until finally, with time running out, the two gunmen had to flee the scene without seeing their main target dead. Afterwards, Torrio was rushed to hospital where police grilled him about the identity of his two assailants. True to gangster form, Torrio wouldn't talk. Instead, it took a bystander at the scene to identify his assailants.

Shown a photograph of O'Banion's pallbearers, he [Peter Veesaert] pointed to Bugs Moran as the first man who shot Torrio. He persisted in his identification when the police brought him face to face with Moran, saying: 'You're the man.'[6]

Moran was later released on bail but, despite Veesaert's identification, he was never indicted. Johnny Torrio recovered in hospital, after which he was sent to Lake County Jail to serve out his nine-month sentence for the Sieben Brewery affair. On his release, he took himself off on a European holiday, leaving Capone in charge of the kingdom. All-out war was about to erupt.

The first hit went to Al Capone. On June 13, 1925, on the corner of Sangamon and Congress Streets, Moran and Drucci were sitting in their car when they were fired upon by men driving past in a black limousine. Badly wounded, they abandoned their vehicle and managed to escape to a nearby hospital where they were laid up for several weeks.

Next on the hit list were Weiss and Drucci, who were shot at twice during 1926, though once again both men survived the attacks. But the gunfight to end all gunfights took place in the Torrio/Capone-run suburb of Cicero on September 20, 1926.

Al Capone was dining at Anton's Hotel early in the afternoon of that day when, according to eye witnesses, a cavalcade of six cars drove down Twenty-Second Street with machine gun barrels poking out of the curtained windows:

The streets were crowded when the shooting started outside of Anton's Hotel. Machine-gun fire raked the windows of Angelo Gurdi's barbershop, where Capone received his daily shave; a delicatessen; a laundry; and the Hawthorne Restaurant. In a final, murderous volley, a man dressed in khaki overalls stepped from the running board of one of the cars and approached the main entrance of the Hawthorne Hotel. With the machine gun resting on his knee, he sprayed the interior lobby the way a gardener might aim the nozzle of a hose at a dry lawn. Then the attack cars sped off, crossing the city limits back into Chicago.[7]

Despite the amount of bullets fired, Capone was unharmed. Naturally, he was enraged at what he saw as a personal assault on his leadership and remained convinced that Moran and Weiss were behind it. Capone was not alone in his assumption, for several historians have since speculated that the two North Siders were almost certainly responsible for plotting the event. Capone, however, tiring of the violence and tit-for-tat shoot-outs, decided a truce should be called. On October 4 in downtown Chicago he sent a representative, Tony Lombardo, to talk to Hymie

Weiss and work out a deal. Weiss, still fuming over O'Banion's murder, demanded that Capone hand over two of the men that Weiss and Moran believed to be responsible for the hit – John Scalise and Albert Anselmi – but when Lombardo relayed this message to Capone, word came back to the effect that he would never betray his men in that manner. Relations between the North Siders and the South Siders were therefore back to square one. War was once again declared and a week to the day after Capone turned down Weiss's offer, Weiss was murdered.

On October 11, 1926, having returned from the law courts where he had been observing the trial of Joe Saltis – a South-Sider whom Weiss had been hoping to persuade to switch allegiances – he entered the North Siders' offices located above Dean O'Banion's old flower shop on State Street. Weiss was unaware that he was being watched from across the road, where two gunmen were waiting to take a shot at their target. Suddenly, the windows of Hymie Weiss's premises were shattered, with glass and bullets flying everywhere, and within moments Weiss was lying on the floor in a pool of his own blood.

With the death of another close friend and business partner, things were not looking good for Moran and the North Siders. It would have been very easy to strike back and continue the feud with Capone, but it was at this point that sense prevailed. Wise counsel came in the shape of another of Moran's friends, Maxie Eisen, who advised him to make peace with Big Al. No sooner was this idea proposed than a meeting was convened at the Hotel Sherman. Every gangland boss in Chicago attended and, again, a settlement was hammered out to everyone's benefit. Yet, just like the peace treaty that had been brokered by Johnny Torrio, this latest settlement was not to last long. On April 4, 1927, Vinnie Drucci was killed by a policeman and Bugs Moran was less than impressed.

Drucci had been killed while attempting the old gangland trick of meddling with an election campaign in an effort to get his candidate, 'Big Bill' Thompson, re-elected. Having decided on a plan that involved the kidnapping of Ward Alderman Dorsey R. Crowe, Drucci was infuriated to find Crowe wasn't in his offices to be abducted, so he beat up a secretary instead. This sent a policeman scurrying upstairs to investigate what all the noise was about. Drucci was arrested and shoved into the back of a police car where he began bad-mouthing the arresting officers, one of whom, Dan Healy, drew his firearm. On being shoved by Drucci, the gun went off, hitting him squarly in the chest and killing him outright.

George Moran had now lost all of his old buddies and, though he was in overall control of the North Siders, he must have felt incredibly isolated. Capone was still a massive thorn in Moran's side, forever encroaching on the North Siders' territory. Consequently, Moran formed an alliance with fellow Irishman, Terry Druggan, who was from the South Side but who had fallen out with Capone. He also struck up an association with a rumrunner by the name of Ted Newberry, as well as with gunmen such as Jake Zuta, Billie Skidmore and Barney Bertsche. Having lost two of his best friends in Schofield's Flower Shop, the premises no longer felt safe, and Moran also

When this photograph was taken in 1932, Prohibition was about to be repealed and, although he had diversified into other businesses, the deceptively relaxed-looking Moran would soon be forced to leave Chicago.

moved offices – after all, everyone knew where to locate him, the name of the flower shop having been mentioned in every newspaper not only in Chicago, but nationwide. Moran relocated the majority of his operation to 127 North Dearborn in the heart of the 'Loop' district. He also conducted some of his business from another premises, the old S-M-C Cartage Co garage at 2122 North Clark Street in Kilgubbin.

At the same time, Moran stepped up operations to stymie Al Capone's enterprises.

Under Bugs Moran, the North Siders were adversaries as formidable as ever they had been under O'Banion, Weiss or Drucci. On the Detroit-Chicago highway they hijacked truck after truck of liquor consigned to Capone by the Purple Gang, and from a Canadian ship moored off the lakeshore they once lifted an entire cargo of whisky meant for Capone.'[8]

Around this time, Moran also began smartening up his entire image, often wearing a pinstriped suit and dark brown fedora to work. Not only that, just prior to taking over as the North Siders' leader, he married a showgirl whose stage name was Alice Roberts. Of Sioux-Indian blood, Alice completely bowled Moran over and she moved in with him in a stylish apartment on Belden Avenue. Afterwards, they moved to rooms at the Parkway Hotel, which was only a short walk away from the S-M-C Cartage garage.

But if his private life was going looking rosy, Moran's business life could not have been more bleak. Al Capone was still his number-one enemy and, with few options left open to him if he wanted to survive, Moran decided to befriend the Mafia in order to be rid of his rival once and for all.

Previously, the Unione Siciliane, which was in effect a Mafia-run organization, had been governed by men like Angelo Genna and Salvatore Ammatuna, men who were business associates of Capone's. Capone, however, being of Neapolitan parentage, was never a member of the Unione Siciliane, so when Frankie Yale took over as president of the Chicago branch, Capone suddenly found he could no longer rely on the Union for support. Yale took an active dislike to Capone. Indeed, ever since Johnny Torrio had handed over his kingdom to Big Al, Yale had watched his former friend grow increasingly arrogant. Capone, realizing he no longer had an ally in the Unione Siciliane, was frantically plotting Yale's downfall. On July 1, 1928, this came to head when Yale was shot to death in New York after leaving a restaurant called The Sunrise Café.

It was at this point that a Mafiosi by the name of Joseph Aiello contacted Bugs Moran to discuss knocking out Tony Lombardo, who was a strong ally of Capone and who had recently taken Yale's place in the Unione Siciliane. Moran jumped at the chance and on September 7, 1928, Lombardo was gunned to death while walking through the Loop. As John Kobler describes it:

> Lombardo left the office at about four-thirty with two bodyguards, Joseph Ferraro and Joseph Lolordo . . . They turned into Madison Street, moving with effort through the dense crowd of shoppers and office workers. As they passed a restaurant midway down the block, Lolordo heard a man's voice behind him saying, 'Here he is,' then four shots. Lombardo pitched forward, half his head torn away by dumdum bullets. Ferraro fell beside him, two bullets in his back.[9]

Although he had seen his assailants, Ferraro would not divulge their names to the police, preferring instead to stick to the Mafia's strict code of silence. Most people have since concluded that one of the gunmen had to be Bugs Moran.

With Lombardo dead, the Unione Siciliane now voted for Pasquale Lolordo (another Capone crony) to take over as leader, but Lolordo's tenure was to be as brief as Lombardo's had been. Once again it is believed that Joseph Aiello contacted Bugs Moran and asked him to prepare a hit. On January 8, 1929, two of Moran's men entered Lolordo's home and shot him eleven times.

Six days later was St Valentine's Day. In retrospect, it seems Al Capone had taken all he was going to take from the North Siders' boss, who had not only involved himself in the murder of two Capone allies, but in the interim had also encroached upon Capone's businesses by taking over a new cleaning and dyeing company in direct competition with Big Al. Enough was enough; something had to be done.

On February 14, 1929, with snow falling heavily in the Chicago area, there were several major traffic jams due to the inclement weather. Motorists could hardly see more than a few feet in front of them and pedestrians were finding it difficult to walk on the icy pavements. In short, apart from the date, it was a typical winter's day in Chicago. But the night before, something fairly untypical had occurred. Bugs Moran had been sitting in his offices when a hijacker called to offer him a truckload of whisky just in from Detroit at a knockdown price of $57 per case. This was an offer too good to refuse. Moran told the caller to deliver it to his warehouse at the S-M-C Cartage Co garage where Moran's men could help him unload. And this indeed is where they were waiting on the morning of 14 February; everyone, that is, except Bugs Moran, who was running late for the appointment. Together with a business associate, Ted Newberry, Moran had left the apartment he shared with his wife at the Parkway Hotel and hurried through the snowy streets of Chicago towards the garage. Meanwhile, a Cadillac pulled up outside the S-M-C Cartage building, out of which stepped several men, some of whom were wearing police uniforms. Slowly, the men made their way into Moran's warehouse/garage where six of Moran's most trusted soldiers were waiting – Frank and Pete Gusenberg, James Clark (Moran's brother-in-law), Adam Heyer, Al Weinshank and Reinhardt H. Schwimmer. Also present was Johnny May, a car mechanic whom Moran had hired for $50 a week. May had brought his Alsatian dog, Highball, along with him for the day and had him chained up to the axle of a truck he was fixing.

The gunmen approached the garage slowly. John Scalise and Albert Anselmi were undoubtedly among their number, while other names put forward as being present have included 'Little Louis' Campagna, Claude 'Screwy' Maddox and Fred Burke from Missouri. Recently Tony Accardo and Sam Giancana have also been mentioned as possible suspects.

Al Capone, meanwhile, had taken himself off to Florida on holiday in order to have a watertight alibi for when the police came knocking at his door. He had left all the details of the hit to one of his most trusted lieutenants, Jack McGurn, who had planned the massacre down to the last bullet. But McGurn hadn't foreseen that Moran might show up late and by the time Bugs arrived, McGurn's men had already entered the garage. Moran and Newberry then spotted McGurn's car, which they immediately decided was a police vehicle. They swiftly turned tail and walked back to the Parkway. Moran's men, on the other hand, were not quite as lucky as their boss.

Also believing that the men who had entered the garage were police, they meekly acquiesced to the demand that all of them line up with their arms and legs outspread, facing one of the garage's walls. Seconds later, all seven men's bodies were riddled with bullets. Blood was spattered everywhere.

> The executioners had been systematic, swinging their machine guns back and
> forth three times, first at the level of the victims' heads, then chests, then
> stomachs. Some of the corpses were held together in one piece only by shreds
> of flesh and bone.[10]

Moran knew exactly whom to hold responsible – Al Capone. But what to do about it, how to hit back? Over the years, Moran had lost Dean O'Banion, Hymie Weiss, Schemer Drucci; now seven of his most loyal men had been gunned down. Moran was, in the words of one commentator, a mobster without a mob.

In fact, after the St Valentine's Day Massacre, Bugs Moran never really recovered his composure, nor his credibility as a leader of men. Until Prohibition was repealed in 1933 he attempted to engineer (with a few loyal hangers-on) various attacks against Capone who had, by this point, taken over completely on the North Side, but none of these accomplished much and by the mid 1930s, Moran decided to leave Chicago altogether.

First he traveled to Wisconsin and afterwards to Minnesota. His marriage to Alice had broken down irrevocably and he had very little money to his name. Desperate times, as the saying goes, call for desperate measures and, reduced to near poverty, Moran decided to seek his fortune in Illinois. Along with a couple of local thugs he began robbing banks and petrol stations. In the 1940s, Moran showed up in Ohio where it is said he became a member of the Virgil Summers-Albert Fouts gang, which also robbed banks and shops. Finally, in 1946, Bugs was picked up by the FBI. Sentenced to ten years in Leavenworth Penitentiary for bank robbery, the moment he finished his sentence he was re-arrested for an earlier bank job and convicted to serve a further ten years. It was during this last stint in prison that George 'Bugs' Moran was diagnosed with lung cancer. He died on February 25, 1957. The Catholic prison chaplain recorded the following:

> George Moran died a peaceful death and was strengthened with the full Last
> Rites (Penance-Extreme Unction-Holy Viaticum-Apostolic Blessing) of the
> Catholic Church while he was fully conscious. This happened some days
> before he died and was not a 'last ditch' stand . . . I am sure that God in his
> mercy was very kind to him in judgement.[11]

1 *Public Enemy Number One*, Alvin Karpis, Bill Trent, 1971.

2 *Guns & Roses: The Untold Story of Dean O'Banion*, Rose Keefe, Cumberland House Publishing, Inc., 2003.

3 *Bloodletters and Badmen*: A Narrative Encyclopaedia of American Criminals from the Pilgrims to the Present, Jay Robert Nash, Natl Book Network, 1995.

4 *The Life and World of Al Capone*, John Kobler, First published by Fawcett Publications Inc. New York, 1972.

5 *Guns & Roses: The Untold Story of Dean O'Banion*, Rose Keefe, Cumberland House Publishing, Inc., 2003.

6 *The Life and World of Al Capone*, John Kobler, First published by Fawcett Publications Inc. New York, 1972.

7 *Return to the Scene of the Crime*: A Guide to the Scene of the Crime, Richard Lindberg, Cumberland House, 1999.

8 *The Life and World of Al Capone*, John Kobler, First published by Fawcett Publications Inc. New York, 1972.

9 Ibid.

10 Ibid.

11 Ibid.

DEAN O'BANION
Chicago's Arch Killer

'You must know that there are two ways to carry out a contest;
the one by law, and the other by force. The first is practised by
men and the other by brutes; and as the first is often insufficient,
it becomes necessary to resort to the second.'

The Prince, Machiavelli

As funerals go, the one that was held on November 14, 1924 in Chicago could well have been organized crime's most extravagant. The body, which had lain in state for three days at the Sbarbaro funeral chapel, was eventually laid to rest in a coffin fit for a king. 'At the corner of the casket are solid silver posts,' wrote the Chicago Tribune. 'Silver angels stood at the head and feet with their heads bowed in the light of the ten candles that burned in the solid golden candlesticks they held in their hands . . . And over it all the perfume of flowers.'[1] On the day of the funeral itself, 'Ave Maria' was played by an orchestra and after the service had finished the coffin was carried out of the chapel by pall bearers who included Hymie Weiss, Louis Alterie, Bugs Moran, Schemer Drucci and Frank Gusenberg. The cortège of twenty-six cars, along with vans to carry all the flowers, drove through crowd-lined streets towards Mount Carmel Cemetery where approximately 5,000 people were waiting. Finally, the coffin was laid to rest while Father Patrick Malloy of St Thomas of Canterbury Church stepped forward and recited a litany, a Hail Mary, and the Lord's Prayer, despite Cardinal George Mundelein's refusal to sanction a full requiem mass on the grounds that the deceased was a 'notorious criminal.' The deceased was Dean Charles O'Banion[2], proprietor of a florist's shop on North State Street in Chicago, but much better known to the public as one of America's leading mobsters, a recidivist par excellence, and the boss of the infamous North Siders gang.

Born to Charles and Emma O'Banion on July 8, 1892 in the small town of Maroa, Illinois (about 150 miles from Chicago), Dean O'Banion grew up in the warmth of both a close-knit community and a loving family. He had one brother, Floyd, and one sister, Ruth. This idyll, however, was not to last long for when Dean was nine years old his mother died from tuberculosis. It was a shock to the young boy, only compounded by the fact that his father now decided to move his family to Chicago to be closer to his wife's family who lived in the North Side district of the city. Originally North Side (some people nicknamed the area Little Hell) was an Irish enclave, housing immigrant workers and their families. Just as Al Capone and the Italian/Sicilian mobsters had grown up in the relative poverty of New York, so Dean O'Banion suffered a similar experience in Chicago. Everywhere the young boy looked he would have seen whorehouses, gambling dens, massage parlours and the like.

Nevertheless, it was into this environment that Charles O'Banion brought his children to live and within a few weeks Dean and Ruth enrolled in the local school while Charles and Floyd took jobs in a manufacturing plant.

At precisely what age Dean received the injuries to his foot that crippled him for the rest of his life is unknown. According to his father, they were the result of a streetcar accident, but whatever the truth behind the incident, one leg was left shorter than the other, causing Dean to walk with a permanent limp (an affliction which saw to it that he escaped being drafted during the First World War). The loss of his mother at such an early age along with the abrupt move to Chicago makes it no surprise that the young boy began displaying signs of bitterness and anger. Life had dealt him a bad hand, so why not deal a bad hand back to life, join a street gang, and create havoc? The bunch of criminals O'Banion chose to join (along with boys such as Vinny Drucci and George 'Bugs' Moran) was the Market Street Gang, who took pride in stealing and shoplifting in order to supply local hoods with merchandise to sell on the black market. The gang was also known for its prowess at jack-rolling, which involved luring drunks into dark alleys where they would be robbed of their wallets and watches at knife or gun point.

By age sixteen, O'Banion was also working for Bob McGovern, proprietor of McGovern's Saloon and Cabaret, where his main job was that of a singing waiter. The job brought him into contact with many famous faces, including those of Hot Stove Jimmy Quinn (a politician of dubious character) and Eugene Geary (a gun-

Dean O'Banion and his wife Viola (third and fourth from left) fled from Chicago with an entourage of bodyguards in October 1924 to escape retribution after O'Banion set up Johnny Torrio for a bootlegging conviction. They are pictured here on a ranch in Colorado.

toting killer). According to Rose Keefe in her book on O'Banion, Dean was Geary's favorite singing waiter:

> The two struck up a friendship with a marked teacher-student aspect. Geary taught O'Banion better marksmanship with a pistol, including the art of ambidextrous gunplay. In all likelihood, O'Banion returned the favor by assisting his mentor as a strongarm whenever Geary encountered resistance in his cigar-sales business.[3]

By age seventeen O'Banion's petty crimes had landed him in jail. Caught breaking into a drugstore and stealing a roll of postage stamps, he was sent to the House of Correction for six months. O'Banion was also jailed less than two years later in 1911 on a charge of carrying concealed weapons. These two sojourns behind bars were to be his only experience of prison. Thereafter, O'Banion, though implicated in hundreds of robberies and no doubt guilty of countless murders, never saw the inside of a cell again. Instead, he returned to his old job at McGovern's Saloon and Cabaret. He continued to commit robberies, normally in association with a handful of the saloon's less savory characters, one of whom was Earl J. Wojciechowski, alias Hymie Weiss, who subsequently became a firm friend. Together they formed a loose type of partnership which, like the later pairing of Meyer Lansky and Bugsy Siegel, proved very fruitful.

Having evaded the draft during the First World War owing to his bad leg, O'Banion now entered a different conflict, one which was being fought by two rival newspapers, William Randolph Hearst's *American* and Medill McCormick's *Chicago Tribune*, both of which were located on O'Banion's front doorstep. The circulation wars between these two publications was fierce and involved each side employing gangs of thugs to beat up newsboys and burn down their rivals' newspaper stands. At this point in his life, O'Banion had resigned from his job as a singing waiter and instead threw himself heart and soul into working for the *Tribune* as a 'slugger' (although soon afterwards he switched his allegiance to Hearst's *American*). It was work he enjoyed and work he did particularly well because both papers supplied their 'sluggers' with guns. But O'Banion was never one to remain satisfied for long and soon began hankering after bigger and better things. He wanted to be the boss, not remain a minion all of his life. He wanted people to respect and look up to him, all he needed was a chance, one lucky break, and on January 17, 1920 one was handed to him when the 18th Amendment of The National Prohibition Law brought the Volstead Act[4] into force. Suddenly, like so many other forward-thinking gangsters of this period (Al Capone and Johnny Torrio to name but two), Dean O'Banion was presented with the ideal opportunity to make substantial amounts of money. Better still, it was the US Government that had presented him with this goose that would lay golden eggs. Losing no time, O'Banion set to work.

Initially, it was the distribution of beer that interested him most, although he would later link up with whisky and gin distributors so as to ensure the supply of alcohol always kept up with the demand. He established brewing contacts in Canada from where the beer would be relayed down to Chicago. O'Banion is also thought to have personally performed Chicago's first liquor hijacking when on December 31, 1919, shortly before Prohibition became law, he spotted a truck loaded up with Grommes and Ulrich whisky. Immediately O'Banion leapt up onto the vehicle's running board and pounded the driver unconscious through the open window, leaving him in the street as he drove the hoard away to hide it in the garage of a friend, the Jewish gangster Samuel 'Nails' Morton.

In fact, it was Nails Morton who encouraged O'Banion (together with Hymie Weiss and Vinny Drucci), to set up his bootlegging business in earnest. Once again, Rose Keefe's book *Guns & Roses* provides invaluable information: 'Under the guidance of Nails Morton, he [O'Banion] invested money in North Side breweries and distilleries operating under the guise of producing legal near-beer and industrial alcohol. He came to an agreement with the owners/operators: They would see to the day-to-day operations and keep the product flowing, and he would pay off the police, deal with interlopers and hijackers, and "take the rap" in the event of a liquor raid.'[5] In this way, all of the North Side speakeasies and after hours clubs were kept in alcohol, in addition to which O'Banion employed hundreds of scouts to drum up new business. He was soon one of the richest men in Chicago, as well as one of the most powerful, with police and government officials on his payroll. O'Banion began dressing in bespoke suits, although he never lost the habit of carrying guns on his person and had all his suits fitted with three extra pockets – one just below the left armpit, a second on the outside left of his jacket and a third centre front of his trousers. Nor did O'Banion curb his temper. As hard-hitting Judge John H. Lyle recalled in his memoirs, *The Dry and Lawless Years*, when a bootlegger by the name of Big Steve Wisniewski hijacked one of his truckloads of whisky, O'Banion had a gang of thugs led by Hymie Weiss track down Big Steve and shoot him in the head.

It has been speculated that by 1922 O'Banion's empire was worth in the region of two million dollars per annum. Everything he touched seemed to turn to gold, yet although he had suffered little or no interference from rival gangs, it wasn't too long before O'Banion heard about two gangsters who were making quite a name for themselves on Chicago's South Side – Johnny Torrio and Al Capone. Keeping a close eye on these two became a full-time job. At the same time, the North Siders began to hijack some of Torrio's trucks just to show who was in charge. Naturally, in retaliation, Torrio started doing the same to O'Banion's vehicles until it became obvious that unless a compromise was reached, all-out war would be the only consequence. In an attempt to avoid this, Torrio met up with all the leading gang bosses in Chicago, including the Genna brothers in Little Italy, the Valley Gang, the Saltis-McErlane gang, the Ragen's Colts, the O'Donnell brothers and Dean O'Banion, to try to thrash out a deal.

'We can't kill each other,' Torrio is said to have told O'Banion, 'there's too much for us both to lose.' In response, O'Banion is supposed to have agreed. Torrio promised that no rival gang would encroach on the North Sider's territory or sell alcohol to any North Side watering hole, but in return O'Banion had to keep to his turf and not hijack any one else's trucks. Indeed, this was the blueprint for all Torrio's negotiations; i.e. that each gang should keep to its own ground and, although there could be a certain amount of trade between rival operations, in general everyone should stick to their own suppliers. For a certain period of time this did seem to work. Everyone stuck to their own territory and relative peace reigned over the city. Around this time O'Banion met and fell in love with a young woman called Helen Viola Kaniff. Less than two months later the two were married at Our Lady of Sorrows Basilica on Jackson Boulevard. It was a perfect match and over the years proved to be one of the most stable of any underworld unions. Viola (as she was always referred to by her husband) was as devoted to Dean as he was to her. Nevertheless, O'Banion's nuptials did not stop his involvement in illegal activities. Only a few months after his wedding he was caught, along with Hymie Weiss, Bugs Moran and Charles Reiser, standing next to an open safe in the offices of the Postal Telegraph

Building on South LaSalle Street. O'Banion and company were arrested and subsequently taken down to the local police station where they were all charged with burglary and with possession of explosives. Bail was set at the nominal amount of $2,000 apiece, but after an outcry by several citizens' groups was later raised, in O'Banion's case, to $60,000. O'Banion swiftly employed a good lawyer who immediately saw to it that the bail was reduced, leaving O'Banion with only one other problem – how to

Dean and Viola O'Banion were married on February 5, 1921. They were to enjoy less than four years together before O'Banion's violent past and scheming ways caught up with him and he was murdered while working in his flower shop.

escape conviction when the case came to court. The solution was to buy off the jury and a 'not guilty' verdict was duly returned not just on himself, but also on his three accomplices, after which everyone retired for a sumptuous meal at the Bella Napoli Café, owned by Diamond Joe Esposito.

Having escaped one rap, O'Banion now successfully evaded several others. He hijacked a truck that was laden with liquor and being driven by Joseph Goodman, who later picked out O'Banion's photograph from a book of mugshots down at the police station. Although he was charged, O'Banion wasn't convicted as Goodman later retracted his statement. This, together with several other narrow escapes from the law, shot O'Banion to fame. Long before Al Capone became a celebrity, Dean O'Banion was the name on everyone's lips.

In 1922, having married Viola, O'Banion decided he needed to demonstrate at least a little bit of respectability and to this end he and Nails Morton bought a controlling interest in William F. Schofield's flower shop, which was located at 738 North State Street, directly across the road from Holy Name Cathedral. O'Banion, in contrast to his gangster credentials, adored flowers and took a hands-on approach to the business, working in the shop every day, arranging bouquets, wreaths and floral tributes. Customers were always treated with the greatest care and kindness and O'Banion's shop employees stated that he was extremely pleasant to work with. Soon, the flower shop was supplying all of the underworld's weddings, funerals and, no doubt, Viola benefited from her husband's passion for all things floral, too.

> On most days, between 9 a.m. and 6 p.m., he could be found in the shop, a sprig of lily of the valley or a white carnation in his buttonhole, happily breathing in the perfumed air as he bustled about, potting a plant here, nipping an excess bud there, arranging a wedding bouquet or a funeral wreath. He became gangdom's favourite florist, a lucrative situation, because underworld etiquette required the foes, as well as the friends, of a fallen gangster – including those who felled him – to honour him with an elaborate floral creation.[6]

But O'Banion's love of flowers did not detract in the least from the more menacing side of his character. He continued to exact revenge on anyone he thought might have crossed him. Into this group fell two brothers, Maxie and Davy Miller. Believing the brothers had snubbed him and made disparaging comments about him, on January 20, 1924 O'Banion decided to act and tracked Davy and Maxie down to the La Salle Theatre where they had been watching a show. In full view of a crowd of spectators O'Banion shot Davy Miller in the stomach and tried to do the same to Maxie, but the bullet ricocheted off his belt buckle. Davy was rushed to hospital where, miraculously, he survived. Davy's recovery was no less miraculous than O'Banion's later escape from justice when, in front of a packed courtroom, he shrugged the whole affair off saying it was simply an act of 'hot-headed foolishness.'[7] O'Banion was found 'not guilty.'

Having escaped yet another rap, O'Banion now set his sights on hijacking a huge consignment (worth in the region of one million dollars) of pre-war bonded whisky.

To pull off the heist he paid several policeman to provide protection while the liquor was being transported from warehouse to warehouse, and the operation ran extremely smoothly. Nevertheless, once the theft was discovered, twenty-six people were indicted, including O'Banion and several high-ranking police and government officials. The case, however, came to nothing and O'Banion once again slipped through the law's net. Only a few weeks later, O'Banion was arrested by police along with Hymie Weiss and a man called Dan McCarthy during yet another heist, and all three were indicted on charges of 'conspiracy to possess, transport and sell intoxicating liquors'. A trial date was set for July 7, 1924 but even before this got underway O'Banion was involved in yet another crime.

On February 21, the body of John Duffy was discovered lying a little way off Nottingham Road. Duffy had been shot three times in the head with a .38-caliber revolver. In fact, Duffy, who originally hailed from Philadelphia, was one of O'Banion's hired guns, having helped him pull off several stunts. Early in February, while heavily intoxicated, he had been involved in a huge fight with his wife, Maybelle Exley. After she had gone to bed, Duffy tried to asphyxiate her by putting a pillow over her face, but then shot her twice in the head. Later – the drink beginning to wear off – he panicked and went in search of a man called Julian 'Potatoes' Kaufman. It was a big mistake, for Kaufman subsequently contacted O'Banion who showed up and assured Duffy he would help him get out of town. The last time Duffy was seen alive was by a witness who saw him climbing into a Studebaker and driving away in the company of his old boss.

With the police eager to question O'Banion in relation to Duffy's murder, the Irishman suddenly disappeared only to turn up four days later after he had consulted with his friend, John Sbarbaro, who was an Assistant State's Attorney. Naturally, O'Banion denied any knowledge of the murder, even going as far as to say that Duffy was completely unknown to him. Infuriatingly for the police, their star witness subsequently developed selective amnesia and when asked to identify O'Banion was unable to do so. Dean O'Banion was once again a free man.

In spring 1924 the small suburb of Cicero on Chicago's south western outskirts was preparing for the upcoming local elections and Al Capone had a vested interest in who would become Town President. Capone wanted Joseph Z. Klenha to be re-elected as he had struck a deal with Capone and Torrio regarding the running of their bootlegging and gambling businesses in Cicero. Bearing this in mind, Capone visited Dean O'Banion with a proposition; if O'Banion could supply Capone and Torrio with a couple of hundred 'heavies' to swing the election their way, he could expand his North Side operations to include Cicero and reap rich dividends. O'Banion jumped at the chance and on the day of the election hundreds of anti-Klenha voters were dragged out of the polling queues and beaten up in front of horrified onlookers. One election official, Michael Gavin, was shot in both legs, an election clerk was effectively kidnapped until after the polls had closed. Four people were killed in clashes with the rival candidate's men. Unsurprisingly, given all of the above, the result went Klenha's way which pleased O'Banion no end. As a bonus, Al Capone's brother, Frank, was killed during the clashes meaning extra revenue for O'Banion as everyone ordered funeral flowers from his shop. Nor was this the end of O'Banion's reward, for part of the deal he had struck with Capone and Torrio had been that, when a Klenha victory was secured, he could run a beer concession in Cicero and take up a quarter per cent share in a popular gambling hall called The Ship. O'Banion swiftly set up the beer concession, but by supplying superior quality beverages to his customers he soon established a much higher revenue than Torrio had ever thought possible, putting a lot of rival suppliers' noses out of joint in the process. Torrio tried to persuade O'Banion to split his profits with those whose businesses he'd affected, but O'Banion laughed this suggestion off, saying he didn't owe anything to anyone. This was perhaps the first nail in O'Banion's coffin. But if O'Banion was encroaching on other gangs' territory, the other gangs now began making incursions into his. The Genna brothers, based in Little Italy, now began sending their men into the North Side.

The Gennas, six swarthy Sicilians who were also known as the 'Terrible Gennas' brewed whisky in basement distilleries which operated out of peoples' homes. It was low-grade alcohol of inferior quality that sold cheaply but quickly. While O'Banion was busy throwing his weight around Cicero, the Gennas began marketing their wares on the North Side. On discovering this, O'Banion was furious and went directly to Johnny Torrio to complain that their former treaty had been broken. Torrio's reaction was nothing if not unhelpful. Having been snubbed by O'Banion when he asked the Irishman to split his beer profits in Cicero, he was in no mood to do him a favor now. O'Banion then took matters into his own hands and hijacked a truckload of the Genna brothers' whisky, worth in the region of $30,000. Now it was the Gennas' turn to be furious. They went to the Unione Siciliane (an organization primarily founded to help Italian immigrants to find housing and jobs in their newly adopted country – but also linked to the mob and believed to be Mafia-owned) to gain permission to kill O'Banion. But the head of this organization, Mike Merlo, preferred (much to the Gennas' disgust) to seek a peaceful compromise. Once again it seemed as though O'Banion had pulled off a narrow escape, but the odds were beginning to stack up against the Irishman, especially as now both the police and gangland had been cheated.

Dean O'Banion's next move was probably the most ill-advised of his life. Still angry at Johnny Torrio's refusal to help him over the Gennas, O'Banion decided to teach Torrio a lesson he'd never forget.

In May 1924 Torrio was visited by O'Banion who imparted some surprising news to his rival – namely that he wanted out of bootlegging – that he'd had enough warring with the Gennas and simply wanted to retire. Would Torrio be interested in buying out his share of a business they both owned, namely The Sieben Brewery, for $500,000? Torrio could hardly believe what he was hearing. After all, with O'Banion out of the picture Chicago would be a more peaceful place, not to mention the business opportunities that might come his way once O'Banion had gone. A deal was struck and Torrio agreed to meet O'Banion at the brewery the next morning to inspect a shipment of beer and pay over the money. On May 19, 1924 Johnny Torrio arrived at Sieben's eager to take ownership, but a surprise awaited him. Not long after he arrived, the police, led by Morgan Collins, raided the premises. Both Torrio and O'Banion were arrested, but O'Banion knew only too well that this would be Torrio's second bootlegging offence. If convicted it would almost certainly mean jail for the Italian. On the other hand, this was O'Banion's first bootlegging offence and, as such, he'd escape prison, if not the whole rap. To add insult to injury, Torrio then learned from one of his insiders that O'Banion had known of the raid in advance – he had set Torrio up right from the start.

Out on bail, O'Banion bolted, along with his wife and a coterie of bodyguards to Colorado, fearful that Torrio, who had also been released on bail, would seek revenge. O'Banion stayed away from Chicago from July through to October, returning on the eve of further local elections. This time O'Banion, despite being courted by the Democrats, decided to back the Republican candidate, once again intimidating voters to achieve the desired result. Meanwhile, the animosity between O'Banion and the Gennas hadn't improved and with the death of Mike Merlo, who had been suffering from cancer, and the subsequent election of Angelo Genna as President of the Unione Siciliane, things began to look increasingly bleak for the Irishman. Never one to look a gift horse in the mouth, however, O'Banion busied himself making up funeral wreaths for the dead man. He and his business partner, William Schofield, spent much of November 9 in this manner, creating all kinds of floral tributes. Johnny Torrio had ordered $10,000 worth of flowers and Al Capone had ordered $8,000 worth of roses. On the evening of 9 November, Jim Genna visited the shop to pay for a $750 arrangement, although in retrospect it is easy to see he was simply casing the place, and memorizing its layout. Later that same evening Frankie Yale (the Unione's national director) also visited the premises, placing an order for $2,000 worth of flowers which he informed the proprietors would be picked up the next day by some friends. O'Banion spent that night out on the town, enjoying the local cabarets with his friend Louis Alterie, but the following day he was back at work, busy once again arranging last-minute orders for the big funeral. Schofield called in to say he wouldn't be in until midday. O'Banion worked on, only to be disturbed yet again by three men, Frankie Yale, Albert Anselmi and John Scalise whom he assumed had come to pick up the $2,000 order Yale had placed the previous day. O'Banion approached the men with a smile and held out his hand – this much was witnessed by one of O'Banion's members of staff, William Crutchfield. Crutchfield then left his boss in the shop while he retired to a backroom. Fifteen minutes later, gunfire started, but by the time Crutchfield reached O'Banion, the Irishman was lying on the floor with a gunshot wound to the back of his head and further bullet holes in his neck and chest. The three assassins had made their escape by way of the front door and disappeared as if into thin air.

Priests from Holy Name Parochial School ran swiftly to the premises, arriving on site even before the police. By this time, a large crowd had also gathered outside the shop so that when William Schofield returned to the premises he could hardly gain entry. Pushing his way through, he demanded to know who could have done such a terrible thing. Nor was he the only one asking for the culprits. The police soon rounded up Johnny Torrio, Al Capone, the Genna brothers, Frankie Yale, the Miller brothers – indeed, anyone who had ever harbored a grudge against O'Banion. Cheekily, Torrio and Capone stated they were good friends of the deceased, pointing to the large amounts of money they had just spent at his shop on floral tributes. In fact, apart from Davy Miller, who stated that he was glad O'Banion had died, everyone swore they'd had nothing to do with the hit. Apart from Frankie Yale, who was charged with carrying a concealed weapon but later released, the police had no evidence on which to hold anyone. Even when they later picked Yale up again, this time at the train station where he had bought a ticket back to New York, there was little or no evidence that could tie him either to O'Banion's murder or an earlier hit in which police believed he had been involved, that of Johnny Torrio's uncle, Big Jim Colosimo. Yale insisted that he had not arrived in Chicago until the day after O'Banion was murdered. Even when William Crutchfield was asked to identify Yale in a police line-up, the result was negative and with no evidence to go on, Yale was once again released.

Controversial in life, O'Banion now became controversial in death. Speculation grew as to whether he had known his assassins. Police Captain William Schoemaker stated that, 'O'Banion, of all things, knew he was marked for death. He knew it might come at any moment. A handshaker, yes, but not with strangers, when any stranger might mean death. He knew them, at least by sight, and he did not suspect them.' Others disagreed and said O'Banion would shake anyone's hand and that the assassins could have been completely unknown to O'Banion.

The feud between the North Siders and the Torrio/Capone camp, as well as the Genna brothers, raged on after O'Banion's demise. Hymie Weiss took over the leadership of the North Siders, swearing revenge for the O'Banion slaying. He was as good as his word.

On 12 January 1925, Al Capone's car was pursued by Weiss's men who proceeded to shoot the driver, Sylvester Barton, dead, and wound the passenger, Charlie Fichetti. Luckily for Capone, he wasn't in the car when the incident took place. Meanwhile, it seemed as if O'Banion would reap his revenge on Johnny Torrio from beyond the grave when, on January 17, 1925 (having enjoyed a brief holiday abroad) Torrio went on trial for the Sieben Brewery case. Withdrawing his not guilty plea, it was only a matter of time before Torrio was sent to jail. In the event, he was given nine months and a $5,000 fine plus court costs. The judge also gave Torrio a few days license before he was sent down, in order to sort out his affairs. It was now that Weiss, Bugs Moran and Schemer Drucci moved in for the kill. Cornering their man as he was about to enter his house with his wife after a shopping trip, they riddled Torrio's body with bullets. Miraculously, he escaped death. In August 1926, Capone hit back

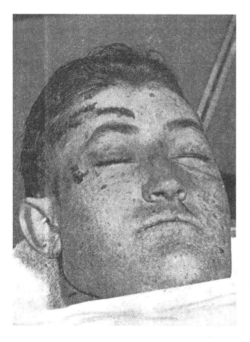

O'Banion lies dead in the morgue. He was shot in the neck and chest as well as receiving one bullet to the back of the head in a brutally efficient execution. No one was ever prosecuted for his murder.

at Hymie Weiss, but missed his target both times. In this way the tit-for-tat continued for months until on 11 October, Hymie Weiss was finally gunned down by 'assailants unknown' while he was in his office located in rooms above O'Banion's flower shop on State Street. No one was convicted for this killing, but most people believe Al Capone was behind the hit. Meanwhile, Police Chief Morgan Collins stated that: 'It isn't over. I fully expect that there will be a reprisal, then a counterreprisal [sic], and so on. These beer feuds go on in an eternal vicious cycle. I don't want to encourage the business, but if someone has to be killed, it's a good thing that the gangsters are murdering themselves off. It saves trouble for the police.'[8]

Perhaps this was Dean O'Banion's greatest legacy. After all, he reveled in bloodshed while he was alive, so it seems only fitting that blood continued to be shed in his name long after his death.

[1] *The Life and World of Al Capone*, John Kobler, First published by Fawcett Publications Inc., New York, 1972.

[2] Newspapers regularly spelt Dean's name 'Dion'.

[3] *Guns and Roses: The Untold Story of Dean O'Banion*, Rose Keefe, Cumberland House Publishing, Inc., 2003.

[4] The Volstead Act was named after Republican congressman Andrew Volstead of Minnesota.

[5] *Guns and Roses: The Untold Story of Dean O'Banion*, Rose Keefe, Cumberland House Publishing, Inc., 2003.

[6] *The Life and World of Al Capone*, John Kobler, first published by Fawcett Publications Inc., New York, 1972.

[7] www.crimelibrary.com

[8] *Guns and Roses: The Untold Story of Dean O'Banion*, Rose Keefe, Cumberland House Publishing, Inc., 2003.

DUTCH SCHULTZ
The Flying Dutchman

'I suppose there ain't no wars around, so they have to put
me on the front page.'

Dutch Schultz, July 1935

On May 13, 1929 at the President Hotel in Atlantic City there gathered together a group of men from cities across America including Chicago, New York and Philadelphia. Their brief, over the next three days, was to discuss the laying down of arms, the cessation of inter-gang warfare and the amalgamation of their respective outfits on a nationwide scale. Another item on the agenda was how organized crime would cope with the inevitable repeal of Prohibition. It was a packed meeting, a meeting which one of the delegates summed up as followed: 'I told them there was business enough to make us all rich and it was time to stop all the killings and look on our business as other men look on theirs, as something to work at and forget when we go home at night. It wasn't an easy matter for men who had been fighting for years to agree on a peaceful business program. But we finally decided to forget the past and begin all over again and we drew up a written agreement and each man signed on the dotted line.'[1] The man who had spoken was none other than Al Capone and numbered among the signatories to the agreement were underworld luminaries such as Frank Costello, Lucky Luciano, Max 'Boo Boo' Hoff, Sam Lazar and a man by the name of Arthur Flegenheimer, better known to most as Dutch Schultz.

Arthur Simon Flegenheimer was born on August 6, 1902 to German-Jewish parents Emma and Arthur Flegenheimer in the Bronx, New York. Emma Flegenheimer attempted to bring her young son up in the Jewish faith and was not entirely unsuccessful for, although in later life Arthur dabbled with both Catholicism and Protestantism, he often returned to his Jewish roots when he was in need of reassurance.

Nevertheless, the biggest influence on his young life was the invironment in which he grew up – the Bergen Street section of the Bronx, a hard area and one which was to be the making of the young boy. At an early age, Arthur joined a street gang, as much for the protection it afforded as for the credibility it gave him among his peer group. Aged fourteen, after his father deserted the family home, he quit school to work in a variety of mundane jobs, but sadly none gave him any real satisfaction, let alone the opportunity to better himself. Instead, he began hanging around the notorious Criterion club, a favorite amongst local hoodlums like Marcel Poffo. Poffo was best known as a bank robber, but Flegenheimer was set to work disrupting crap games that wouldn't pay a percentage of the profits to Poffo. From then on, Flegenheimer entered a life of crime receiving, aged seventeen, his first and only prison sentence for taking part in a burglary of an apartment in the Bronx. Sent to prison on Blackwell's Island (known today as Roosevelt Island), the teenager, far from being rehabilitated, mixed with hardened criminals and soon made himself extremely unpopular with the prison guards. As a consequence he was transferred to an even more brutal prison regime at Westhampton Farm. On his release, he returned to the Bronx, twice as violent and antisocial as he had ever been before. It was also around this time that his old Bergen Street gang are thought to have nicknamed him 'Dutch Schultz' – although quite why has never properly been established.

By 1920, with the passing of the Volstead Act and the beginning of Prohibition, Schultz, like nearly all his fellow gangsters, saw an ideal opportunity to make substantial amounts of money in a short space of time. Initially, he went to work for the legendary Arnold 'The Brain' Rothstein, who had also been a fundamental part of the early careers of, among others, Lucky Luciano, Jack 'Legs' Diamond, Meyer Lansky and Waxey Gordon. Prohibition was the making of Schultz not only financially but also as a strong-arm man, a man whose name became synonymous with danger and violence. Early in 1928, Schultz went into business with an old friend from childhood, Joey Noe. The two set up several speakeasies throughout the Bronx and established their own beer-running operation with alcohol bought from Frankie Dunn, who owned a brewery in New Jersey. Soon both Schultz and Noe realized that they could further their takings if they began supplying rival outfits with their beer, an operation they ensured was water-tight by threatening speakeasy proprietors with violence if they didn't purchase their wares. Two of the latter, Irish brothers by the name of Joe and John Rock, soon discovered the consequences of such foolish behavior. One night Joe Rock was kidnapped by men working for Schultz and Noe, after which he was severely beaten and then hung by his thumbs from a meat hook. Legend also has it that a piece of fabric that had been smeared with the discharge from a gonorrhea victim was laid over Rock's eyes, resulting in him later becoming blind. Eventually, however, Joe was released after his family paid out an estimated $35,000 in ransom money.

Events such as this served to create a tough-guy image for Schultz, the image of a man with whom no one should mess. Consequently, he and Noe found it easy to take over the majority of beer franchises within the Bronx. Their empire also began to extend into Washington Heights and Harlem, so Schultz and Noe moved to new offices in Manhattan. They also began employing several more henchmen, including Abe 'Bo' Weinberg, 'Fatty' Walsh and Edward 'Fats' McCarthy. However, by moving the centre of their operation from the Bronx into Manhattan, Schultz and Noe stepped on the toes of rival gang leader, Jack 'Legs' Diamond. On October 15, 1928, in response to the encroachment on his territory, Diamond sent men to ambush Noe as he exited the Chateau Madrid nightclub on West 54th Street. A gunfight ensued with Noe firing off at least as many shots as his assailants, although he was wounded in the chest and spine. One of Diamond's gunman also fared badly. Police later discovered the getaway car abandoned by the side of a road with the body of Louis Weinberg on the back seat. Meanwhile, Joey Noe was rushed to hospital but, despite surviving the journey he lived only for a further three weeks. He died on November 21. 'There is no question that Schultz was crushed,' writes Paul Sann in his biography of Dutch Schultz, *Kill the Dutchman!* 'Noe was the closest intimate of all his days. He might have drawn some inspiration from a hoodlum like Marcel Poffo, but Noe, who always called him Arthur, as when they were kids on the street corner without a care in the world, put him on the golden highway. When Noe was with him, he could give the armed guard the night off, and Noe for that matter, was the only one he ever took along when he went to see his mother.'[2]

The City of New York Police Department issued this notice, which was distributed to other law enforcement agencies and prison authorities, for the arrest of Dutch Schultz for income tax offences in 1934. Under pressure to find cash to fend off the IRS, Schultz shot Julius Modgilewsky.

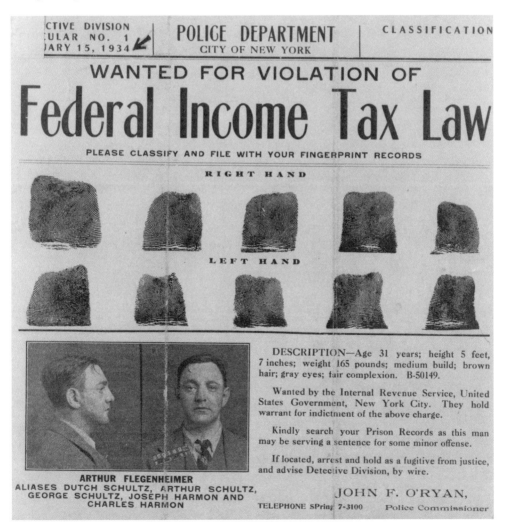

Devastated by Noe's death, Schultz, like the good friend that he was, vowed revenge. Less than three weeks later on Sunday November 4, Arnold 'The Brain' Rothstein, having spent the early part of the evening gambling at Lindy's received a phone call, the nature of which sent him scurrying towards the Park Central Hotel. Later that same evening, Rothstein was discovered slumped outside the employees' entrance with bullet wounds to his stomach. Rothstein died two days later and, although the police were able to question him about his assailants, like the true criminal he was, he refused to give them any information.

Most people believe Rothstein was killed due to gambling debts which he was refusing to pay, but in some quarters it was alleged that Schultz was connected with his death. Rothstein had been a close friend of Legs Diamond, and to Schultz his death would have amounted to the perfect payback. Whatever the case, Rothstein was dead and when, a few years later in 1931, Legs Diamond was also killed, Dutch Schultz certainly shed no tears.

Now alone, Schultz had twice as much work on his hands running the business. He did, however, attend several meetings hosted by Lucky Luciano during which plans were discussed to establish a national organized crime network. Shortly afterwards, the Atlantic City Conference took place. Just when it seemed as if the underworld was beginning to knit itself into one amorphous unit, 'Castellammarese War' broke out between Joe 'The Boss' Masseria and Salvatore Maranzano of the Castellammarese Family. According to John Kobler in his book *The Life and World of Al Capone*, Masseria was hell bent on taking over Maranzano's Family, even arranging the murder of Tom Reina, one of Maranzano's top men. In retaliation, Maranzano killed one of Masseria's closest Family members and had another Family boss, Peter Morello, who was a staunch supporter of Masseria, knocked off. The result was all-out war during which it is estimated that over sixty men lost their lives.

Lucky Luciano was, in the beginning, a Masseria man and honoring his working relationship with Luciano, Dutch Schultz followed suit. Luciano, however, grew tired of Masseria's old-world ways and switched allegiances Maranzano. Luciano, with Maranzano's blessing, set Masseria up and had him gunned down at a Coney Island restaurant (see chapter on Lucky Luciano). Having rid Maranzano of his greatest enemy, one might have thought Luciano's star would be in the ascendant, but legend has it that Maranzano now drew up a list of men he wanted killed in case they challenged his authority. On this list were Frank Costello, Vito Genovese, Lucky Luciano and Dutch Schultz. Suddenly, the tables were turned and Luciano had to act swiftly. On September 10, 1931, Maranzano was gunned down in his office; one of the hit men was allegedly Bo Weinberg, Dutch Schultz's right-hand man.

Another Schultz foot soldier, however, was not displaying quite the same loyalty as Weinberg. Earlier in the year Vincent 'Mad Dog' Coll, who was best known for his prowess with a gun (according to Lucky Luciano, Coll had been hired by Salvatore Maranzano to kill Lucky around 1931), announced he wanted to become Schultz's business partner. Unimpressed with the way Coll was throwing his weight around,

Schultz refused the request after which Coll stormed out and set up a rival gang, taking several of Schultz's men with him. Subsequently, Coll was indicted on charges of carrying a concealed weapon. Bail was posted at $10,000, a sum that Schultz, in an overwhelming act of generosity, put up. Ungrateful to the last, Coll is then said to have skipped bail, failing to show up for his trial and thus forfeiting Schultz's money. Incensed by what he saw as a betrayal of his trust, Schultz responded in the only way he knew how; he had Coll's brother, Peter, murdered. Of course, given that this was gangland, Coll then retaliated, killing several of Schultz's men. But this, sadly, was not where the warfare ended.

Vincent Coll, now in desperate need of funds, kidnapped George Jean 'Big Frenchy' DeMange, a close associate of Owney 'Killer' Madden, the owner of the infamous Cotton Club. Coll demanded a $35,000 ransom, a sum that Madden dutifully paid, but afterwards he began plotting Coll's downfall. The result was one of the most notorious underworld massacres in history. On July 28, 1931, gunfire could be heard on East 107th Street as five men suddenly opened fire on Dutch Schultz's associate, Joey Rao. But instead of hitting their target, the gunmen shot five children, killing a little boy called Michael Vengali and wounding his seven-year-old brother as well as another child who was asleep in a pushchair. Two further children suffered less serious wounds. Five days later, a witness to the crime came forward by the name of George Brecht, who identified Vincent Coll and another man, Frank Giordano, as two of the gunmen. Coll immediately went into hiding, only to be arrested on October 4, 1931 at the Cornish Arms Hotel near Eighth Avenue. When the case finally came to trial in late December, Coll was defended by top-of-the-range lawyer Samuel S. Leibowitz who ripped George Brecht's evidence to pieces. In another blow for the prosecution, by the end of the trial Brecht was found to be suffering from a mental disturbance and was subsequently incarcerated at Bellevue psychiatric unit. Both Coll and Giordano were acquitted and released.

The following year started equally badly for Dutch Schultz, for in the ongoing war between himself and Vincent Coll, four of Schultz's gunmen shot down an innocent victim, Louis Basile, while attempting to kill Coll. The hit took place on Commonwealth Avenue in the Bronx, but Coll only arrived half an hour after the shooting had taken place. Coll's luck was not to last for ever, though, as eight days later, on February 9, 1932, while standing in a telephone booth (allegedly having a conversation with Owney Madden) in a drug store on 23rd Street, Coll was gunned down. He was hit by between twenty to fifty rounds from a sub-machine gun. Afterwards, the gunman left the premises quickly and jumped in to a waiting car driven by Bo Weinberg.

Vincent Coll's funeral was not a large affair, especially when compared to other underworld send-offs, with less than a hundred people in attendance. Coll had left his mark, however, especially on Dutch Schultz, who had lost several of his key men, during the fued. He had also lost numerous consignments of beer to hijackers and a fair proportion of his speakeasies had been raided and ransacked. But perhaps the

This court appearance, one of many, in 1931 was the least of Dutch Schultz's problems that year. Along with Frank Costello, Vito Genovese and Lucky Luciano, Schultz was under sentence of death from Castellammarese Family boss Salvatore Maranzano.

greatest loss Schultz suffered during 1931 was that of his close friend and hired gun, Danny Iamascia.

At the time, Schultz was living in a Fifth Avenue apartment where he was being staked out by two New York detectives, Stephen DeRosa and Julius Salke. On spotting the policemen, Schultz, Iamascia and two others left the apartment to confront their stalkers. DeRosa ordered Schultz and his men to raise their hands but on going for his gun he spooked Iamascia into reaching for his own weapon. DeRosa had no alternative but to fire, wounding Iamascia in the stomach and wrist. Schultz fled the scene with Salke in hot pursuit. Eventually, Salke caught up with his prey and together with DeRosa they rushed Iamascia to hospital. In the car, DeRosa claims that Schultz tried to bribe him and his partner with a $50,000 pay-off plus a house each.

The following day Iamascia died from his wounds while Schultz was charged with assault and carrying a concealed weapon. Unlike Vincent Coll's funeral, Iamascia's was a huge affair with a procession of some 125 cars, 35 of which were used solely to carry floral tributes. Schultz ultimately stood trial for the above offences but, as so many hoodlums had done before him, he escaped conviction, the jury finding that there was insufficient evidence to show that he had pulled his gun on the detectives. As for the charge of carrying a concealed weapon, Schultz proved that he had a permit so to do. Once again, he was a free man.

After the Coll/Schultz war drew to a close, Dutch Schultz concentrated on his business interests. In particular, he had set his heart on breaking into some Harlem 'numbers' or 'policy' rackets – a type of illegal lottery game. Realizing early on, however, that more was needed than just strong-arm tactics, Schultz began buying off not only the police, but also such notable figures as the politician James J. 'Jimmy' Hines and attorney-at-law Richard J. 'Dixie' Davis. In his book, *Twenty Against the Underworld*, Thomas E. Dewey – New York's Special Prosecutor with responsibility for rackets – says of Dixie Davis that he, '. . . was an improbable figure to be a top commander of a New York racket. He [. . .] worked his way through Syracuse Law School and was admitted to the Bar in 1927. This made him the professional contemporary of many of the men on our staff. Davis was given a clerkship in an honored law firm, but soon he went into business for himself.'[3] This business included representing members of the mob when they were in court and he soon became known by them as 'the Boy Mouthpiece.'

When Schultz decided to push into the Harlem numbers racket, Dixie Davis gave him invaluable support, in particular because Davis represented several of Harlem's black policy operators – who were astute businessmen but hardly hardened street criminals. With Davis's help, and backed up by his own muscle, Schultz soon began making inroads into Harlam's policy rackets working out agreements with people whom he promised to protect in exchange for large payouts. Soon Schultz had the three largest numbers operators on his payroll, but there was one last controller, Stephanie St. Clair (better known to most as 'Madame Queen') who wasn't so easily brought into line. On being approached by Schultz and subsequently intimidated by his men, she went straight to the police and the newspapers to expose Schultz's operational methods. Unfortunately, there was little anyone could do to help her and eventually Schultz put Madame Queen out of business by having the remainder of the black policy operators squeeze her out.

Dutch Schultz was now making good money and this only improved when Otto 'Abbadabba' Berman, who was something of a mathematical genius, approached Schultz around 1932 with an offer he couldn't refuse. Berman had come up with a way of fiddling the numbers racket so that those numbers which were most played in any given game would never come up as winners, thereby saving Schultz from ever having to pay out. Initially, it is said that Schultz turned Berman's offer down, but finally with huge tax demands to pay off, he eventually decided to employ Berman to 'fix' the racket. Suddenly, Schultz's profits shot through the roof and some people have estimated that his yearly income was between twelve to fourteen million dollars. But Schultz still wasn't satisfied and now turned to another racket, this time involving the restaurant industry.

Julius Modgilewsky, one of Schultz's most trusted men, bought a small café/diner in order to become a member of Local 16, the Hotel & Restaurant Employees Alliance, an operation that dealt with all restaurant waiters in Manhattan. Modgilewsky's employees, with Schultz's help, then put themselves forward as union officials, rigging the ballot boxes to ensure desired results. Schultz made it his business to take over another Restaurant Union Alliance, Local 302, only this time, instead of relying on the ballot box, he simply told the union's bosses to join up with him or face the consequences. Schultz then established the Metropolitan Restaurant & Cafeteria Owners Association, an outfit set up with the sole intention of collecting protection money from the catering industry. The real beauty of the whole operation was the fact that Schultz himself remained a shadowy background figure employing others to threaten and bully. Still, there were some owners who refused to pay up. Hyman Gross, having invested heavily in his business didn't want to have to pay out more money to gangsters. Of course he immediately regretted his decision as one night several highly effective stink bombs were dropped down the chimneys of his restaurant. The bombs contained acid which burnt all the fixtures and fittings, as well as making the carpets and other soft furnishings smell foul. The restaurant needed a complete re-fit, something Gross couldn't afford and consequently he lost his business.

But Hyman Gross had, in fact, escaped lightly. In March 1935, Schultz showed his true colours in an incident involving Julius Modgilewsky. Embroiled in a tax fraud case, Schultz had ordered Modgilewsky to bring him $21,000 in cash from the takings at Local 16. On arrival at the hotel where Schultz was staying, Modgilewsky was accused by his boss of stealing in the region of $70,000. The argument that ensued was witnessed by two men, one of whom was Dixie Davis.

> Dutch Schultz was ugly; he had been drinking and suddenly he had his gun out. The Dutchman wore his pistol under his vest, tucked inside his pants, right against his belly. One jerk at his vest and he had it in his hand. All in the same quick motion he swung it up, stuck it in Jules Martin's [Julius Modgilewsky's alias) mouth and pulled the trigger. It was as simple and undramatic as that – just one quick motion of the hand. The Dutchman did that murder just as casually as if he were picking his teeth.[4]

With Martin dead, the restaurant racket grew from strength to strength until a shadow loomed on the horizon in the shape of one Thomas E. Dewey. Suddenly the future didn't look so rosy after all. Dewey soon arrested ten of Schultz's men who stood trial on 18 January 1937.

Dewey, as is mentioned elsewhere in this book, had entered the State Attorney's offices with one mission in mind; to rid the city of organized crime. Early in the 1930s, he prosecuted several racketeers, including Wilfred Brunder and Henry Miro, on charges of tax evasion, though his most famous case to date was against Irving Wexler (also known as Waxey Gordon) on charges of bootlegging. Waxey had been found guilty and sent down for ten years. Not wishing to follow in Waxey's footsteps, Schultz, who was facing up to forty-three years in prison if found guilty of tax evasion, decided to go into hiding. The first year passed smoothly enough; Schultz hardly bothered to conceal his location and often visited his wife, Frances, and lawyer Dixie Davis, in broad daylight. But in 1934 the newly elected mayor, Fiorello 'Little Flower' La Guardia, was determined to cleanse his city of 'underworld scum' and to this end teamed Dewey up with the FBI Director of Operations, J. Edgar Hoover.

On November 28, 1934 Dutch Schultz, after spending twenty-one months as a fugitive, gave himself up to the authorities and was subsequently indicted on the charges of tax evasion. His bail was then set at $50,000, although shortly afterwards it was doubled. Suddenly, Schultz was behind bars, a situation he had not found himself in since he has been a teenager. Dixie Davis soon sorted the situation out, and had the bail reduced to $75,000. Schultz's trial began in Syracuse on April 16, 1935 with John H. McEvers handling the prosecution. He and his team subpoenaed twenty witnesses to give evidence for the prosecution, although it was hardly surprising that none of them appeared too willing. Indeed, a couple of men decided it was preferable to go into hiding than face Schultz's mob, while others conveniently developed selective amnesia. Bo Weinberg, on the other hand, pleaded the Fifth Amendment.

The defense team's case proved a far quicker affair, taking in total just over three hours and calling only three witnesses who stated that Schultz had been legally advised that he wasn't required to pay tax on his illegal earnings. When Schultz discovered that he did have to pay, he tried to make amends but stated that the government had declined his offer. The jury were sent away to assess all the evidence but, having spent two days deadlocked, the judge discharged them from duty. A second trial was then set, only this time it would be heard in Malone, a small town near the Canadian border.

Canny as ever, Schultz made certain he arrived in Malone a week earlier than the trial was due to start, in order to show the townsfolk what a regular type of guy he was – he even attended a local game of baseball with the Malone mayor and when the trial did begin, Schultz's defense team hired a local attorney to represent their client, believing this would play well with the jury. As for the prosecution, they stuck pretty much well to their original case, calling the same witnesses to the stand including Bo Weinberg. On August 2, the jury returned a 'not guilty' verdict. The judge was incensed and, turning to the jury, spouted the following:

> You have labored long and no doubt have given careful consideration to this case. Before I discharge you I will have to say that your verdict is such that it shakes the confidence of law-abiding people in integrity and truth. It will be apparent to all who have followed the evidence in this case that you have reached a verdict based not on the evidence but on some other reason. You will have to go home with the satisfaction, if it is a satisfaction, that you have rendered a blow against law enforcement and given aid and encouragement to the people who would flout the law. In all probability they will commend you. I cannot.[5]

Relieved, and feeling like the luckiest man alive, instead of returning to New York

(where a federal warrant had been issued for his arrest on further charges of tax evasion), Schultz set up residence in the Stratfield Hotel in Bridgeport, Connecticut. Unknown to him, however, it wouldn't be too long before his luck changed irrevocably.

Wined and dined in Connecticut as a celebrity, it is not entirely clear why, on September 24, 1935, Schultz decided to head for New Jersey, where he was immediately arrested on suspicion of being a fugitive. Once again, Dixie Davis posted bail, this time for $50,000, after which Schultz moved into the Robert Treat Hotel in Newark.

Having failed to convict the Dutchman in either the Syracuse or the Malone trials, Thomas E. Dewey was not about to let Schultz walk for a third time, and instead intended to put him on trial not only for tax evasion but also for running illegal policy rackets. Before this could occur, a federal grand jury indicted Schultz on the same charges for which he had previously been tried – tax evasion. Eventually an agreement was reached which saw him indicted on lesser charges of failing to file tax returns over a three-year period.

By now hounded not only by the IRS but also by the FBI and the Mob itself, Dutch Schultz was a troubled man when this photograph was taken in 1935 shortly before he was murdered.

Not one to take kindly to being pursued in this way, albeit by the FBI instead of Dewey, Schultz vented his anger on Dewey, who then became the target of death threats. The truth about how close Dewey came to being assassinated did not become apparent until 1940, five years after Schultz's death, when Abe 'Kid Twist' Reles related how Albert Anastasia had been asked by Schultz to 'take out' the Special Prosecutor.

But, according to Lucky Luciano, what happened next ran contrary to everything Schultz wanted. A meeting was convened between some of gangland's most influential members during which it was decided that the Dutchman was becoming a liability and therefore should be taken out. 'His own mob was sick of him,' wrote Hickman Powell in his book on Lucky Luciano. 'His own men were sore at all the publicity he had been getting . . . and the big shots generally had decided he was no longer an asset to the underworld. The Dutchman had been out of his mind, practically crazy, for several months, and had killed too many people for anyone to like him very much.'[6]

Contrary to this version of events, another explanation is that, having gone to the mob with a request that Dewey be hit and having been told that it wasn't the mob's job to shoot government officials, Schultz became angry and said he would take Dewey out himself. It was at this point that Luciano, together with several others, decided the Dutchman had to go. Whichever version you believe, the end result was the same – Luciano ordered the mob's special hit squad, Murder Inc., to take out Dutch Schultz. On October 23, 1935, Charles 'Charlie the Bug' Workman and Emanuel 'Mendy' Weiss entered the Palace Chop House and began firing at the table at which they both thought Schultz was seated. Three of the Dutchman's companions, Abbadabba Bermen, Lulu Rosencrantz and Abe Landau were wounded, but Schultz himself (there are several different versions to this story) was in the men's room. Charlie the Bug then tracked him down and shot him, afterwards rifling through his clothes for any spare cash. Meanwhile Landau, though wounded in his right arm, is said to have given chase to the assailants, shortly followed by Rosencrantz who had also been wounded, but both men soon collapsed. Schultz, on the other hand, made it as far as the restaurant table where he is said to have shouted for a doctor – an order that the barman swiftly fulfilled. All four men were rushed to Newark City Hospital. Abbadabba Berman was the first to die, followed by Landau and then Rosencrantz. But these three hoodlums weren't the only ones to lose their lives on October 25. It is believed that Murder Inc, desperate to cleanse the mob of all Dutch's associates, also took out Marty Krompier (a Schultz associate in the numbers racket) while he was having his haircut at the Hollywood Barber Shop on Seventh Avenue. Wounded alongside Krompier was a hoodlum by the name of Sammy Gold.[7]

Meanwhile, back at Newark City Hospital, Schultz had been operated upon and was fighting for his life. He was put in a small side ward and surrounded by police who were trying to establish who had shot him. Father Cornelius McInerney was called in to give the Dutchman the last rites, as it appeared Schultz wanted to die a

Catholic. In fact, it took Schultz several excruciating hours to expire, during which it is said he rambled incoherently while drifting in and out of consciousness. Dutch Schultz died at 8.35 a.m. on October 26. He was buried at the Gate of Heaven Cemetery on October 28, with only his mother, his sister and his wife, Frances Flegenheimer, together with Father McInerney and two state troopers in attendance. Murdered by the mob, none of their number deigned to attend the funeral in order to pay their last respects. Only four floral tributes arrived, something of a snub to a man who had once been such a major figure in organized crime.

1 *The Life and World of Al Capone*, John Kobler, First Published by Fawcett Publications Inc., 1972.

2 *Kill the Dutchman!*, Paul Sann, New York: Popular Library, 1971.

3 *Twenty Against the Underworld*, Thomas E. Dewey, New York, Doubleday, 1974.

4 www.crimelibrary.com

5 Ibid.

6 *Lucky Luciano: The Man who Organized Crime in America*, Hickman Powell, Barricade Books Inc., 2000.

7 Both Krompier and Gold survived the attack.

BENJAMIN 'BUGSY' SIEGEL

The King of Las Vegas

'Leadership is the art of getting someone else to do something
you want done because he wants to do it.'

Dwight D. Eisenhower

By the time Benjamin Siegel had reached his early twenties he already had a reputation as a vicious villain, having been involved in extortion, robbery and even murder. Nicknamed 'Bugsy' (an appellation he loathed), Siegel was always willing to step in to sticky situations and was labeled a sociopath for his apparent nonchalance when committing even the most heinous of crimes. Apart from Al Capone, Bugsy Siegel is the man who perhaps best sums up the image of a prototypical underworld gangster. Tall, with a shock of dark hair, piercing blue eyes and a penchant for wearing sharp suits, he was a hugely popular with the ladies and, unlike several of his counterparts, enjoyed the limelight to the extent that he hobnobbed with movie stars, making Hollywood his second home. But perhaps, more than anything else, Siegel will be best remembered for having been the man who transformed a small, desert town called Las Vegas into the world's most glitzy gambling Mecca.

Like practically all of Siegel's gangster contemporaries, he was born into poverty, the son of immigrant parents. The section of New York in which he was raised in the early 1900s, the Williamsburg quarter of Brooklyn, was a melting pot of impoverished Italian, Jewish and Irish men and women all struggling to make a life for themselves in their newly adopted country. Siegel's father worked in the garment industry, but barely brought in enough money to feed his growing family, a fact that was enough to persuade Siegel he wasn't going to follow in his father's footsteps; that he was going to do better, be richer, achieve more.

Early on in his life he befriended a boy called Moey Sedway and together Siegel and Sedway set up a small-time extortion racket that targeted street vendors. One of the boys would demand that the vendor give them a dollar and when the man declined the other boy would splash his stall with kerosene and set it alight. The next time the boys asked for money, payment was nearly always forthcoming. It was while running this scam with Sedway that Siegel met another boy who had also decided a life of crime was better than a life of drudgery, Meyer Lansky.

Lansky, like Siegel, was from an immigrant background and wanted nothing more than to make money and leave his past behind. There are several stories about how the two met, but the most popular one (though no doubt apocryphal) is that Siegel had been visiting a prostitute who was in the employ of Lucky Luciano, but had not been paying for her services. Luciano, on hearing this, burst in on Siegel and the girl and began attacking them, at which point Lansky entered the room and broke up the fight. Afterwards, so the story goes, the three hoodlums became firm friends. The biographer Robert Lacey tells a different version, however, in his book *Little Man: Meyer Lansky and the Gangster Life*. Lacey maintains that Lansky was busy watching a street-corner crap game when a fight broke out and a gun fell to the ground. Siegel immediately picked the gun up and was on the point of shooting the gun's owner when the police showed up and Lansky, always a quick thinker, knocked the gun out of Siegel's hand, hustling him away from the brawl. Afterwards, according to Lacey, the two became best buddies. 'Violent and irrational, generous and charming, Benny Siegel shivered with an exuberance and vitality that Meyer found difficult to generate on his own account. His smile was devastating, his rages quite mesmeric.'[1]

Siegel's other friends at the time also proved significant later in life and included Lepke Buchalter who organized 'intimidation hits' in the garment trade and who, in March 1944, became one of the few gangster bosses to be sent to the electric chair. Siegel also hung around with a youth named Arthur Flegenheimer, who was later better known as Dutch Schultz, while other friends included Jacob 'Furrah' Shapiro and Abner 'Longie' Zwillman. But it was Meyer Lansky who really made the difference to the young Siegel, and together the two of them started setting up small-time protection rackets, illegal crap games and many other scams that came to mind. Lucky Luciano was also part of this scene; in fact it was Luciano who instigated Siegel's first murder.

Sent to prison for peddling both heroin and morphine at the age of eighteen, when Luciano re-emerged on the streets he was intent on revenge. He wanted to kill the person responsible for shopping him to the police, but Lansky (always cool under pressure) told him that he and Siegel would take care of the matter. A year went by, after which Lansky told Luciano to take a holiday and find himself a strong alibi. In the meantime, Siegel and Lansky kidnapped the person Luciano had named as the stool pigeon – the nineteen-year-old son of a Brooklyn policeman – and the boy was never seen alive again.

Having committed his first murder, Siegel now felt he was invincible, and together with his number-one partner-in-crime, Meyer Lansky, he concentrated on running crap games and organizing robberies. Soon he also had a reputation for being adept with both a knife and with his fists, and by the end of the First World War, he and Meyer had joined forces with Luciano and another young thug, Frank Costello. At the time this was a fairly unusual union as Costello and Luciano were Italian, whereas Meyer and Siegel were Jewish. Nevertheless, the combination worked well, especially when it came to running protection rackets, which they proceeded to set up all over the city.

Siegel also found his future bride around this time, a young woman called Estelle Krakower. The two would be married in 1927 and three years later Estelle bore Siegel a little girl whom they named Millicent. Several years later Estelle then had a second daughter, Barbara.

As they entered the Roaring Twenties, Lansky and Luciano had amassed quite considerable sums of money from their crap games and protection rackets. They were looking for somewhere to invest their capital and Lansky is said to have asked Siegel to go check out a bank with an eye to placing their funds there. Siegel, so the story goes, returned only to inform Lansky that the bank was unsafe, that anyone could go in and steal the takings. Two weeks later the Bugs/Meyer mob (as it was then known) did precisely that: they broke into the bank, tied up the elderly security guard and stole over $8,000.

But if jobs like this were relatively easy, Lansky, Siegel and Luciano knew that in order to break into the big time they were going to have to diversify. All three began buying into New York's bookmaking operations as well as bankrolling both the Lower East Side police and those politicians who were most easily corrupted. And it was this that first brought Siegel and Lansky to the attention of Arnold 'The Brain' Rothstein. Rothstein was one of the early twentieth century's first urban criminals; he was Mr Organized Crime itself, a shtadlan (fixer), a terrifying figure who had achieved mythic status at least a decade before Al Capone arrived on the scene.

With the Volstead Act and the passing of Prohibition as law in 1920, Arnold Rothstein had developed his business empire to include bootlegging on a grand scale. In fact, no other law in America had (or has) been flouted so aggressively as that of Prohibition, with speakeasies and gin joints springing up all over America. Police would regularly turn a blind eye to these illegal activities with the result that, for underworld bosses, Prohibition was a license to print money. But Rothstein didn't want to go it alone; he needed good, reliable men around him. He sought out and employed Lansky, Luciano and Siegel. By this time Lansky and Siegel, together with Siegel's childhood friend, Moe Sedway, had also set up a truck rental business in a garage on the Lower East Side. It acted as a good front for their new bootlegging activities as well as being a legitimate truck rental business.

> Rothstein proposed that under the direction of the Bugs and Meyer mob – specifically Lansky (he had no patience for a man of Bugs' temperament) – Dutch Schultz would take over the New York bootlegging operation and Longie Zwillman, Lansky's close friend and kindred intellectual spirit, would run North Jersey. Other men who were later brought into the operation included the dapper Giuseppe Doto, a.k.a. Joe Adonis, Carlo Gambino (the future head of the Gambino crime family), Vito Genovese, Gambino's predecessor as godfather, and the sinister Albert Anastasia.[2]

A great deal of careful organization was required to keep their operations running smoothly and it was Lansky who took care of the business side of the venture. Siegel concentrated on the actual bootlegging and hijacking of other gangs' whisky. It was a match made in heaven; the brains and the brawn, the hot head and the cool, calculating mind acting in unison. It was also around this period that Siegel met up with an old friend from his days back in the Williamsburg district of Brooklyn, Al Capone. Capone wasn't part of the Bugs/Meyer mob, preferring instead to work for his boyhood hero, Johnny Torrio. Nevertheless, he had always kept in touch with Siegel and when he needed help hiding from some thugs who were threatening to kill him, Siegel obliged, finding Capone a safe house in which he could lay low. Afterwards, Capone followed Johnny Torrio to Chicago where Torrio's uncle, James 'Big Jim' Colosimo ran several gambling and prostitution rackets. Big Jim was a legend in his own lifetime, but when Prohibition became law, rather than view it as another opportunity to make money Colosimo wanted nothing to do with rum-running. Infuriated by what he saw as his uncle's short-sightedness, Johnny Torrio is thought to have been behind Big Jim's murder on May 11, 1920. However, there was also a rumor that the Bugs/Meyer gang might have sent one of their own, Frankie Yale, to kill Big Jim because they were fearful that his reluctance to embrace bootlegging would allow other, less friendly gangs, to operate in Chicago, thus freezing them out. But, if Bugsy wasn't directly involved in Big Jim's murder, the same cannot be said for the next killing, which turned out to be one of the biggest hits in the history of organized crime.

In New York two Italian/Sicilian Mafia families had been warring for years over who should be the 'boss of bosses.' One of the two men was Joe 'The Boss' Masseria, the other was Salvatore Maranzano. Lucky Luciano belonged to the first group, but Maranzano was quietly winning him over to his side and sometime in 1931 a deal was struck to the effect that he could join Maranzano – alongside Jewish friends such as Siegel – so long as he organized the killing of Masseria. Luciano arranged a lunch for Joe 'The Boss' at his favorite restaurant, the Nuova Villa Tammaro on Coney Island. Vito Genovese and Ciro Terranova also attended the meal, but they both excused themselves early, leaving Masseria alone with Luciano. The two proceeded to finish the meal and (so legend has it) then began playing cards. Half-way through the game Luciano visited the men's room, after which four gunmen burst into the restaurant and pumped Masseria's body full of bullets. The man in charge of the assault was allegedly Benny Siegel, alongside Albert Anastasia, Joe Adonis and Vito Genovese who only minutes before had been dining alongside his boss. Masseria was said still to have been clutching the ace of diamonds when he died. It has further been reported that after the hit, all four gunmen ran out to the getaway car which was being driven by Masseria's other dinner guest, Ciro Terranova, but because he was so nervous he kept stalling the vehicle, leading Siegel to shoot him in the head and take over the controls.

Siegel and his pals seemed to revel in the viciousness of the crimes they committed. One veteran New York detective serving at the time said: 'For a sawbuck that gang would break the arm of a man they'd never seen. They'd kill a stranger for less than fifty dollars. If you can believe it, Bugsy preferred to do the job himself. He wasn't content just to give the orders and collect the fees. He enjoyed doing the blasting personally. It gave him a sense of power. He got his kicks out of seeing his victims suffering, groaning, and dying.'[3]

It comes as no surprise, then, that Siegel didn't balk at the prospect of murdering one of his childhood friends, Bo Weinberg, when Dutch Schultz hired him for the hit. Weinberg had upset Schultz by taking over some of his businesses while Schultz had been lying low, trying to avoid prosecution for tax evasion. Eventually, Schultz did appear in court and was (thanks to a bought jury) found not guilty. On his release, Schultz hired Bugsy to execute his former buddy, a job that Siegel approached like any other. Siegel called on Weinberg and the two went out for dinner, but all the time that Bugsy was driving to the restaurant he was looking for a convenient spot in which to pull the car over. As soon as he found such a place, Bugsy got out of the vehicle and walked round to Weinberg's side of the car where he proceeded to pistol whip his old pal. After that, Bugsy is believed to have stabbed Weinberg in the throat and the abdomen before throwing the corpse into the East River. Bo Weinberg's body was never recovered.

By this time the Bugs/Meyer partnership was causing waves throughout the underworld and not long after the death of Joe Masseria, Siegel found himself involved in a near-death experience himself. A couple of brothers called the Fabrizzos broke into the Bugs/Meyer offices and planted a bomb in the fireplace. Both Meyer Lansky and Bugsy were in the building at the time the bomb was supposed to be detonated, but Bugsy spotted the device and is said to have thrown it out of the window. The ensuing blast injured him (Lansky remained unhurt) and he had to be taken to hospital. On his release, he vowed revenge and subsequently Andy Fabrizzo's body was found in New Jersey, while Louis Fabrizzo was gunned down in Manhattan. This wasn't quite the end to the Fabrizzo/Siegel feud as there was still one more brother, Tony Fabrizzo. Terrified that he would be accused of the attempted murder of Bugsy, he let it be known that not only wasn't he involved, but that he would be penning a memoir (with a whole chapter devoted to what he knew about Bugsy) which, after he was finished, would be given to his lawyers so that if anything happened to him, everyone would know who was to blame. Bugsy was said to be furious and, in order to give himself an airtight alibi, he booked himself in to a hospital for a few days 'rest.' On the second night he was there, he told the nurses not to disturb him, before creeping out to where a couple of his gang were waiting for him in a car. The threesome then drove to Tony Fabrizzo's house where Siegel shot Fabrizzo in full view of his elderly parents. Afterwards, Bugsy drove back to the hospital and returned to his 'sick' bed.

By 1935 the net was beginning to tighten around New York's gang bosses, mainly due to the tenacity of one man, Thomas E. Dewey, who had been appointed the city's special prosecutor with particular responsibility for racketeering. Dutch Schultz was at the top of Dewey's hit-list, but after Schultz was gunned down in October 1935, Police Commissioner Lewis J. Valentine speculated on whom he thought would replace Schultz:

The new combination consists of gangs headed by six notorious racketeers: Charles Lucky Luciano, Charles (Buck) Siegel, Meyer Lansky, Louis (Lefty) Buckhouse, Jacob (Furrah) Shapiro, and Abe (Longie) Zwillman, the last one of Newark.'[4]

In 1944, when Bugsy Siegel (left) appeared in court on charges connected to illegal gambling, his childhood friend, Georgie Ranft testified on his behalf. Having changed his name slightly, Georgie was by then better known as Hollywood star George Raft.

Despite Siegel's name appearing on this list, he had already decided to leave New York; the only question was where to go next. The obvious choice would have been Chicago where he'd already made inroads with Capone and Torrio, but instead Siegel decided that his future lay further afield in California. At this time, California was relatively gang free, although there was one outfit operating in the area headed by Jack I. Dragna who was president of the Italian Protective League. The IPL was supposedly an organization set up to help Italian immigrants, but instead operated mostly as a protection racket intimidating the very people it was established to defend. Dragna also ran a bootlegging operation and several gambling businesses, so it seemed only proper that before Siegel went out West someone warned Dragna of his impending visit. This role fell to Lucky Luciano who was at the time serving a long prison sentence in Dannemora State Penitentiary. From his prison cell, Luciano got in touch with Dragna and told him that his Syndicate was moving in to the West and he could either run with the big boys or effectively be trampled. Sensibly, Dragna decided to cooperate although it was said that he resented a Jewish boy stepping on to his territory.

On his arrival in California Siegel, with his wife and two daughters, immediately rented a huge, white-brick mansion, complete with massive swimming pool, owned by the Metropolitan Opera Singer Lawrence Tibbett. Siegel also reacquainted himself with another of his old childhood friends, Georgie Ranft, now better known as George Raft, the Hollywood screen actor.

Raft, more than anyone else or anything Bugsy himself had done in this first weeks and months in Hollywood, helped create the mystique that was soon to surround Siegel. 'He's a big man from back East,' Raft would confide to intimates, exhaling the words out of the side of his mouth. The whispers could not help but circulate and soon Siegel was a glamorous and much sought-after companion of the movie colony's faster social set. He made friends by the dozens, generating the image he had set out to establish for himself.[5]

With his social life taken care of, Siegel now set about organizing his new business ventures. Sensibly, he allowed Dragna to continue handling the gambling side of things, while Siegel targeted the unions. In particular, he began with the film extras union, and together with Moey Sedway he muscled in on the scene, extracting money from the movie moguls who needed extras in order to make their films.

Riding on a high both socially and professionally, Bugsy is said to have had several affairs during this period, including a wild romance with an actress called Ketti Gallian. More famously, though, he was also linked to Jean Harlow and doubtless had flings with several other young starlets. Although his glamorous romantic liaisons might have suggested a softer side to his character, where Bugsy was concerned murder and mayhem were never too far away, the glitz and glamor of Hollywood making little difference to this deeply sinister side of his activities.

Back home in the East, Lepke Buchalter had become Thomas Dewey's latest target and Buchalter, paranoid that an associate of his, Harry 'Big Greenie' Greenberg, was going to spill too many beans to New York's special prosecutor, tracked Greenberg down to California. A hit man by the name of Allie 'Tick-Tock' Tannenbaum was contracted to kill Big Greenie with the assistance of none other than Bugsy Siegel. Other men involved in the hit were Whitey Krakow (Siegel's brother-in-law), Frankie Carbo and Sholem Bernstein. Big Greenie was tracked down to 1904 West Vista Del Mar in Los Angeles and put under surveillance. A couple of days later, returning to his house after buying his daily newspaper, he was gunned down on the street by Tick-Tock. With another killing under his belt, Siegel now set about assisting his East Coast syndicate friends, together with Sam Giancana in Chicago, in another business venture; that of the bookmakers' wire service. The only legal wire service in operation in the early 1940s was Western Union, but they were restricted by law as to the sort of information they could transmit over the airwaves. There were, however, two illegal services – the first called the Continental Press, which was owned by James Ragen, and the second known as Trans American, which was owned by Syndicate-backed men. It was Siegel's new job to begin 'persuading' all of California's bookies to switch allegiance to Trans American, thereby freezing out James Ragen, who eventually handed his business over to Sam Giancana. It was a job well done, but when the East Coast men informed Siegel that from then on they would be handling the proceeds from Continental, Bugsy threw a fit. According to several documents, he was raking in over $25,000 per month from the service's operation in Las Vegas, so he wasn't about to hand over the business to anybody, no matter what their credentials. It was a bad move; one that in the space of a few years would return to haunt Bugsy in a manner even he couldn't have foreseen. But first there was Vegas.

Bugsy Siegel did not, contrary to popular opinion, build Las Vegas or invent it. He never had a dream to establish an American Monte Carlo in the middle of the Nevada desert, nor did he foresee what a success such a venture would be. What he did do was to come across a small, run-of-the-mill gambling operation that was being run out of a no-hope town and decide to make it his own.

At that time in America, Nevada had one thing in its favor; unlike any other state in the country, it was legal to gamble there. Having suffered from a massive loss of revenue during the depression, the State Legislature had legalized gaming and off-track betting on horse races in order to be able to collect taxes on gambling. Several mob bosses, including Meyer Lansky and Bugsy himself, already owned and ran carpet joints and floating casinos, but Bugsy knew that if he could build an upmarket club in Las Vegas, it would give him a legitimate place of business as well as a huge income. He found himself a partner, Billy Wilkerson (the founder of the Hollywood Reporter and the brains behind the Café Trocadero), who had already begun building a luxurious hotel complete with swimming pools and air-conditioning, but who needed extra cash to finish the project. Siegel bought a controlling share in the business, but soon afterwards he too ran out of money (the project was costing millions of dollars) which led him to beg and borrow funds from numerous contacts, including Meyer Lansky, Frank Costello and Lucky Luciano. Eventually, the hotel's gambling casinos were up and running (the hotel rooms were to be left until later) and Siegel named the establishment The Flamingo – some think after his new girlfriend, Virginia Hill. But the hotel became a millstone around Bugsy's neck. The money didn't appear to be rolling in in the way that Bugsy had predicted. Lansky and Costello alongside other, smaller investors grew disillusioned with the Californian golden boy who had promised quick profits, none of which seemed to be appearing. It has also been reported that Meyer Lansky called a meeting in Havana, Cuba, attended by the likes of Vito Genovese and Frank Costello, during which Lansky revealed that Bugsy had been appropriating money due to the mob and hiding it in overseas bank accounts.

It is not known whether there is any truth to this story, but what isn't in doubt is that Bugsy's old friends were growing increasingly disenchanted with him. Although they were prepared to wait and see if The Flamingo could recoup their investment, realistically it seemed only a matter of time before Bugsy blotted his copy book one time too many.

Although he had a wife and two daughters when he moved from Chicago to California, Bugsy's infatuation with leading a glamorous lifestyle led to him taking several mistresses, among them Virginia Hill.

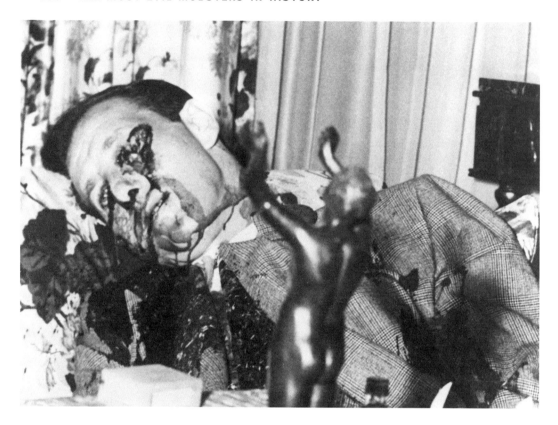

Bugsy had argued with Virginia Hill and she had left to travel to Paris by the time Bugsy settled down on the couch in her house to read the Los Angeles Times *on the evening of June 20, 1947. He never finished his newspaper.*

When The Flamingo opened, Bugsy lined up a series of top acts, including Jimmy Durante, to make the show go with a bang. The guests were also high caliber, with Clark Gable and Joan Crawford in attendance, but despite this glamorous line-up, the locals weren't drawn to the casino. Unfamiliar with this type of Hollywood glitz, they preferred more down-to-earth establishments. The weather didn't help. The desert town was unusually damp and rainy and after the second day most of the celebrities headed back to Los Angeles. Suddenly, Siegel was on the ropes again, with all of his old friends baying for blood. All, that is, except Meyer Lansky who, for a second time, persuaded Siegel's enemies to give him another chance, let him finish the hotel and see if he could then turn the business around. The pressure was now on and Bugsy is said to have worked round the clock to ensure that the hotel's bedrooms were finished before its second grand opening on March 1, 1947. The floorshow for this extravaganza had as its top-billed act the incredibly popular Andrews Sisters. Bugsy is also said to have initiated mid-week bingo sessions to entice the reluctant locals out of their homes. All his hard work did seem to reap dividends as by May The Flamingo was shown to be making a profit. Siegel started to relax and his friends began recouping their investment, but then Billy Wilkerson decided he wanted to pull out of the project. Bugsy didn't see this as a problem long as Wilkerson agreed to sell his shares for a price that Bugsy could afford. But Wilkerson wouldn't cooperate and, as his attorney Greg Bautzer recalls, Bugsy began threatening his former partner. '"You give me the thirty-three and a third and get paid for it,"' shouted Bugsy, '"or I don't think any place you live will be healthy for you."'[6] Naturally, Bautzer was unimpressed and told Siegel that if anything happened to his client, he would hold Bugsy personally responsible. On top of this, Bautzer was going to prepare an affidavit detailing the threat and forward this to both the police and FBI. Bugsy was being played at his own game and he hated it. For days afterwards he was apparently so angry that no one dared go near him.

Nevertheless, with the pressure slowly easing in relation to The Flamingo, Bugsy returned to Los Angeles from where he wired his mistress, Virginia Hill, who was staying out of town having had a fight with Bugsy, asking her to return home. Virginia did as she was bid and the two were reunited, but shortly afterwards the two lovers fell out yet again, only this time Virginia flew to Paris via Chicago and New York. Bugsy stayed behind in Virginia's house on North Linden Drive in Beverly Hills.

On June 20, 1947, having returned from an early evening haircut, Bugsy Siegel was resting on a downstairs sofa, reading the *Los Angeles Times* and chatting to another West Coast gangster, Alan Smiley, when nine bullets were fired into the room from a .30 caliber army carbine. The first shot hit Bugsy in the head, blowing out his eye, which was later found fifteen feet away from his body, while the next four bullets ripping through his ribs and lungs. Bugsy Siegel, 42 years old, was dead. The following morning his slaying made all the front pages and the story was invariably accompanied by a photograph of his blood-stained body. Ironically, given the problems he had been having with The Flamingo, Bugsy's death helped to make the casino a roaring success. After his murder, the hotel became synonymous with all that was wicked and wild, and people flocked to see it for themselves.

His funeral was a small affair, attended by relatives only. Meyer Lansky, perhaps his closest friend, was apparently in Havana at the time. As for his Hollywood buddies, not one of them found it within themselves to attend the service.

There are several theories relating to who actually killed Bugsy Siegel, the most popular being that Siegel's business partners in The Flamingo, who included Moe Sedway, Lucky Luciano and a man by the name of Gus Greenbaum, had him killed for non-payment of debts. 'Benny had spent a lot of their money,' said Harold Conrad (an East Coast sportswriter who was friends with Meyer Lansky), 'and money was what counted with those guys.'[7] Meyer Lansky, on the other hand, flatly denied any involvement in the slaying and, despite the police's best efforts, no one was ever charged with his death.

Today Las Vegas is as big and as brash as ever, but the fate of The Flamingo is much like that of Bugsy himself. After a period of success generated partly by its notoriety, the hotel was taken over in the 1980s by the Hilton Corporation which has swept away the establishment's shady past, understandably preferring not to dwell on the story of Bugsy Siegel who, after all, was nothing but a hoodlum, a thief and a cold-hearted murderer.

[1] *Little Man: Meyer Lansky and the Gangster Life*, Robert Lacey, Little Brown Inc., 1991.

[2] www.crimelibrary.com

[3] *Bugsy: The Godfather of Las Vegas*, George Carpozi Jr, Everest Books Limited, 1976.

[4] *New York Times*, October 26, 1935.

[5] *Bugsy: The Godfather of Las Vegas*, George Carpozi Jr, Everest Books Limited, 1976.

[6] *Little Man: Meyer Lansky and the Gangster Life*, Robert Lacey, Little Brown Inc., 1991.

[7] Ibid.

Picture Acknowledgements

The Mario Gomes Collection at www.alcaponemuseum.com: pp. 25, 28, 33

Rose Keefe at www.deanobanion.com: pp. 157, 160, 166

Rose Keefe at www.bugsmoran.net: pp. 145, 148, 151

©Bettmann/CORBIS: Joseph Bonanno pp. 13, 16   Paul Castellano pp. 39, 42, 44
Frank Costello pp. 52, 56   Carlo Gambino pp. 61, 67   Vito Genovese pp. 71, 76, 78
Sam Giancana pp. 83, 88, 90   John Gotti p. 102   Lucky Luciano p. 140
Bugsy Siegel pp. 184, 187, 188

© CORBIS SYGMA: Carlo Gambino p. 65

© NORCIA/NEWYORK POST/CORBIS SYGMA: Sammy Gravano p. 108

© Ed Quinn/CORBIS: John Gotti p. 95

© Reuters/CORBIS: Sammy Gravano pp. 113, 117   John Gotti p. 99

© Arthur Rothstein/CORBIS: Joseph Bonanno p. 21

TopFoto: Meyer Lansky p. 130

Library of Congress, Prints & Photographs Division, NYWT & S Collection:
LC-USZ62-120716 p. 55,   LC-USZ62-120717 p. 120,   LC-USZ62-120723 p. 125,
LC-USZ62-114640 p. 135,   LC-USZ62-124983 p. 169,   LC-USZ62-124980 p. 172,
LC-USZ62-124966 p. 176

Acknowledgments

The author would like to thank Margaret Soper for all her help
with the research for this book and extend her gratitude to the
designers at D23, Rod Green and the whole editorial team at
Michael O'Mara Books for all their help and support.